Oct. 1986

The Gnostic Dialogue

Theological Inquiries

*Studies in Contemporary
Biblical and Theological Problems*

General Editor
Lawrence Boadt, C. S. P.

PAULIST PRESS
New York • Ramsey • Toronto

The Gnostic Dialogue

The Early Church and the Crisis of Gnosticism

Pheme Perkins

PAULIST PRESS
New York • Ramsey • Toronto

Library of Congress
Catalog Card Number: 80-81441

ISBN: 0-8091-2320-7

Published by Paulist Press
Editorial Office: 1865 Broadway, New York, N.Y. 10023
Business Office: 545 Island Road, Ramsey, N.J. 07446

Printed and bound in the
United States of America

Contents

PART THREE
Religious Issues in the Gnostic Dialogue

Preface

This book is both conclusion and beginning. As conclusion it draws together over fifteen years of reflection on the problems of gnosis, both ancient and modern. As beginning, it suggests paths for further exploration that will, in all likelihood, occupy twice that many years. One learns only to find more questions. I had begun reading Jung as a high school student. A Friday night lecture by Hans Jonas when I was an undergraduate at St. John's led me to his *Gnostic Religion* and thence back to the Gnostic element in Jung's thought and to Eric Voeglin on modern Gnostic political thought. Thanks to the generosity of Prof. James M. Robinson of Claremont and the continual patience and enthusiasm of Prof. George W. Mac-Rae, S.J. of Harvard, I began studying some of the new revelation dialogues as the project for a Ph.D. dissertation at Harvard. Though that dissertation has long since gone the way of my undergraduate musings on gnosis, into the ash can of preliminary beginnings, my fascination with the Gnostic phenomenon has not. More than anyone, Prof. MacRae has suffered the deluge of lecture, typed page, and printed word that has resulted. To him go my thanks, but no promises of a respite.

Not even this "concluding pause" in my reflection would have come about without a Fellowship from the *National Endowment for the Humanities*, which enabled me to do nothing else during a sabbatical year in 1978/79 than think, talk and write about Gnostic revelation, both here at home and in Egypt and Israel. I cannot begin to say how much their confidence that there was something worth pondering in these ancient texts and the leisure to do so have meant to me. Both the conclusions and the beginnings are in no small way indebted to them. I should also thank certain individuals and groups, whose deadlines for learned articles and talks pushed me through the detailed research on specific areas that underlie this more comprehensive discussion: W. Haase; the Institute for Philosophy and Religion at Boston University; the Greater Boston Human Relations Council. My thanks to Dave Toolan, S.J. of *Commonweal* for the review copy of Pagel's *Gnostic Gospels*, which has quite a different approach to the issues discussed in Part Three; and to the editor of this series at Paulist Press, Larry Boadt, C.S.P. (maybe now that the book is finished I'll make good on the Indian Pudding).

Finally, I would like to dedicate this book to an unfailing friend and spiritual guide through all these years, whose sudden death in August 1979 has spared her the labor of reading yet another book, Mother Marie Assumpta, O.S.B.:

> *Super omnes docentes me intellexi:*
> *quia testimonia tua meditatio mea est.*

Yom Kippur, 1979
Boston College

Abbreviations

Standard scholarly abbreviations are employed for biblical books and patristic writings. The following codex numbers and abbreviations for the Coptic texts from Nag Hammadi have been suggested by the Claremont Coptic Gnostic Project.

I,1	Prayer of the Apostle Paul	PrPaul
2	Apocryphon of James	ApocryJas
3	Gospel of Truth	GTr
4	Treatise on the Resurrection	DeRes
5	Tripartite Tractate	TriTrac
II,1	Apocryphon of John	ApocryJn
2	Gospel of Thomas	GTh
3	Gospel of Philip	GPhil
4	Nature of the Archons	NatArc
5	On the Origin of the World	OrigWld
6	Exegesis on the Soul	ExSoul
7	Book of Thomas the Contender	ThCont
III,2	Gospel of the Egyptians	GEgypt
3	Eugnostos, the Blessed	Eug
4	Sophia of Jesus Christ	SJC
5	Dialogue of the Savior	DialSav
V,2	Apocalypse of Paul	ApocPaul
3	First Apocalypse of James	1 ApocJas
4	Second Apocalypse of James	2 ApocJas
5	Apocalypse of Adam	ApocAd
VI,1	Acts of Peter and the Twelve Apostles	AcPet12
2	Thunder, Perfect Mind	Thund
3	Authoritative Teaching	AuthLog
4	Concept of Our Great Power	GrPow
VII,1	Paraphrase of Shem	ParaShem
2	Second Treatise of the Great Seth	GrSeth
3	Apocalypse of Peter	ApocPet
4	Teachings of Silvanus	Silv

5	Three Steles of Seth	3StSeth
VIII,1	Zostrianos	Zostr
2	Letter of Peter to Philip	PetPhil
IX,3	Testimony of Truth	TestTr
X,1	Marsanes	Mar
XI,3	Allogenes	Allog
XIII,1	Trimorphic Protennoia	TriProt

(References to these writings are prefaced by CG, which is followed by codex number, the page number as established by the Facsimile Edition of the codices, and then the line numbers.) The following writings from the Berlin Codex 8502 are also cited:

BG,1	Gospel of Mary	GMary
2	Apocryphon of John	ApocryJn
3	SJC	SJC

(In the table BG=GMary. References to the BG version of ApocryJn and SJC are to be distinguished by the BG preceding the page and line reference.)

Finally, Pistis Sophia is abbreviated PS.

Bibliographical Note

The reader will find a selected bibliography at the end. The following indicates convenient editions of the basic writings discussed in this book, which the reader may wish to have at hand.

The most important reference is the Claremont Project's one-volume translation of all the Nag Hammadi writings and of the *Gospel of Mary*. We would strongly urge readers to obtain a copy of this work:

James M. Robinson, ed. *THE NAG HAMMADI LIBRARY IN ENGLISH*. San Francisco: Harper & Row/Leiden: E.J. Brill, 1977. (=*NHLE*)

An extensive collection of the patristic accounts of Gnosticism may be had in:

W. Foerster. *GNOSIS 1: PATRISTIC EVIDENCE*. Oxford: Oxford Univ., 1972. (This book also contains a translation of the Berlin Codex version of the ApocrynJn=short version, which can be compared with the long version from CG II in *NHLE*.)

A new text and translation of Pistis Sophia has recently appeared:

C. Schmidt & V. MacDermot. *PISTIS SOPHIA*. NHS IX. Leiden: E.J. Brill, 1978.

CHAPTER ONE

Gnosticism in Its Context

Before we turn to analyze those Gnostic writings which report a dialogue between a Gnostic hero and a revealer from the heavenly world, we need to orient ourselves to the religious context of these dialogues. Because Gnostic myths describe this world as the work of an ignorant creator who desires to keep humanity from realizing that its true home lies in a divine world (the pleroma) beyond this cosmos, Gnosticism is commonly described as pessimistic, as an anti-world dualism that represents widespread alienation. Yet the writings in which these stories have come down to us circulated during the years of the Antonine peace. Those who read them were the same people who had most benefited from the imperial order. Is it sufficient to call them a harbinger of social evils to come in the third century, as E. R. Dodds has done?[1]

We may begin by observing that the bias in favor of "this world-ly" religion is a modern development. It derives from secular scientific ideology, which has endowed the created universe with an order and predictability quite unthinkable in earlier days. The ancient argument, epitomized in Plotinus (Enn. II, 9), ran differently.[2] Philosophers asked whether or not the beauty and order of the divine, intelligible world could be reflected in a material world fraught with change. Followers of Plato tried to elaborate on his doctrine of forms to describe the order of the universe. Their chief opposition came from Stoics, whose doctrine of a universe run by an immanent divine

---

[1] See E. R. Dodds, *Pagan and Christian in an Age of Anxiety* (Cambridge: Cambridge University, 1965), 4.

[2] See the discussion of Plotinus in my "Deceiving the Deity: Self-Transcendence and the Numinous in Gnosticism," *Proceedings of the Tenth Annual Institute of Philosophy and Religion, Boston University, 1979*, forthcoming.

Logos (word) seemed to many people to force the cosmos into a deterministic straightjacket. Some Gnostic writers entered into this debate.[3] At the same time, they tried to combine the philosophical perception of the divine as an "ordering intelligence" with the common stories about God in the various mythic traditions and in traditions of the Bible. There, they learned that the will and purposes of God transcended the stable, intelligible order of the cosmos. Gnostic attempts to render the two visions of God coherent are only the smallest beginning of a combination that will lead to theologies and philosophies which stress the primacy of will over intellect.[4] Gnostic writings are difficult to interpret precisely because they do not argue in the analytic terms established by the philosophical schools. Rather, they tell stories which mix archaic myth, biblical exegesis, and philosophical terminology. One must enter into all the complexities of religious discourse in the second and third centuries in order to understand them.

AN ECUMENIC CULTURE IN TRANSITION

A. D. Nock subtitled his classic study of conversion: *The Old and the New in Religion from Alexander the Great to Augustine of Hippo.*[5] The context of our story fits into the changes from the classical city states and ancient Near Eastern empires through the ecumenical period of Roman dominion to the sack of Rome near the end of Augustine's life, that harbinger of mortality for a civilization so ancient that people had thought it would endure forever. The traditions of apocalyptic prophecy, interpretation of old myths, and scientific speculation about the universe, which are taken for granted in

---

[3]See the examples in my "On the Origin of the World (CG II, 5): A Gnostic Physics," *VigChr* 34 (1980), forthcoming.

[4]See the illuminating comments by Hans Jonas, "Jewish and Christian Elements in Philosophy," *Philosophical Essays: From Ancient Creed to Technological Man* (Englewood Cliffs: Prentice Hall, 1974), 27–44; and the discussion of the stoic discovery of will as "that which is in our power" in H. Arendt, *The Life of the Mind. Vol. II: Willing* (New York: Harcourt, Brace, Jovanovich, 1978), 76–84. Such speculation becomes important in ascetic traditions, which emphasize the individual's ability to control, consolidate, and ultimately forge a new identity for the self.

[5]A. D. Nock, *Conversion: The Old and the New in Religion from Alexander the Great to Augustine of Hippo* (London: Oxford University Press, 1933).

Gnostic authors, developed in Hellenistic wisdom circles.[6] By the end of Augustine's life, Manichaeism, the last powerful manifestation of Gnostic spirituality in the ancient world, had spent its force. It was ill-adapted to the new world that was emerging. It would not reappear until the neo-Manichaean movements of the twelfth century that accompanied a new expansion of the West into the East.[7]

In these centuries of sweeping change, the East became the mentor of the West.[8] Socially, the traditional aristocracies tried to hold onto their accustomed forms of privilege. But neither the empire as a whole nor local societies continued to be dominated by the traditional families. New sources of wealth and new outlets for individual ambition and preferment through patronage and imperial service enabled "new men" to enter the small elite that represented power and status in Late Antique society.[9] Money was not a sufficient condition for entry. One had to share a common culture of "higher edu-

---

[6]See the discussion of the relationship between apocalyptic and scribal wisdom traditions in J. Z. Smith, "Wisdom and Apocalyptic," *Religious Syncretism in Antiquity*, ed. B. Pearson (Missoula: Scholars Press, 1975) 131–56. Such movements are probably behind the traditions G. Quispel finds in *Thunder, Perfect Mind* (VI, 2), "Jewish Gnosis and Mandean Gnosticism: Some Reflections on the Writing *Bronte*," *NHS* VII, ed. J.-E. Menard (Leiden: E. J. Brill, 1975), 82–122. His suggestion that the work originated in Alexandrian wisdom circles may be supplemented by referring to a Ptolemaic "brontology" that was attributed to Hermes Trismegistes. This universal prophecy indicated the significance of thunder, month by month. July, the most Egyptian in content, emphasizes the reversals of fortune and cosmic confusion that will redound to the glory of Egypt; quoted in P. M. Fraser, *Ptolemaic Alexandria* (Oxford: Clarendon Press, 1972), Vol. I, 437f; Vol. II, 633f. Codex VI contains several hermetic writings. The subtitle of *Thunder*, "perfect mind," is typical of hermetic writings. Thus, we find Quispel's turn toward Eastern Semitic traditions less likely than an understanding of Thund as a Gnostic elaboration of Alexandrian, pseudo-scientific wisdom traditions. Similar astrological speculation was probably the source for the pattern of the archons in ApocryJn. See A. J. Welburn, "The Identity of the Archons in the Apocryphon of John," *VigChr* 32 (1978), 241–54.

[7]See the challenging and perceptive discussion in Peter Brown, "The Diffusion of Manichaeism in the Roman Empire," *Religion and Society in the Age of Augustine* (London: Farber, 1972), 94–118. Brown rejects approaches which simply correlate the various doctrines of a syncretistic religious phenomenon with the groups to which they might appeal. He tries to understand how Late Antique religions fitted into and reacted to the pressures of the wider social environment.

[8]See H. Jonas, *The Gnostic Religion*, rev. ed. (Boston: Beacon Press, 1963), 3–27.

[9]See Peter Brown, *The World of Late Antiquity* (New York: Harcourt Brace, 1971, 34–40; no matter how tight the stratification of society, it never became impenetrable. Also see R. MacMullen, *Roman Social Relations* (New Haven: Yale, 1974), 88–120.

cation," schooling in rhetoric and philosophy, and have attained sufficient family pedigree. One also needs to remember that despite the travel and trade generated by the imperial order, no one was anonymous. People lived in a face-to-face society where neighbors and peers monitored every step. What is obvious for villages is also true of the cities. People lived close together among fellow countrymen or fellow tradesmen[10]—just as they do today in old Jerusalem or Cairo.

Even the third century was not one of unmitigated crisis.[11] The traditional society of the ancient world resisted change. "The new" was no virtue. Its visionaries did not seek to bring into being a new and glorious future but to recover a revered and glorious past. Modern authors sometimes think that Christians were an exception with their apocalyptic visions of the future. However, an ancient man would read those same visions with his focus on the key themes from the past that were to be realized in their true splendor: creation, paradise, exodus, new covenant, entry into the land, new (heavenly) temple. Recovery of one's origins, not movement to a radically different future, is the key.[12] Since people sought to recover the past, their tradition, and since they did not have print and electronic media documenting every change of style, they perceived much less discontinuity between themselves and their past than we do. Whatever one's group or society said/felt to be in continuity with the tradition

---

[10]Brown protests against the view that people were subject to alienation, rootlessness and loneliness. Their problems were more often those of close living and constant observation by one's peers, claustrophobia, and interpersonal tensions that often led to violent eruptions of anger; see *The Making of Late Antiquity* (Cambridge: Harvard University, 1978), 4. MaMullen, *Roman Social Relations*, 97f, points out that although merchants and artisans traveled, it was considered an ill to be avoided—as was changing the occupation into which one was born.

[11]From P. Brown, "Monks and Philosophers in Late Antiquity," lecture, Harvard University, March 5. 1979.

[12]The view that the future as a category can impinge on the present—rather than simply be the object of imaginative speculation and prophecy—is the creation of the modern reduction of the world to scientific law. Statistical models applied to problems of sociology, economy and ecology are expected to yield precise information about future conditions. See the attack on the pervasive use of "the future" as a category by E. T. H. Brann, *Paradoxes of Education in a Republic* (Chicago: University of Chicago, 1979), 140.

would be perceived as such by an individual regardless of what modern social historians might think.[13]

Historians have also commonly considered the increasing fascination with esoteric revelation and the influx of mystery cults, which archaeology shows to have hit the empire in the second century A. D., as symptoms of a decline in rationalism.[14] They suppose that this decline was the result of anxieties generated by massive social change. Again, this generalization derives from modern preoccupations. Peter Brown has shown the ancient situation to have been more complex.[15] He points to several common errors in the interpretation of ancient religion:[16]

(1) Because modern thinkers identify religion with the subjective, scholars have focused on the experience of unusually gifted individuals and have tried to translate ancient religious writings such as Gnostic myths into subjective experiences.[17] This approach runs counter to the realism shown by the ancients in their dealings with the divine.

(2) Since people assumed that the world was shared with invisible as well as visible beings and that one had the same sort of obligations to the invisible ones as to the visible, the pressures of dealing with the divine were not emotionally different from those of dealing with neighbors.

(3) Religion was taken absolutely for granted. People did not have to defend its possibility.

(4) Ancient religion was resolutely "upper worldly." This

---

[13]Brann, *Paradoxes*, 78f, suggests that our own sense of change is falsely exaggerated, since we mistake quantitative accumulation for qualitative alteration. Erosion of the sense of a usable tradition by academic historiography has intensified the illusion of "newness."

[14]A. J. Festugiere, *La Revelation d'Hermes Trismegiste, Vol. I,* rev. ed. (Paris: Gabalda, 1950), 1–18. M. Hengel, *Judentum und Hellenismus* (Tübingen: J. C. B. Mohr, 1969), 381–94, surveys these developments and their relationship to Jewish apocalyptic.

[15]See the discussion of Dodds' *Pagan and Christian* by P. Brown, "The Religious Crisis of the Third Century A.D.," *Religion and Society,* 79–84.

[16]Brown, *Making,* 9–20.

[17]Also see P. Berger, *The Heretical Imperative* (New York: Doubleday, Anchor, 1979), 32–54. Berger remarks that subjective experience is only a part of religious reality even for "moderns."

world, the sublunar, is riddled with tensions and change. The divine, above, contains what is unchanging, stable and true.

(5) Divine power and guidance were considered to be readily available. The educated with a secure tradition of learning and philosophy may have considered much religion superstition, but most people sought to distinguish between miracle and magic in terms of the source of divine power. Claims to divine power required careful social scrutiny.

(6) In the second century the boundary between human and divine was very fluid. Even educated men like Galen found dreams a valuable source of divine guidance.[18]

(7) Third-century people began to locate contact with the divine within the structure of the personality. Above the various layers of soul associated with the body, a "divine core" linked one to the divine. People began to claim personal, divine protection through this higher spirit, and, not surprisingly, status in the social hierarchy was correlated with that in the divine.

(8) The easy access to the divine of these centuries closes down in the fourth and fifth centuries. Philosophic emphasis on the transcendence of the divine had left the intellect as man's faculty for coming into contact with it. But Christianity's focus on will and sin as it was institutionalized in the ascetic movement stressed the difficulty of genuine contact with God. Divine power became limited to ascetic heroes and to special institutional channels, ecclesial office, Scripture and sacrament.

All these forces are felt in the Gnostic writings that we shall be studying. One must remember that they belong to the larger religious context of the Late Antique world and are not peculiarities of Gnostic speculation.

Religious changes begin to be felt at the end of the second and the beginning of the third centuries. The bearers of change are not the educated elite but the vast, diverse mass of humanity between them and the poor and rural peasant. (If one calls this group "middle class," one should remember that they do not share common characteristics beyond not belonging to the other groupings.) These are the

---

[18]See the discussion of Galen's approach to dreams in G. Bowersock, *Greek Sophists in the Roman Empire* (London/New York: Oxford, 1969), 73f.

people who have benefited most from the imperial order—merchants, businessmen, freedmen, administrators, and women from such families.[19] These demographic considerations have two important consequences. First, it is unlikely that people turned to religion out of feelings of personal helplessness and failure. People assumed that divine protectors acted much as powerful human patrons did. A person with the combination of drive and good fortune to obtain a powerful divine patron would be successful.[20] The negative images used for the state of those without gnosis in Gnostic myths should not be read as indices of private despair. Rather, they serve as an appropriate foil for the preaching of a saving revelation which its adherents felt to be an unexpected stroke of good fortune.[21]

Second, these people were not in a position to suffer a "decline of rationalism," since the leisured pursuit of philosophic learning had never been theirs to enjoy. Their traditions, knowledge, customs and beliefs were still embodied in oral traditions—in words, skills, and stories passed from one person to another. What is true is what has been passed down in story, proverb, maxim, and fable—in short, in what people say. It does not have to be discovered by the rigorous logic of analytic reason. Reasoning of that sort is a skill which only developed with the advent of literacy and which was not even then spread throughout the society.[22] For many, literacy was still a "craft," a skill learned by some whose services could then be pur-

---

[19]Brown, *World*, 62–68.

[20]See Brown's discussion of the Thessalos story in *Making*, 64f.

[21]Nock, *Conversion*, 9 (commenting on *Poimandres*), notes that any religion with a prophetic message must create the awareness of the need it is going to fulfill. Those who are said to be "asleep" or "drunk" are not aware of any need for the assistance of a heavenly revealer.

[22]See the important studies of the development of literacy and abstract cognition in E. Havelock, *The Origins of Western Literacy* (Toronto: Ontario Institute for Studies in Education, 1976), 18–21. Havelock argues that the flexibility of the phonetic alphabet in Greek was required to make a genuine popular literacy possible. He suggests that the repetitive, stilted character of Semitic epic derives from the necessity of enabling readers to make certain guesses as to meaning from a system of writing that does not completely render the spoken language. His *The Greek Concept of Justice* (Cambridge: Harvard, 1979) traces the development of "justice" from concrete examples of just behavior in Homeric epic to the abstract concept in Plato. He argues that a concept of "justice" was only possible once widespread literacy had made it possible for people to conceptualize "justice" as an entity by associating it with the written, visible word.

chased. If a community lost or forgot its stories, its identity and even its technical knowledge would be gone forever. People in the world we are studying were subject to mixed influences. "Philosophic culture" and its literacy were widely admired. People sought to possess trappings of it. The old religious traditions were being copied and written down in various forms. We find, for example, collections of oracles, apocalyptic visions, magic spells and formulae. Once written, these traditions circulated outside the guilds of religious practitioners who would have kept these things to themselves in earlier times. Gnostic writings mix such old oral and guild-oriented traditions with the abstract, analytic vocabulary of philosophy. This mixture does not represent a falling away from reason but a groping for truth and authority under the impact of literacy and analytic thought. Old myths, formulae, writing, and abstract philosophical terms all carried the aura of authority and, for the time being at least, it was not clear who the victor would be.

The traditions of a society which is completely oral are changed as they are retold so that they fit their context. People are not aware of such changes. But writing turns the tradition into a "past" which individuals can perceive as different from themselves.[23] Greek-speaking peoples experienced this phenomenon when they learned Homer. Every school child learned differences in vocabulary and some minimal interpretations of the Homeric text. For Jews, the Torah was becoming a "text" that required its own special class of interpreters. In both cases, a person could treat the interpretations given by the teacher as more "oral tradition." The individual did not have to adopt the radically different style of analytic thought and self-awareness that was initiated by literacy and would be brought to its apex by print media.[24] The attentive reader will notice that when the Gnostic interprets the Bible, he uses another story, his own myth of the origins. The Gnostic does not allegorize by turning the Bible or other stories about the gods into philosophic statements about the

---

[23]See J. Goody and I. Watt, "The Consequences of Literacy," *Language and Social Context*, ed. P. Gilioli (Baltimore: Penguin, 1972), 340.

[24]See the discussion of the history of media and its relationship to psychological structures in W. Ong, *The Presence of the Word* (New Haven: Yale, 1967), and his discussion of the oral character of biblical narrative in *Interfaces of the Word* (Ithaca: Cornell, 1977), 230–70.

soul and its progress toward perfection as Philo does, for example. A Gnostic does not discover the truth about the soul through an analytic description of its faculties and their interrelationships. Rather, he or she hears a story of its origins and destiny. Yet, the prestige of philosophical language makes this a hybrid story. The particularity of gods and goddesses vanishes behind a cosmology in which the operative agents are often abstract terms. Abstract terms sometimes appear in oral poetry as well. Just because a person uses them does not mean that he or she had made the transition to analytic thought. When a person who is non-analytic uses them, they appear as the subject of active verbs rather than as part of an argument that uses "is" to tie them to equally abstract predicates.[25] Gnostics generally use their abstractions in the oral, narrative mode rather than in the philosophic, analytic one.

Thus, we can see that any religion had to meet a number of issues. Increasing pressures of literacy were leading to the conversion of oral religious traditions into texts. Judaism and Christianity were able to accommodate the shift by developing a normative religious text, Sacred Scripture, and by developing ways of interpreting and hence living with a fixed canon. The shifting and fluid boundaries between human and divine made contact with it a live issue. How did a person best take advantage of the divine aid to be gained in this world or for the next? Ritual, magic, dream, a philosophic "turning around" within the soul, and, in time, even the sacred texts themselves emerge as candidates. Nock has pointed out that for the average person cultic and religious practices were considered a matter of individual inclination so long as public traditions and commitments were not threatened. But Judaism and, even more intensely, Christianity introduce a note of urgency lacking in polytheistic paganism. One is told that one must convert or break with a sinful past or be lost. This urgency would later appear in thoughtful pagans as they tried to shore up flagging traditions.[26] Association with Christianity seems to have altered the position of Gnostics. Some writings show the common pagan tolerance; others show all the urgency of Christian preachers.

---

[25]Havelock, *Justice*, 221–24, 307–29.
[26]Nock, *Conversion*, 10–16.

WHO ARE THE GNOSTICS?

We have already observed that Gnostic literary remains suggest that the movement comprised members of the growing "middle class" who sought an authority equivalent to educated discourse without having made the conversion to analytic thought. Esoteric and pseudo-scientific traditions, which had developed as "scribal wisdom" in the Hellenistic period, seem to have enjoyed wider diffusion in the second century. Gnostic evidence suggests that they followed the unstructured form of association typical of many Graeco-Roman cult associations.[27] Such groups had no fixed dogma. They used diverse rituals in different areas and drew on the leadership of individuals who had begun the asssociation—though leadership could be passed from father to son. A religious cult which had been transplanted from its native soil was quite different from the same cult back home. For such cults, sacred places cease to be important. Since the kind of traditional, large-scale, public ceremonial available at home cannot be transplanted into the foreign environment, the focus of the cult shifts to the relationship between the individual and the deity. Though Gnosticism did not derive from such a transplanted cult, it exhibits features common to them to an extreme degree: allegorical esotericism, freedom from any ties to place, and emphasis on individual transcendence.[28] Gnostics reject gods and religious traditions that are tied to this cosmos in any way at all! Thus, Gnostic mythology often seems devoid of ties to place or time. Such intensification of the tendencies of Hellenized cults suggests that the religious sensibilities and expectations of those who joined had already been formed in the milieu of Hellenized rather than of native traditions. Irenaeus' account of the varied opinons about ritual among Gnostics

---

[27]Brown, *World*, 62f; MacMullen, *Social Relations*, 82–87; R. Wild, "Diversification in Roman Period Isis Worship: The Nile Water Pitcher," *Society of Biblical Literature 1977 Seminar Papers*, ed. P. Achtemeier; Missoula: Scholars Press, 1977), 145–54.

[28]See the discussion of native and diaspora cult forms by J. Z. Smith, "Native Cults in the Hellenistic Period," *HistRel* 11 (1971), 236–49. The usual denial of nationalism in diaspora cults may have been intensified in Gnostic assertions that they are a "race without a king" and will "reign over the All."

(AdvHaer. I, 21) not only serves the rhetorical function of casti-
gating one's opponents for their inconsistency,[29] but it also suggests
the type of cultic variation one would expect in the Graeco-Roman
period.

Although we know the names of a few revered Gnostic teachers
like Basilides, Isidore, Valentinus, Heracleon, Marcus and possibly
Concessus and Macarius,[30] Gnostic writers show no interest in their
lives, authority or personalities. The heroes in the Gnostic dialogues
are either figures from primordial times or apostles and others from
the New Testament. Several dialogues clearly indicate that these
New Testament figures belong several generations in the past.[31] For
the Gnostic, then, contact with the divine is mediated through the
primordial revelation or through the rituals of the cult and not
through its association with particular, contemporary teachers, seers
or holy men. In this respect, the Gnostics remain firmly rooted in the
second century. They do not share the movement which will come to
associate divine power on earth with a limited number of exceptional
human agents.[32] Though Gnostic writings provide very few indications of time or place, we do find occasional hints as to their relationship with other groups. One writing even attacks other Gnostic

---

[29]See my "Irenaeus and the Gnostics," *VigChr* 30 (1976), 193–200.

[30]P. Bellet, "The Colophon of the *Gospel of the Egyptians:* Concessus and Macarius of Nag Hammadi," *Nag Hammadi and Gnosis,* NHS XIV, ed. R. McL. Wilson
(Leiden: E. J. Brill, 1978) 44–65, argues that Gnostics used "eugnostos" as a title for a
revered teacher. The "Concessus" of the colophon would have been such a teacher.
And—if "eugnostos" is indeed a Gnostic title—the treatise in Codex III, *3* and V, *1*
commonly called "Eugnostos, the Blessed *(macarios)*" should be called "eugnostos,
Macarius."

[31]See the discussion of the Apocryphon of James in Chapter Eight. Both Jewish
and pagan apocalyptic traditions claimed to derive from great figures of the past. The
revelation dialogues with the apostles as subjects come to play an important role in the
conflict between Gnostic and orthodox Christians over Church authority and individual access to the divine. See E. Pagels, "Visions, Appearances, and Apostolic Authority," *Gnosis. Fest. Hans Jonas,* ed. B. Aland (Göttingen: Vandenhoeck & Ruprecht,
1978), 415–30.

[32]Brown, *Making,* 32. Brown goes on to point out that the rise of the Christian
Church was directly tied to this shift. It focused divine power in a series of individuals:
apostles, martyrs, the ascetic heroes of the monastic movement, and, finally, the powerful ascetic bishops. These individuals were felt to be the link between heaven and
earth.

teachers by name—Valentinus, Isidore, and Basilides—apparently for not insisting on the stringent ascetic life favored by its author.[33] Since he is without ties to a particular place or nation, the Gnostic author does not feel compelled to locate his revelation within the history of a particular people as Christians had to do with respect to Judaism, for example.

Gnostics first appear as an identifiable group when they are attacked by Christian heresiologists in the second century. Until the discovery of the collection of Gnostic writings known as the Nag Hammadi codices,[34] only a few Gnostic writings were known. One had to rely on the heavily polemicized accounts given by their Christian opponents. Even from those sources, it was clear that Gnostics considered themselves members of the larger Christian community. They claimed to have a "higher, spiritual" interpretation of what Christians believed and of what they read in the Gospels and in the letters of Paul.[35] We also know from Plotinus' writing against the Gnostics that some Platonists from his own circles had adopted Gnostic teaching. His editor and biographer, Porphyry, mentions the titles of several writings read by these people. Two of them, *Allogenes* and *Zostrianos*, appear in the Nag Hammadi collection. Zostr is a revelation dialogue which we will be studying in Chapter Five. Both these writings and two others from the Nag Hammadi corpus, *Three Steles of Seth* and *Marsanes*, contain close parallels to metaphysical

---

[33]The *Testimony of Truth* (CG IX, *3*). See B. Pearson, "Anti-Heretical Warnings in Codex IX from Nag Hammadi," *Essays on the Nag Hammadi Texts, NHS* VI, ed. M. Krause (Leiden: E. J. Brill, 1975), 145–54, and K. Koschorke, *Die Polemik der Gnostiker gegen das kirchliche Christentum, NHS* XII (Leiden: E. J. Brill, 1978), 91–174.

[34]J. M. Robinson gives a short account of the discovery in *The Nag Hammadi Library in English*, ed J. M. Robinson (San Francisco: Harper & Row, 1977), 1–25. Further information is promised in the introductory volume to *The Facsimile Edition of the Nag Hammadi Codices* (Leiden: E. J. Brill), forthcoming. The general reader might also consult such general accounts of Gnosticism and the Nag Hammadi discoveries as J. Dart, *The Laughing Savior* (New York: Harper, 1976), and E. Pagels, *The Gnostic Gospels* (New York: Random House, 1979).

[35]See the discussion of Valentinian exegesis by E. Pagels, *The Johannine Gospel in Gnostic Exegesis* (Nashville: Abingdon, 1973), and *idem, The Gnostic Paul* (Philadelphia: Fortress, 1975). In the latter, she tries to reconstruct Gnostic interpretations for some Pauline texts.

language used by Plotinus. Thus, we gain a first-hand look at what a Gnostic Platonist considered to be the truth of that tradition.[36]

Codex VI contains a number of hermetic writings which seem to have developed out of the pseudo-scientific speculation that flourished in Hellenistic Alexandria. Hermetism constituted an identifiable strain of esoteric wisdom which Festugiere thinks was handed on in "schools" similar to those formed by various philosophical groups.[37] The Nag Hammadi hermetica suggest that some of these groups also had cultic practices such as prayer and had been influenced by the language of the mystery cults.[38]

One must remember that although we speak of the Nag Hammadi library, codices or corpus, these writings did not form a Gnostic sacred scripture like the various writings in our Bible. The very diversity of writings and doctrines represented in the collection has led some scholars like the late J. Barns to suggest that the collection was made for heresiological purposes. He points, for example, to the scribal colophons attached to the hermetic writings. The scribe apologizes for having copied a writing that the recipient might already possess. He refers to an hermetic prayer as something that "they said."[39] The hermetic traditions are sufficiently close to Gnostic concerns that they could have been used either by someone who wished to expose false gnosis or by someone who was a Gnostic collecting esoteric writings, even though they are best considered an independent religious development.[40]

---

[36]See the discussion of the relationship between these writings in J. M. Robinson, "The Three Steles of Seth and the Gnostics of Plotinus," *Proceedings of the International Colloquium on Gnosticism*, ed. G. Widengren (Stockholm: Almqvist; Leiden: E. J. Brill, 1977), 132–42; B. Pearson, "The Tractate Marsanes (NHC X) and the Platonic Tradition," *Gnosis. Fest. Hans Jonas*, 373–84; P. Perkins, "Deceiving the Deity."

[37]See Festugiere, *Revelation Vol. II* (1949), 28–50.

[38]See K. W. Troger, "On Investigating the Hermetic Documents contained in Nag Hammadi Codex VI. The Present State of Research," *Nag Hammadi and Gnosis*, 117–21 and the literature cited there.

[39]See J. Barns, "Greek and Coptic Papyri from the Covers of the Nag Hammadi Codices," *Essays on the Nag Hammadi Texts*, 9–18, and the discussion of the possibility that the collection was made by an heresiologist in T. Save-Soderbergh, "Holy Scriptures or Apologetic Documents? The 'Sitz im Leben' of the Nag Hammadi Library," *Les Textes de Nag Hammadi*, 3–14.

[40]See, for example, J. P. Mahe, "Les sens des symboles sexuels dans quelques textes hermetiques et gnostiques," *Les Textes de Nag Hammadi*, 123–45.

Finally, there is an unresolved question as to the relationship between the actual codices and early Christian monastic settlements in the region where they were found. Materials used in the cartonage, such as old letters, date from the mid-third century. They refer to figures in the Pachomian movement—perhaps even to Pachomius himself.[41] This evidence has been variously assessed. Robinson and Wisse suggest that the monastic movement was so amorphous that Gnostics, whose ascetic convictions are well documented now, could have joined it. They may have been driven to do so as formal persecution increased in the villages.[42] After all, Athanasius' biography of St. Anthony praises him for not associating with Manichaeans *except to convert them* (Vit. Ant. c. 68)! Save-Soderbergh rejects this suggestion because the lives of Pachomius stress the founder's hostility to Gnosticism (and Origenism). He does admit, however, that one cannot be sure that the authors have not idealized the "orthodoxy" of their founder to suit somewhat later standards.[43] The "monastic rabble" was highly suspect among both pagan and Christian members of the Egyptian "upper classes." The two groups easily joined forces against them.[44] Investigation of the early monastic movement suggests that organization into hermitic and cenobitic types was quite diverse in the third and early fourth centuries. The master-disciples style of ascetic life had engendered a number of variations, and a single individual might move from one to another.[45] Thus, while some caution is in order, it is possible to consider the Nag Hammadi codices to have been the possession of ascetics who found such gnosis suitable to their spirituality rather than something to be attacked. We can only hope for further archaeological or papyrological evidence to help us understand the context in which the collection was made.

---

[41]See Barns, "Greek and Coptic Papyri," 13–17.

[42]Robinson, *NHLE*, 16–21; F. Wisse, "Gnosticism and Early Monasticism in Egypt," *Gnosis. Fest. Hans Jonas*, 431–40.

[43]Save-Soderbergh, "Holy Scriptures," 8–11.

[44]P. Brown, "Monks and Philosophers"; P. Rousseau, *Ascetics, Authority and the Church* (London: Oxford, 1978), 9–11; and on the problems in dealing with the Lives of Pachomius, *ibid.*, 17f.

[45]Rousseau, *Ascetics*, 33–49, points out that there was a range of monastic lifestyles from hermit to master and disciples to cenobitic community.

The reader will have noticed that in all these instances Gnostics come into view as the "underside" of a larger religious movement. They claim to have the deeper wisdom of Christianity, hermetism, Platonic mysticism, and perhaps, even, of ascetic withdrawal. Both. Christian and philosophical opponents of Gnosticism assume that members of their circles could easily slip into the movement. Outsiders would probably identify people we would call Gnostics simply as Christians, hermetists, Platonists, or monks. They may well have described themselves in the same fashion. Thus, when we use the term "Gnosticism," we should remember that it was not a neatly defined sociological entity.[46] Rather, gnosis seems to flourish as a religious or intellectual movement which claims to give the deeper significance of a tradition held by members of a larger group to which the Gnostics also belong. They developed modes of interpretation that enabled them to maintain this identity—at least until their efforts to win others over evoked sufficient attention and/or persecution to force them out of that larger group.

For the most part, the mythic and revelatory traditions used by Gnostic authors are similar to other Hellenistic reworkings of ancient Near Eastern mythologies and to the pseudo-scientific lore of astrology and medicine. Some writers also know the scientific debates of the second century and reformulate what they know as Gnostic cosmological tradition accordingly.[47] This "underside" of the Hellenistic achievements in philosophy and science may have originated in Alexandria, but it had probably spread in the other eastern cities known for their centers of learning. It would appeal to those who sought more than the cultic immortality promised by a mystery religion (an immortality also promised in ritually oriented Gnostic sects). They sought the authority and prestige of "knowledge."

While we have discussed the relationship between Gnosticism

---

[46]This plurality is one of the major difficulties in pursuing a quest for Gnostic origins, as the papers from the Messina Congress made clear: *Le origini dello gnosticismo* (Supplements to *Numen* XII), ed. U. Bianchi (Leiden: E. J. Brill, 1967). Even the limitation of the term "Gnosticism" to the sociologically identifiable groups of the second century does not resolve all the problems raised by the diversity within the Nag Hammadi corpus.

[47]See my "On the Origin of the World."

and pagan cults, Christianity, and philosophy, we have not yet touched one of the most puzzling aspects of Gnostic writings—their consistent antipathy toward the Jewish Creator God.[48] Several Gnostic writings make little or no reference to Christianity, but hardly a single one can tell the story of origins without reference to the God of the Old Testament. Hans Jonas has described this strain of revolt at/against Judaism as "a kind of metaphysical anti-Semitism." He does not think it likely that this sweeping condemnation, which belongs to the most archaic levels of Gnostic myth, originated with Judaism. But it suggests that these traditions were formed by people who lived in close vicinity to Judaism and in reaction against it.[49]

Several examples of what appear to be Jewish midrashic traditions inverted by Gnostic exegesis appear in the Nag Hammadi writings. Some of them even depend upon an Aramaic or Hebrew text.[50] Gnostic stories portray the Old Testament God as vain, ignorant, envious, and jealous—a malicious Creator who uses every means at his disposal to keep humanity from attaining its true perfection. For example, one Gnostic tradition says of him:

> What kind of God is he? First, he envied Adam that he ate from the tree of knowledge. Second, he said to Adam, "Where are you?" God has no foreknowledge, since he did not know that. Afterward, he said, "Let us cast him out of this place so that he will not eat from the tree of life and live forever." Thus, he has shown that he is a malicious envier. What kind of God is this? (Those who read and do not

---

[48]The many articles in the Messina volume which treat parallels between Gnosticism and Judaism show how extensive the relationship is. In addtion, see W. C. van Unnik, "Gnosis und Judentum," *Gnosis. Fest. Hans Jonas*, 65–86, and G. MacRae, "Nag Hammadi and the New Testament," *ibid.*, 144–50, who uses the same contacts to argue for the existence of a pre-Christian Gnosticism.

[49]H. Jonas, "Delimitation of the Gnostic Phenomenon," *Le origini*, 101f. We doubt that he is correct in attributing hatred of Judaism to the latter's "this worldly" attitude. There is no ancient evidence for such a charge against Judaism.

[50]See the discussion of the Gnostic use of Jewish haggadah in B. Pearson, "The Figure of Norea in Gnostic Literature," *International Colloquium on Gnosticism*, 143–52; *idem*, "Jewish Haggadic Traditions in the Testimony of Truth," *Ex Orbe Religionum. For G. Widengren* (Supplements to *Numen* XXI), ed. J. Bergman (Leiden: E. J. Brill, 1972), 457–70; *idem*, "Biblical Exegesis in Gnostic Literature," *Armenian and Biblical Studies*, ed. M. Stone (Jerusalem, 1976), 70–80.

recognize it are blind indeed!) He said, "I am a jealous God. I will bring the sins of the fathers on the children to the third and fourth generation." And he said, "I will harden their hearts and blind their minds so that they will neither know nor understand the things that are said." But he said these things to those who believe in and serve him![51]

Such sentiments are common in Gnostic writings. While they may represent an attack on Judaism by outsiders who had access to the Scriptures as Jonas has suggested, other scholars find the evidence so overwhelming that they postulate a revolt within Judaism itself. George MacRae thinks that Gnosticism arose as a revolutionary movement within Hellenized Jewish wisdom and apocalyptic circles. The movement then found a natural affinity with Christianity, since it also arose as a set of Jewish heresies.[52] Many Gnostics claim to be descended from Seth.[53] This identification would seem odd in a group without any ties to Jewish tradition. Klijn finds the exegetical background for the Gnostic claim that Seth was a "different seed" in Philo.[54] Study of the dualistic heresy of "two powers in heaven" that appears in second and third heterodox Judaism has shown that before that time the problem of anthropomorphism had led Jewish interpreters to a doctrine of a "second god" of "divine power" to be the subject of anthropomorphic statements in Scripture.[55] The passage we have just read could well stem from a catalogue of such texts.

We are inclined to a slightly different reading of the evidence than either Jonas or MacRae. The traditions underlying such passages must, it seems to us, be Jewish in origin. However, that origin

---

[51]TestTr, CG IX _3_ 47, 14–48, 15. Author's translation from the photographs published in J. M. Robinson, ed., _The Facsimile Edition of the Nag Hammadi Codices. Codices IX & X_ (Leiden: E. J. Brill, 1977).

[52]MacRae, "Nag Hammadi and the New Testament," 150.

[53]See A. F. J. Klijn, _Seth in Jewish, Christian and Gnostic Literature_ (Leiden: E. J. Brill, 1977), for a useful survey, though we question his Christian Gnostic reading of ApocAd, pp. 90f; G. MacRae, "Seth in Gnostic Texts and Traditions," _SBL 1977 Seminar Papers_, 17–24; B. Pearson, "Egyptian Seth and Gnostic Seth," _ibid._, 25–43.

[54]Klijn, _Seth_, 25–27; Philo, _Post. Caini_ x. 42, 124f, 173f, 177.

[55]A. Segal, _Two Powers in Heaven. Early Rabbinic Reports about Christianity and Gnosticism_ (Leiden: E. J. Brill, 1978).

does not mean that there was a Jewish Gnosticism as such in the first century. The "powers in heaven" and "seed of Seth" traditions belong to the general line of esoteric interpretations that cuts across many religious movements in the period. Perhaps Alexandrian Jews are responsible for both. If we follow MacRae's suggestion that "Gnostics" and Christians both represent Jewish heresies, one has to remember that Christians remained within Jewish circles for much of the first century—at least in some areas. Both they and Jews interested in such interpretations were forced out when Judaism began to consolidate its tradition and to draw back from its more radical ventures into cultural accommodation. Johannine scholars have shown that expulsion from the synagogue left deep scars on the language tradition of that group of Christians.[56] We suggest that the hostility and ambivalence toward Judaism in Gnostic writings—so similar to the Johannine version that some have taken it as evidence of Gnostic influence on John—seem to us to derive from a similar experience in which the Jewish community acted violently and decisively against such speculation. The end of the first century would seem to have been the period in which such "tightening up" occurred. It seems probable that some of these heterodox Jews would find their way into Christian circles where Jewish tradition is both accepted and rejected. It is possible that this is the context in which what we know as characteristic Gnostic exegesis of the Old Testament arose. The esoteric and perhaps philosophizing interpretations of the Old Testament were turned against that tradition and its God. Those who moved into Christian circles gained confidence for their attack from the Christian view that God had rejected the unbelieving Jews in favor of a new people of God. When Christians refused to accept the Gnostic readings of the Old Testament, a whole new area of controversy arose. This controversy is the one for which we have evidence in patristic writers and, from the Gnostic side, in many Nag Hammadi writings.

Obviously, there is no simple account of the origins of Gnosticism. Traditions of esoteric and pseudo-scientific interpretation had been developing in different quarters throughout the Hellenistic peri-

---

[56]See the groundbreaking work of J. L. Martyn, *History and Theology in the Fourth Gospel*, rev. ed. (Nashville: Abingdon, 1979).

od. The original interpretations may even have been more sophisti-cated than the versions we find embedded in mythological stories. By the time we find them in Gnostic writers, we are not dealing with di-rect readings of the Bible but established Gnostic traditions which are being reworked and reinterpreted. The Gnostics never take the further step achieved by both Judaism and Christianity—that of can-onizing certain written embodiments of their tradition as Sacred Scripture.

THE GNOSTIC DIALOGUE

Our discussion so far has shown that Gnostics thrive on "dia-logue" in the widest sense. Their very existence demands that they appropriate the originating insights of other traditions. Anyone who is to possess the "deeper truth" must stand over against some esoter-ic tradition. No great religious leader or prophet, no Moses or Jesus, no great philosopher, no Heraclitus, Plato or Aristotle, stands at the source of Gnosticism. Instead, the movement seems to have emerged from the popularization of scribal wisdom and pseudo-scientific lore in the Graeco-Roman period.

Many Gnostic writings adopt the dialogue as part of their literary form.[57] Unlike the lively drama of the Platonic dialogue or the more pedantic style of the philosophic dialogue employed by a Cicero or Augustine, the Gnostic dialogue does not aim at an exchange of ideas and an examination of philosophical positions. The Gnostic dialogue sets off statements of Gnostic myth and teaching. The artifi-ciality of some of the questions suggests that the protagonists never represent a real alternative. They merely provide the revealer with an opportunity to discharge his mission. Thus, the philosophic dialogue tradition can hardly have been a source for Gnostic composition. Other types of dialogue may represent more proximate models. Jew-ish apocalypses routinely have heavenly journeys or visions in which

---

[57]See the discussions of the Gnostic revelation dialogue by K. Rudolph, "Der gnostische Dialog als literarische Genus," *Probleme der koptischen Literatur* (Wiss. Beitr. Martin-Luther Univ., Halle-Wittenburg, 1968/1 K2), 85–107, and P. Perkins, "The Gnostic Revelation Dialogue as Religious Polemic," *Aufstieg und Niedergang der romischen Welt II, 22,* ed. W. Haase (Berlin/New York: Walter de Gruyter), forthcoming.

the seer questions an angelic guide about what he has seen. Gnostic revelation dialogues contain examples of this type of questioning. The esoteric, pseudo-scientific traditions also cast some revelations as dreams or visions in which the teaching comes through conversation with the deity. Hermetists cast such lore into the form of a teacher/pupil dialogue. They were less interested in the magic and astrological concerns of such writings than in a philosophical description of reality and of the soul's divinization.[58] Other interpreters think that the Gnostics followed the *erotapokriseis* model.[59] This type of writing is frequently used to give questions and answers to problems of Homeric exegesis or of jurisprudence. Thus, it is primarily instructional but lacks the introductory "setting" characteristic of Platonic and other philosophical dialogues.[60] Most Gnostic revelation dialogues invoke New Testament stories to provide a setting for the dialogue. Thus, they are not simply *erotapokriseis*, though some of their question/answer content may derive from such a source. A post-resurrection scene is most popular. We also find allusions to the opening chapters of Acts and to the farewell discourses in John. Just as the origins of Gnosticism seem to come from diverse sources, so also their dialogues seem to have drawn on a variety of models. The settings to the dialogues often provide important clues about an author's opponents. They have a polemic edge which sets them apart from the more irenic instructional dialogues.[61]

Two passages in non-dialogue writings may refer to the revelation dialogue. *Great Power* (VI, 4) says of the revelation which comes after Jesus has apparently died and has descended to Hades:

And after these things, he will appear ascending. The sign of the aeon to come will appear, and the aeons will dissolve. Those who understand these things which have been told

---

[58]Festugiere, *Revelation Vol. I*, 312–54.

[59]See H. Dorrie, "Erotapokriseis," *Realexikon fur Antike und Christentum 6* (Stuttgart: Hiersemann, 1967), 342–48.

[60]Thus, Rudolph, "Dialog," 89f, rejects Dorrie's claim that *erotapokriseis* was the prototype for the Gnostic writings. However, his own preference for the hermetic model does not encompass all the examples either.

[61]Education itself was always carried on in a polemical vein. One arrived at the truth by taking a side and defending it, not by impartial analysis.

them will be blessed. They will appear, and will be blessed, since they will know the truth; since you (pl.) have found rest in the heavens.[62]

This passage seems to refer to the type of dialogue in which Jesus instructs disciples in gnosis before his ascension. Those instructed are then sent out to preach. The second example comes from a very fragmentary treatise, *Melchizedek* (IX, 1).[63] A reference to the resurrection precedes the comment: ". . . holy disciples. And the Savior will reveal to them the word that gives life to the All" (4, 4–6). The next page tells us that the preaching of Jesus has been perverted:

> They will come in his name. They will say that he was not begotten, though he was begotten; that he did not eat, though he eats; that he did not drink, though he drinks; that he was uncircumcised, though he is circumcised; that he was not in the flesh, though he came in the flesh; that he did not come to suffering, though he came to suffering; that he did not rise from the dead, though he rose from the dead.[64]

You will notice that some of the doctrines attacked here were commonly upheld in other Gnostic circles. If more of the surrounding pages had survived, we might have been able to figure out the role played by the reference to the revelation dialogue in what seems to have been a dispute between different groups of Gnostic Christians. The author seems to be appealing to the instructions for preaching given by the risen Jesus. This example also warns us that Gnostic thinkers are as diverse in their views as early Christians were.

After discussing the common elements of structure, composition and content in the revelation dialogues in Part One, we will analyze the major types of dialogue in their polemic context in Part

---

[62]GrPow, CG VI *4* 42, 18–31. Author's translation from the text in M. Krause and P. Labib, *Gnostische und Hermetische Schriften aus Codex II und Codex VI* (Gluckstadt: J. J. Augustin, 1971).

[63]See Pearson, "Anti-Heretical Warnings," 147.

[64]Melch, CG IX *1, 5,* 1–11. Author's translation from the photographs in the *Facsimile Edition Codices IX & X.*

Two. Part Three returns to a more synthetic discussion of Gnosticism as a specific mode of religious and theoretical speculation. In this last part, we will be dealing primarily with the interaction between Gnosticism and Christianity, since the evidence of the revelation dialogues, at least, suggests that that is the context in which their thought took shape.

PART ONE

Literary Characteristics of the Gnostic Dialogue

CHAPTER TWO

Techniques of Dialogue Composition

We have seen that Gnostic authors had a variety of dialogue models to follow. Pedagogical question-answer dialogues, philosophical dialogues, and dialogues that occur as part of a revelation by a heavenly being were all well-known. At the same time, the frequency with which Gnostics set their dialogues into a post-resurrection appearance of Jesus suggests that they considered that a distinct type of dialogue. It seems to have formed an important part of the Gnostic debate with Christianity. Such dialogues sought to establish the claim of Christian Gnosticism to be the true intention of the revelation in Jesus. Although these dialogues sometimes contain revelations of an apocalyptic type, they do not follow the angel-seer model of the Jewish apocalypses.[1] Nor does one find the deity-devotee of the pagan esoterica. In many instances, the teacher-pupil mode of *erotapokriseis* is appropriate to the content of these dialogues. But since the risen Lord often stands in the position of "teacher," characteristics of the heavenly, angelic revealer also appear in the descrip-

---

[1]See the study of the apocalypse as a genre, ed. J. J. Collins, *Apocalypse: The Morphology of a Genre*, *Semeia* 14 (Missoula: Scholars Press, 1979). The volume contains a helpful survey by F. Fallon, "The Gnostic Apocalypses," 123–58, which tries to classify all the various Gnostic revelations according to a scheme worked out by Collins on the basis of Jewish apocalypses. Fallon's study does not deal with such independent sub-types as the revelation dialogue and has modified the "master paradigm" to fit the anomalies of the Gnostic case. See my comments in "The Rebellion Myth in Gnostic Apocalypses," *Society of Biblical Literature 1978 Seminar Papers*, ed. P. J. Achtemeier (Missoula: Scholars Press, 1978), 15f, 27. The two Gnostic revelation dialogues in which the revealer is not Jesus, NatArc and Zostr, both have ties to Jewish models. The questions posed in the former concern Gnostic teaching and the fate of

tion. This type of dialogue is widespread enough and stable enough in its characteristics to be recognized as an independent literary genre.[2] The relationship between this tradition and the two revelation dialogues which are not overtly Christian, NatArc (II, 4) and Zostr (VIII, 1), must be assessed in the context of their interpretation. Those who hold that these writings also come from Christian Gnostic circles would consider them further examples of the genre. On the other hand, if one considers them the product of non-Christian Gnostic groups, then one has two alternatives. They may have been influenced by the Christian Gnostic dialogue, or they may reflect an independent formulation of the revelation dialogue on the basis of Jewish models, which were also influential in the Christian Gnostic type.

THE GNOSTIC REVELATION DIALOGUE AS A LITERARY GENRE

The revelation dialogue seems to have been as characteristic of Christian Gnostics as the Gospel was of orthodox Christians.[3] However, as PetPhil (CG VIII 2 133, 15–17) shows, Gnostics would eventually be forced to ground their claims in the teaching of the earthly Jesus as well as that of the Risen One.[4] Our perception of the

---

the Gnostics. The latter contains a heavenly journey but the angels concern themselves with a mystic soteriology, not with visions seen by the seer. Collins, "Jewish Apocalypses," *Apocalypse*, 33–35, notes that the dialogue in 2 Bar and 4 Ezra takes a more dogmatic turn, since those writings are concerned with theodicy. 4 Ezra may also be directed against other-worldly mysticism. This turn may represent a more general second-century shift toward the revelation of more speculative knowledge. Within Jewish circles the concern with theodicy may not only have been a reaction to the fall of Jerusalem but a way of participating in the larger cultural debate over the order of the cosmos that had been precipitated by Stoic discussions of determinism and human freedom.

[2]So Rudolph, "Dialog," 89. Further evidence that the revelation dialogue was recognized as a powerful weapon in the Gnostic debate with orthodoxy may be inferred from the *Epistula Apostolorum*, which seems to be an orthodox attempt to use the genre against Gnostic opponents by presenting the content of post-resurrection revelation as identical with the teaching of the canonical Gospels. See M. Hornschuch, *Studien zur Epistula Apostolorum*, PTS 5 (Berlin: Walter de Gruyter, 1965).

[3]See J. M. Robinson, "On the Gattung of Mark (and John)," *Jesus and Man's Hope Vol. I*, ed. D. Miller (Pittsburgh: Pittsburgh Theological Seminary, 1970), 114–17.

[4]*Ibid.*, 114.

genre of any writing is an important help in interpreting it. The implication of particular details may change radically if we change our view of a writing's genre.[5] Thus, some hypothesis as to genre is a necessary heuristic tool for the interpreter.

The interrelationship between interpretation and genre also means that our description of the Gnostic revelation dialogue as a literary genre cannot help but be dependent upon our interpretation of some of their traits. Hirsch suggests that the best way to describe a literary genre is to study the common features of texts that have established historical relationships, such as is clearly the case with the Gnostic writings.[6] New literary types do not spring into being out of nowhere. They invoke metaphor and the ability of the imagination to embrace novelty by analogy with the familiar. New types commonly result either from expansion of an existing type or from the amalgamation of two older types.[7] Even with fairly formal literary canons, no single instance of a genre will exhibit all the traits of the type. The interpreter must evaluate such departures from type. Is the genre so well known that certain traits may be taken for granted without being developed? Has the author chosen to focus only on a particular aspect of the genre in question? Or is the author deliberately suggesting an established genre in order to depart from it in a new direction? We cannot always reach a consensus on such questions, and interpretations of a text will vary accordingly.

When M. Krause compared DialSav with other revelation dialogues, for example, he developed the following outline as a definiton of the genre: (1) setting: post-resurrection; (2) question/dialogue; (3) action; (4) conclusion.

Of the group he studied, DialSav is the only one which lacks a

---

[5] See the general discussion of genre in E. Hirsch, *Validity in Interpretation* (New Haven: Yale, 1967), 70–90, and the telling discussion of "spiritual and symbolic interpretations" in the analysis of a contemporary novel by F. Kermode, *The Genesis of Secrecy* (Cambridge: Harvard University, 1979), 1–21. The problem of interpretation is even more difficult when dealing with Gnostic texts in which there is no shared world of literary discourse to guide the analysis. The caricature of the Jewish God in many Gnostic accounts may be intended as irony. See my discussion of the problem of irony in ApocAd in my "Genre and Function of the Apocalypse of Adam," *CBQ* 39 (1977), 382–95.

[6] Hirsch, *Validity*, 110.

[7] *Ibid.*, 105.

setting. Krause also notes that the function of the dialogue varies widely in the group. There is no other dialogue exactly like DialSav.[8] Depending upon the number of details taken into account in the analysis, the same might be said of any of the other revelation dialogues. The interpreter must then decide whether the author is simply presuming a feature, the setting, as seems to be the case with DialSav, has dropped it for some other reason, or is trying to operate with a different genre. That last assumption underlies the claims of other scholars that DialSav has expanded a dialogue source that consisted of an interpretation of sayings of Jesus like GTh.[9]

SOURCE AND REDACTION CRITICISM

The hypothesis that DialSav has redacted an earlier dialogue points to a further complication in understanding these writings. Krause points to different ways in which the dialogue is related to its context.[10] Two examples will make this difference clear. The first exchange is typical of dialogue on the meaning of Genesis in ApocryJn:

> And I said to the Savior, "What is 'sleep'?" And he said, "Not as Moses wrote, what you have heard. For he said in his first book that he laid him down; but (it is) in his perception. For he said through the prophet, 'I will harden their hearts so that they do not understand or see.'"[11]

---

[8]M. Krause, "Der *Dialog des Soter* in Codex III von Nag Hammadi," *Gnosis and Gnosticism*, NHS VIII, ed. M. Krause (Leiden: E. J. Brill, 1977), 20–22. It will be obvious from Chart One that we disagree with his claim that only DialSav lacks a setting. We find close analogies between it and ThCont, also without a setting, which suggests that they are a sub-group that has developed in a very special situation; see Chapter Six. We also would not include GTh as a revelation dialogue, though it does derive from the same context as these other two writings. See E. Pagels and H. Koester, "Report on the Dialogue of the Savior," *Nag Hammadi and Gnosis*, 67f.

[9]So Pagels-Koester, *loc. cit.*

[10]Krause, "Dialog des Soter," 20. There is no real dialogue in GTh. ThCont and SJC seem to have inserted or used dialogue for aesthetic reasons. There is no real relationship between the dialogue and the content. PetPhil uses a set list of Gnostic questions to create a dialogue. The exchanges in DialSav and GMary, on the other hand, do serve to advance the discussion and to introduce new material.

[11]CG II *1* 22, 21–28; author's translation from the text in M. Krause and P. Labib, *Die Drei Versionen des Apokryphon des Johannes*, ADAIK 1 (Wiesbaden: Otto Harrassowitz, 1962).

The general form of this type of dialogue is *erotapokriseis*. It is introduced by the question, "What does the text mean by 'x'?" The content and concern with biblical interpretation are indebted to Jewish haggadah so that the passage might be assigned to the more limited type "midrash."[12] However, as in the example from TestTr above, the passage turns midrash against itself. It argues for a rejection of the authority of the common sense of Scripture. Now consider the opening of the Genesis exegesis section in DialSav:

> Judas said, "Tell us, Lord, before heaven and earth were, what was?" The Lord said, ". . . heaven and water and spirit over them. I tell you that what you are seeking and asking about is within you and . . . of the power and . . . the spirit so that . . . the wickedness which comes from the mind and . . ."[13]

Here Judas' question leads first to an affirmation of the opening of Genesis. Then the importance of such speculation is rejected. The disciple is not to be concerned with the external spirit and its role in cosmology. What counts is an understanding of the spirit within.[14] Such concerns are characteristic of the milieu from which DialSav comes. Its dialogue seeks information about Gnostic teaching rather than interpretation of Scripture against a Jewish or Jewish-Christian tradition of interpretation.

---

[12]Pearson, "Haggadic Traditions," 208–11.

[13]CG III *5* 127, 19–128, 9; author's translation from the photographs in the *Facsimile Edition: Codex III* (1976).

[14]Pagels and Koester, 66f, also note the difference in type of dialogue between DialSav and ApocryJn. They suggest that DialSav is not as hostile to Jewish traditions as ApocryJn, but it does undercut the "plain sense" of the tradition. The fragmentary condition of the manuscript makes interpretation of DialSav difficult. The continuation of this passage includes statements about the positive action of the logos in the cosmos despite the negative forces to which it is subject. This evaluation of the logos is similar to that in TriTrac. Both these interpretations differ from Philo—to whom Pagels and Koester appeal—in that they continue to use personified, mythic language about the logos. They do not use a systematically articulated philosophical doctrine to interpret the creation story as Philo does. Nor do the Gnostic writings evidence a clearly defined doctrine of the relationship between mind, soul and virtue such as we find in Philo. Thus, the "spiritual meaning" of the text is always in terms of another story rather than of a psychological process.

The usual analyses of Nag Hammadi texts have taken them apart into sources, which are then painstakingly stitched together by the redactional work of one or more authors.[15] The account of their structure is then modeled on some overarching claims about revelatory genre,[16] focused on their dogmatic content so that some of the revelation dialogues have been characterized as "like dogmatic manuals,"[17] or described in terms of a theological position as in the discussion of DialSav as an "interpretation of baptismal salvation in terms of a Gnostic future eschatology."[18] Instead, we need to attend to the genre requirements that bring together a number of common elements in a collection of dialogues whose content suggests that they derive from different contexts and hold diverse theological views. Chart One picks out major features of structure and content which occur in at least sixty percent of the examples known to us.

Study of the details of setting and content in the next two chapters will attend to features shared by fewer dialogues. Analysis of individual texts will deal with the particular omissions of individual works. The first section of the chart shows that the incidents of angelic appearance, I AM predications, and rebuke of the fearful disciples belong together. One may legitimately ask whether cases in which one of the three is missing expect the audience to supply the missing item. Similarly, it seems clear that Gnostic writers identify appearances of the Risen Lord with the commissioning scenes that we find in the canonical Gospels. By associating their teaching with the Risen Lord the Gnostics not only avoided the problem of deriving it from the traditional teaching of the earthly Jesus but were able to claim it as the true, definitive revelation of the Savior. We see that whenever the text emphasizes the hidden character of what is revealed, it mentions persecution of the Gnostics in a fashion which suggests that more is involved than a normal skepticism at such preaching. While there are various kinds of dialogue in these writ-

---

[15]See J.-E. Menard, "La Lettre de Pierre à Philippe: sa structure," *Nag Hammadi and Gnosis*, 103–107, who speaks of many Nag Hammadi texts as fragments of traditional materials with glosses.

[16]As in Fallon, "Gnostic Apocalypses," 124–26, despite his modification of the "master paradigm."

[17]Menard, "Lettre," 107.

[18]Pagels-Koester, "Report," 68–71.

CHART ONE

Features Common to Gnostic Revelation Dialogues

	I,1	II,1	II,4	II,7	III,4	III,5	V,3	VI,1	VII,3	VIII,1	VIII,2	BG	PS
setting						–							
risen savior			–							–			
revealer's appear.													
angelic	–			?		–	–	–					
I AM proclam.	–			–		–							
rebuke discip.	–			–		–		–	–				
opponents mentioned													
are to preach gnosis					–	?		?					
to face persecution					–	?		–	–	–			
revelation hidden						?							
post-resurrection commission			–	–		?				–			
questions													
listed	–					–	–	–	–				
erotapokriseis	?												
CONTENT													
Sophia myth	–			–		–		–	–				
ascetic preach.		–	–				?		–				
ascent soul			–	–					–	–			
Xt=Gnostic sav.													
Chr'n-Gnostic doctrine			–					–		?			

– means that feature is missing in the work in question. ? means that feature is subject to interpretation of difficult or fragmentary text.

ings, almost all contain questions of the *erotapokriseis* type. A large number also include lists of Gnostic questions addressed to the revealer in a block. Some do contain lengthy descriptions of the highest God and the pleroma. But the common practice is to deal with the Sophia myth, soteriology, ascent of the soul, asceticism and the true interpretation of Christianity.[19] Whatever sources an individual author may have used for the various elements in his work, there does seem to have been a common pattern in the composition of revelation dialogues.

CHARACTERISTICS OF ORAL COMPOSITION

We have seen that the Gnostics still operate within the conventions of a world of oral tradition. Ong has shown that throughout the patristic period writing is dominated by oral patterns of composition, since literacy has not yet been deeply interiorized.[20] Written compositions were often conceived of as spoken performances—just as education retained its ties with the oral world by focusing on recitation.[21] Those who heard a text related to it by repeating it and thus "hearing the word" even while reading alone. For the ancient, unlike the modern, reading was a participatory experience. This observation has important consequences for composition. Minimally, the tight linear organization of argument or of modern narrative plot is out of

---

[19]Fallon's attempt to make present salvation through knowledge the defining characteristic of the Gnostic apocalypses, "Gnostic Apocalypses," 125, is too broad to fit the genre. Many Gnostic writings are engaged in intense debate over present and future salvation both with Christians and with other Gnostics. Contrast the judicious observations about eschatology in DialSav made by Pagels-Koester, "Report," 68–71, with Fallon's outline of the same work, *op. cit.*, 141.

[20]Ong, *Interfaces*, 271.

[21]Ong, *ibid.*, 259–66. This overlap in media and corresponding types of consciousness must be taken into account in the various debates over "oral tradition and the Gospels." C. Talbert's response to A. Lord, "Oral Literature and the Gospels," *The Relationships among the Gospels: An Interdisciplinary Dialogue*, ed. W. O. Walker (San Antonio: Trinity University, 1978), 93–102, provides many examples of how such modes of thought have been translated into the literary style of educated writers like Plutarch who at the same time use written sources in their composition. The mixture of styles used by Gnostic writers is even less dominated by the conventions of literacy.

the question. Pursuit of novelty also falls by the wayside. The repetitious, traditional and familiar are appreciated in such a context.

Whenever we analyze "sources" in such a work, we must be careful not to impose overly modern criteria of plotting. We must not assume that repetition, starting over with slight variation, and the like automatically mean that an author has hung two independent pieces together. Variation on a theme and repetition are formal requirements of oral composition. Similarly, reading as recitation requires units or breaks in the narrative. Writing followed the episodic character of oral recitation. Further, an oral poet never has complete control of his narrative sequence. Lapses in temporal sequence and beginnings *in medias res* are almost assured by the episodic character of recitation. What is missing must be made up by flashbacks.[22] The revelation dialogue in NatArc constitutes such a flashback.

The interiorization of literacy that resulted from print media has also changed our ideas of memory and verbal identity from what is typical of the ancient period. We expect a person who has memorized something to reproduce the words fixed on a printed page. However, anthropologists have shown that if sixty percent of the words of two recitals of a story are identical in an oral culture, those who hear the two performances will say that the two are the same. Though themes and formulae remain much the same, they will be put together differently each time a work is recited.[23] Thus, two versions of a myth or story which an ancient reader might consider identical appear different to those whose perceptions have been formed by the habits of print literacy.

Other peculiarities of oral narrative are also typified in Gnostic writing. Adversary relationships are *de rigueur* throughout the culture. All information to be learned was attached to some pole or value judgment. Even scientific information is transmitted as part of a universe of warring elements or as the combat of humors within the body.[24] Wars and dangerous journeys are typical forms of narrative.

---

[22]Ong, *op. cit.*, 253f.

[23]*Ibid.*, 251f. Ong points to the fact that the words of institution are never reported the same way twice in the New Testament as an example of such oral conventions.

[24]Havelock, *Justice*, 50–106.

Abstract nouns appear as agents who either act or have something done to them. They do not figure in the logical sequences of philosophical argument.[25] Both abstraction and dualistic polarization appear in Gnostic stories. Wars are less common, though we do hear of opposition against evil powers who rule the cosmos and of the hazardous journey that the soul takes out of the cosmos. But the most common feature of such discourse is personification of abstract nouns. Gnostics personify abstractions to an unparalleled degree. Since all ancient writings conceive truth as something to be won from an opponent, one must be particularly careful in evaluating what a group says about outsiders. Such information as they give is dominated by the rhetoric of "for us" or "against us." This rhetoric plays a valuable role in establishing the identity of a group, especially in the case of Gnostics who typically define themselves over against a larger religious or philosophical tradition. But abstraction and dualistic polarization also mean that all the language appropriate to one's bitterest enemy or to evil itself is fair game. To modern interpreters used to a more irenic, "objective" neutrality such writing inevitably seems more hostile and negative than it would to those for whom such exchanges are part of everyday discourse.

Modern interpreters also tend to reduce religious narrative to statements of principle—or even non-principle, a reflection of the absurdity of life! Such statements of principle require the kind of cognitive abstraction that develops with deeply ingrained habits of literacy. Oral narrative properly deals in concrete examples of actions and their results, not in general principles.[26] Despite its peculiarities, Gnostic narrative is framed along these lines, but the Gnostic also lives in a world of developing abstraction. Statements of philosophical theory about the origins of the cosmos appear in some writings only to be rejected in favor of a narrative account of the unfolding of the pleroma.[27] When not telling such stories, Gnostic writers are sermonic or proverbial. They rarely exhibit sustained philosophical analysis.

---

[25]*Ibid.*, 42.
[26]*Ibid.*, 50–54.
[27]As in Eug, CG III *3* 70, 1–72, 2.

However, Gnostic writing would not have been possible without the explosion of literacy, which led to the writing down of old traditions from the various wisdom schools in the Hellenistic period. This literature made widespread dissemination of foreign myths and religious traditions possible. Gnostic writers sometimes take over blocks of such material. Our most striking example is the use of another Gnostic treatise, Eug, for the content of a revelation dialogue in SJC. Eug seeks to enumerate the various beings of the pleroma as a Gnostic answer to philosophical opinions about the order of the cosmos. Its personification of abstract terms for the aeons resembles oral personification. But unlike genuine stories, these abstractions have no personality. The sheer size of the Gnostic list also suggests the kind of information pile-up made possible by literacy. Sometimes Gnostic writers refer readers to other works (e.g., CG II *1* 19, 8–10). Such references may serve a "decorative" function, to place the writing at hand within the larger context of esoterica. This "mixed media" situation creates problems for the interpreter. One cannot assume that everything we might think to be a source derives from a written text. Nor can we assume that such authors considered texts as fixed documents in which every word counts. They are more likely to have perceived them as cues to words of a spoken revelation. Discrepancies in wording may not have been perceived with the same seriousness that modern redaction critics have attributed to them. We are faced with the problem of determining when there is a sufficiently consistent pattern of alteration to suggest purposeful activity on the part of an author beyond the usual rearrangements of oral recitation. Certain lapses, discontinuities and repetitions must be accepted as part of the oral mode of composition.

THE COMPOSITION OF GNOSTIC TEXTS

In conclusion, Gnostic authors show a variety of written and oral traditions that have been pulled together into the revelation dialogues. The traditions that have been identified behind DialSav are characteristic:[28] apocalyptic vision (134, 24—137, 3), creation myth

---

[28]Pagels-Koester, "Report," 72–74.

(127, 23—131, 15), dialogue source,[29] journey of the soul through the spheres (121, 5—122, 1), and wisdom list (133, 16—137, 3). These may have been derived from written compendia, though they are all short enough to have been part of the oral tradition of a Gnostic community. We frequently find smaller independent units in Gnostic writings. Many seem to be liturgical in character—for example, the opening prayer in DialSav (121, 5—122, 1); the creed which underlies a sermon attributed to Peter in PetPhil (CG VIII, *2* 139, 15-21),[30] the hymnic praise of the saving activity of Sophia in ApocryJn (CG II *1* 30, 11—31, 25)[31] or the various I AM predications of the Gnostic revealer (e.g., NatArc, CG II *4* 93, 8—10).[32] Citations from the New Testament form another category of liturgical tradition. Since we are dealing with texts that have been translated from Greek into Coptic, it is not always possible to tell if the author was quoting from memory or using a text.

All these elements would have been familiar to an author's audience. In many instances, we have to infer that they were expected to recall a more extended version of a myth or story than that actually given by the author. These traditions are assembled in a rather loose order in the revelation dialogues. In general, the authors do not seem to be using them as a source for speculative elaboration of Gnostic doctrine—something we do find in treatises like the *Tripartite Tractate* (CG I *5*), *On the Origin of the World* (CG II *5*), or *De Resurrectione* (CG I *4*). Nor do these texts provide for liturgical use like the *Three Steles of Seth* (VII *5*). Nor are they elementary expositions of gnosis like the *Letter of Ptolemy to Flora*. Rather, their overriding concern is apologetic. The revelation dialogue locates the Gnostic over against the wider religious milieu—usually to show that gnosis is the higher wisdom revealed at the source of the tradition in question.

---

[29]If the suggestion that DialSav is dependent upon a tradition of interpretation of sayings of Jesus like GTh, so Pagels and Koester, "Report," 67f, is correct.

[30]See G. P. Luttikurzen, "The Letter of Peter to Philip and the New Testament," *Nag Hammadi and Gnosis*, 101.

[31]See G. MacRae, "Sleep and Awakening in Gnostic Texts," *Le Origini*, 499-502.

[32]See G. MacRae, "The Ego Proclamation in Gnostic Sources," *The Trial of Jesus*, SBT, ser 2, 13, ed. E. Bammel (London: SCM, 1970), 129-134.

CHAPTER THREE

The Narrative Setting
of the Gnostic Dialogue

The diverse contents of Gnostic dialogues are held together in a narrative setting which introduces the recipients and commissions them to transmit the revelation to those for whom it is intended. Although the setting is usually a small part of the whole, it authenticates the contents as the true teaching of the traditions its authors seek to appropriate. The various contents of the dialogues are not new. They are found in other Gnostic writings. But by setting them within such a narrative, the author makes them the message which the disciples of Jesus or other religious heroes were commissioned to preach to humanity.

THE HEAVENLY REVEALER AND THE RISEN JESUS

With the exception of NatArc and Zostr, the recipients are either disciples (James, John, Thomas, Peter) or the disciples plus women or "the twelve." Christian Gnostics claimed that Jesus taught gnosis after his resurrection as Irenaeus reports:

> He remained eighteen months after his resurrection, and when perception descended into him, he taught what is clear. But only to a few of his disciples whom he knew to be capable of such great mysteries did he teach these things. (AdvHaer I 30, 4)

The revelations which center on the figure of Peter are the only exceptions to the discontinuity referred to in the Irenaeus passage. They assume a continuity between the teaching of the earthly and the risen Jesus.[1]

Gnostic authors focus on the elements of commissioning in the canonical resurrection stories for the settings of their dialogues, since they claim that the preaching mandated by the Lord was gnosis, not the doctrine of their opponents. Any Gospel reader knows that the commissioning scenes in the canonical Gospels are very brief. C. H. Dodd picks out five elements in the "concise" type of account: (1) situation of the followers without the Lord; (2) appearance; (3) greeting; (4) recognition; (5) word of command.[2] A majority of Gnostic works depart from this pattern (see Chart One). The luminous appearance of the Lord is frequently followed by rebuke and an I AM predication. The revelation dialogue itself is precipitated by a list of questions. Opposition from non-Gnostics and directions for protecting the revelation often appear. Pagels suggests that the Gnostics were developing the "circumstantial" type in which Jesus' appearance to one or a few followers will culminate in recognition of the Lord (Jn 20:14–18; Lk 24:13–35; Ac 9:3–7). She thinks that the Gnostics picked these stories to contrast with orthodox emphasis on stories proving the bodily reality of the risen Jesus and his appearance to the whole group.[3] However, Gnostic stories do not focus on recognition as the climax of the scene. Instead, the appearance is the opening for a new revelation which is the source of genuine apostolic authority.[4] We do agree that important issues of revelation and religious authority are addressed in the setting of the revelation dialogues—issues to which we shall be returning in Chapter Nine. But the Gnostic emphasis on the commission to preach gnosis—even if that preaching is limited to a small circle—and the various accounts

---

[1]PetPhil makes this point explicitly (CG VIII 135, 5f). AcPet 12 implies some continuity. The disciples are told to focus their mission on "the poor" but are not given any new, Gnostic teaching.

[2]Cf. Mt 28:16–20; C. H. Dodd, "The Appearances of the Risen Christ," *Studies in the Gospels: Essays in Memory of R. H. Lightfoot*, ed. D. Nineham (Oxford: Blackwell, 1967), 9–55.

[3]E. Pagels, "Visions," 417–19.

[4]*Ibid.*, 419–22.

that are given of "the twelve" in relation to that message show that Gnostic writers have the commissioning type of appearance in mind. Whenever the revelation is not to the twelve, the group is either expanded by inclusion of the women[5] or has the recipient—either himself or through another disciple as recorder[6]—transmit the revelation to the rest. Frequently, the other disciples reject that revelation, but it is never the case that "the twelve" have not heard Gnostic preaching.

The various allusions to the transfiguration in Gnostic literature suggest that they were also conscious of orthodox claims that the resurrection stories prove the bodily reality of the Risen One.[7] SJC verifies its claim that the form of the Risen Jesus was not like that of the earthly one by appealing to the transfiguration. There the Savior demonstrated his "purified flesh" (CG III 91,10–20). Similar arguments appear in two other Gnostic writings. DeRes says that the transfiguration proves that the resurrection was spiritual, not physical (CG I 48, 5–19). GPhil interprets the transfiguration as a demonstration of Jesus' true, non-fleshly nature (CG II 57, 35–58, 10). These passages suggest that there was a common Gnostic interpretation of the transfiguration. They show that the authors were aware of differing claims about the real significance of the resurrection. Since SJC is not concerned with resurrection as a theme, the passing allusion to the transfiguration argument shows that that interpretation was the general consensus of the author's community.

However, the transfiguration "epiphany" does not account for all the differences between Gnostic and orthodox appearances. Other

---

[5] A presence given explicit legitimation in 1 ApocJas (CG V 38, 15–24).

[6] As in ThCont, where Matthias acts as scribe to take down the dialogue. J. Turner, *The Book of Thomas the Contender* (Missoula: Scholars Press, 1975), 105–111, considers this passage a late addition. However, it fits into the polemic construction of the revelation dialogue by providing additional apostolic testimony. On Matthias as transmitter of words of Jesus see Papias in Eusebius *HistEccl* III 39, 16, Basilides in Hippolytus *Ref* VII 20, 1, and Clement of Alexandria *Strom* III 4, 26. 3.

[7] J. M. Robinson, "Gattung," 116f, considers the transfiguration the norm for resurrection appearances and probably a displaced resurrection account (referring to 2 Pt 1:16–18). He argues that Gnosticizing interpretation led to the suppression of such accounts. However, the Gnostic evidence that we have in the Nag Hammadi materials shows that Gnostics, too, considered the transfiguration an event in the life of the earthly Jesus.

traditions about the appearance of the heavenly revealer are also involved. There are formal parallels between the setting of revelation
dialogues with Christ as revealer and those with an angelic revealer
coming to a primordial ancestor of the Gnostics. The recipient in
NatArc, Norea, the sister of Seth/wife of Noah, has a checkered history in Jewish haggadah. She is frequently the epitome of wickedness
and is sometimes the consort of the "sons of God."[8] Here, on the
other hand, she resists their advances and is being persecuted by
them. The angelic revealer rescues this ancestress of the Gnostic race
from their clutches.[9] NatArc has clearly reversed the Jewish tradition. Thus, it is not surprising that its description of the appearance
of the revealer has parallels in Jewish accounts of angelic messengers.

Zostr is directed against the mystic Platonism at Alexandria.
The circles from which it comes were fascinated by the possibilities
of heavenly journeys. Jewish parallels to this work may indicate that
these circles also had access to Jewish speculations about the heavenly world. Several later Jewish apocalypses supplement the more normal concerns for the fate of Israel with interest in the nature of the
cosmos and eschatology.[10] These interests fit into the larger picture
of esoteric wisdom in Alexandria. Another Gnostic writing from the
same circles as Zostr, Allog, reports a heavenly journey and includes
elements from the esoteric tradition in its conclusion: the revelation
is to be written in a book hidden on a mountain and protected by a
curse invoking the Guardian, the Dreadful One (CG XI 68, 16–23).[11]
Both are attacks on Platonic mysticism.[12] It would seem that the
group among which they arose were also fascinated by esoteric Jewish traditions. Zostr is the only revelation dialogue, which is entirely
set in the context of a heavenly journey. There are some other indica-

---

[8]See Pearson, "Norea."

[9]ApocAd has a variant of this story. There, the seed of Seth must be rescued from
the flood by angels on light clouds. The Creator God had directed the flood against
the Sethians. In both stories, Noah remains the pious servant of that God.

[10]For example, TLev ii–v, 2 En and 3 Bar. See Collins, "Jewish Apocalypses,"
36–44.

[11]Hidden books are a common feature of esoteric tradition. For Jewish examples
see D. S. Russell, *The Method and Message of Jewish Apocalyptic* (Philadelphia: Westminster, 1964), 108f; for the hermetica, Festugiere, *Revelation I*, 318f.

[12]See the discussion of this debate in Perkins, "Deceiving," and *idem*, "Gnosis as
Salvation: A Phenomenological Inquiry," *ANRW* II, 22.

tions that such traditions influenced Gnostic writers. Book IV of the *Pistis Sophia* includes a heavenly journey in which the various types of souls and their fate are revealed. 1 Jeu has a vision of various heavenly treasuries, and DialSav has an apocalypse in which the disciples are taken to the ends of the earth to see the fate of the soul.[13] Since the Nag Hammadi writings provide many examples of esoteric Jewish traditions, the affinities between Gnostic dialogues and Jewish apocalypses probably indicate the genera in which those traditions were handed on in Gnostic circles. We cannot say how the first Gnostic revelation dialogue came into being. All the surviving examples seem to be operating with a genre which they expect their readers to recognize. Perhaps Jewish circles had developed apocalypses whose content consisted of cosmology, exegesis of the Genesis *Urgeschichte,* and eschatological prediction similar to NatArc or to the non-dialogic testament, ApocAd. Christians, for their part, may also have been speculating about what had transpired between the Risen Jesus and his disciples.[14]

NARRATIVE SETTING OF THE GNOSTIC REVELATION DIALOGUE

Charts Two and Three indicate the major features in the setting of revelation dialogues. The opening narratives are more uniformly stylized than the concluding ones. The locale, names of the recipients, their activity and mental disposition—usually grief or perplexity—are common features which correspond both to Dodd's description of the introduction to resurrection accounts and to the opening of Jewish apocalypses.[15] Occasionally—as is usual in Jewish revelations—the recipient is praying to God.[16] Assimilation to the resurrection appearance stories may have led to the omission of

---

[13]The journey in ApocPaul is a means of authenticating his Gnostic authority: Pagels, "Visions," 425.

[14]Ac 1:6 assumes that the disciples had been questioning Jesus; so Pagels, 419. However, we cannot concur with her conclusion that this passage indicates that a dialogue tradition has been suppressed.

[15]See the chart in Collins, "Jewish Apocalypses," 28.

[16]For example, TLev ii–v; 2 Bar, 3 Bar, and 4 Ezra. Prayer is part of both non-Christian Gnostic dialogue settings.

CHART TWO
Opening Narrative of the Gnostic Revelation Dialogue

	I,1	II,1	II,4	II,7	III,4	III,5	V,3	VI,1	VII,3	VIII,1	VIII,2	BG	PS
LOCATION													
mountain		x	x		x		x				x		x
Jerusalem/temple		(x)							x				
other		x						x		x			
TIME	x						x						x
RECIPIENTS													
non-Christian	x	x								x			
a disciple(s)		x	x	x			x						
"the twelve"								x	x		x		
"the 12" & women					x	x						x	x
THEIR ACTIVITY													
are persecuted		x[1]	x										
preaching								x		x	x		
writing/discussing Jesus' words											(x)		
other	x					x	x			x			x
MENTAL STATE													
grief/troubled		x					x			x[2]			x
ponder/perplexed		x		x	x					x		x[3]	
prayer				x			x			x			

REVEALER APPEARS						
cosmic signs						x
luminous	x	(?)	x	x	x	(?)
child				x		
pluriform	x		x	x		x
REVEALER'S ADDRESS						
I AM	x	x	x			
purpose	x	(?)	(x)	x	x	x
	x	x	(x)			
rebuke	x	(x)	(x)	(x)	x	x
LIST OF						
QUESTIONS	x[4]	(x)	x[4]	x[4]	x	(x)
mode of revelation in addition to dialogue	x	(x)	(x)	x	(x)	x

(x) = feature implied later in dialogue; barely mentioned.

(?) = feature subject to interpretation of a difficult or fragmentary text.

[1] if one understands the challenge by the Jew as persecution along the Johannine model.

[2] see discussion; the text seems to imply that the seer is willing to commit suicide.

[3] displaced until after the dialogue to make the transition to Mary's revelation and further dialogue among the disciples.

[4] list occurs prior to the revealer's coming as the object of seer's perplexity

CHART THREE
Concluding Narrative of the Revelation Dialogue

	I,2	II,1	II,4	II,7	III,4	III,5	V,3	VI,1	VII,3	VIII,1	VIII,2	BG	PS
COMMISSIONING													
preach (to Gnostics)	x	x		(x)[1]	x[1]	(x)	x	x	x	x	x[1]	x[1]	(x)
preserve revel'n	x	x					x	(x)[2]		x			
benediction			x	x		x	x		x		x	x	
predict future	x		x				x					x	
ASCENSION	x	(x)									x		
SEER RETURNS													
to preach	x	x			x		x[4]			x	x		[5]
to tell disciples[3]	x	x									x		
to a place	x									x	x		
MENTAL STATE													
joy/thanks	x				x			(x)			x		x[6]
distress												x	
ADDITIONAL NARRATIVE													
example of preaching										x	(x)		
other	x						x				x	x	

(x) = feature implied later in dialogue; barely mentioned.

(?) = feature subject to interpretation of a difficult or fragmentary text.

1 though there will be opposition, preaching in these writings is directed to the world at large and not limited to the Gnostics.

2 if one understands the prohibition against association with the rich as a variant of instructions for preserving the revelation.

3 except in ApocryJn, this motif implies rejection and division among the disciples.

4 the text is fragmentary; it seems that James "rebukes" the other disciples.

5 a late ending to PS supplies the motif of the disciples going to preach.

6 "peace and joy" occur as a mental state in the opening of PS, since the Risen Lord has been present for years; cosmic signs change that to fear.

prayer in the Christian dialogues. It appears in 1 ApocJas, since it is typical of the apocryphal James tradition.

The luminous descriptions attached to the revealer may have condensed the standard Jewish picture of angels as appearing in white and gold or as the sun with the Gnostic dogma of the pleroma as the light world. The revealer's opening address is also stylized. The combination of rebuke and I AM predication seems to be peculiarly Gnostic. Gnostic writings frequently use I AM formulations. We find discourses in that style and hymnic materials which seem to have been developed from Hellenistic I AM aretalogies.[17] The recipients then initiate the dialogue with a list of questions, unless that list has occurred earlier as the object of their perplexity.

The conclusion usually contains some statement of the recipients' activity after the revelation. Some conclusions include further narrative. The departing revealer usually commissions the recipients to preach gnosis. When that commission is lacking, as in NatArc, the predicted future of the Gnostic race indicates that the revelation is authoritative for the author's generation. In such cases, Jewish apocalyptic judgment scenes in which the wicked and righteous are separated are reapplied to the non-Gnostics (opponents) and Gnostics.[18] Jewish apocalypses also contain brief conclusions. But the canonical resurrection stories are probably behind the simple "he disappeared" indication of the revealer's departure. The announcement that Jesus is ascending to the perfect Aeon in ApocryJn (CG II 31, 26f) seems to be a conflation of Johannine sayings, probably Jn 20:17 with 17:4–6. Jewish apocalypses typically speak of the seer's awakening or his return to earth as we find in ApocPet and Zostr.[19] ApocryJas and PetPhil, on the other hand, have elaborated the ascension tradition with elements from the "taking up" of Jewish seers.[20] These various parallels are sufficient to indicate that the audi-

---

[17] See Fallon, "Gnostic Apocalypses," 142–45; MacRae, "Discourses of the Gnostic Revealer," *International Colloquium on Gnosticism*, 111–122.

[18] See the discussion of such scenes in a variety of Gnostic writings in my "Apocalypse of Adam," 389–91, and "Rebellion Myth," 20–24.

[19] For example, the final commissioning, return to earth and awakening of Levi in TLev v, 2–7.

[20] Compare the ascension of Enoch in 2 En lxvii. After his heavenly journey, the seer preaches to the people. Then he is taken up into the presence of God.

ence who heard these dialogues were on familiar ground. They would know from the outset that the revelation came from divine sources to the heroes of the tradition who passed it on to them.

INTRODUCTORY EPISTLE

Since the epistolatory introductions are secondary to the revelation dialogue, they are not included in the analytic charts. Three of the dialogues are introduced by such an epistle. ApocryJas also contains an epistolatory conclusion. Its epistle has the following parts:

(a) *Opening* (1, 1–14):
Greeting (11. 1–7): "James to . . . peace."[21]
Introduction (11. 8–14): The introduction establishes the letter as a cover letter answering a request for a book, a well-known literary topos.[22]

(b) *Body* (1, 15–28):
The issue at hand is stated in this section of the letter: the secrecy and limited nature of Gnostic revelation. The addressee is entitled to the revelation because he is to be a Gnostic teacher in the succession of the author. Not all claims to apostolic tradition are to be accepted. The argument concludes with a benediction on the Gnostics (11. 26–28) such as one might expect at the conclusion of a letter.

(c) *Addendum* (1, 29–35):
The addition to the body refers to books the author had already sent. Letters typically refer to past or future contacts between the

---

[21]I am not persuaded by the arguments for reconstructing the addressee as "Cerinthos." The Nag Hammadi writings have such a variety of names that one cannot assume that all names are those from patristic sources. For a defense of the Cerinthos hypothesis, see J. Helderman, "Anapausis in the Epistula Jacobi Apocrypha," *Nag Hammadi and Gnosis*, 37f. Helderman also tries to recontruct π] pnnϵ, "child", in the opening instead of †] pnnϵ, "peace." This reconstruction violates the parallelism of the lines in the greeting and the "pseudo-letter" genre of the passage.

[22]G. Kennedy, *The Art of Rhetoric in the Roman World* (Princeton: Princeton University, 1972), 253f.

two parties at this point. This section presents the following revelation as part of a larger group of esoterica.

(d) *Conclusion* (16, 12–30):
    The conclusion repeats the concerns of the body of the letter. The recipient is commissioned as a Gnostic teacher and is warned to restrict the teaching to those worthy of it.

The opening letter in PetPhil forms a striking contrast to ApocryJas. The latter had claimed that only some disciples received gnosis. PetPhil, on the other hand, stresses apostolic unity (CG VIII 132, 10–133, 8). Peter requests that Philip join the others in coming together and preaching as the Lord had commanded. Philip responds enthusiastically. Thus, both pseudonymous letters deal with the proper recipients and carriers of Gnostic teaching. ApocryJas evidences the more common Gnostic claim that the revelation was only given to a few. PetPhil, on the other hand, emphasizes the unity in the preaching activity of all the twelve.

The introduction to NatArc belongs to a different type of letter. The author does cite Paul as a textual authority for the Gnostic struggle against the powers of the cosmos. The concluding sentence (CG II 86, 26f) follows the pattern of a dogmatic letter in answer to a question about a particular doctrine. DeRes is the best-known Gnostic example. Like ApocryJas, DeRes divides people into those who can receive the revelation ("have faith") and those who cannot (CG I 43, 24–44, 12; 49, 37–50, 16). Eug, the treatise on the true heavenly world, which seems to have been used as the content for much of the revelation dialogue SJC, also begins as a dogmatic epistle (CG III 70, 1–71, 13). Once again the Gnostic "few" receive the revelation while the "many" including the revered philosophers do not know the truth.

TIME AND LOCATION

Occasionally one finds an indication of the time that has elapsed since the resurrection. The "few days" of 1 ApocJas fits the ambiguity of the canonical traditions. Jn 20 has eight days between appearances; Ac 1:3–9 has forty, which is the only longer period. Heracleon does not specify the length of time (Comm. Jo. xiii, 52). PS has the longest period with eleven years. The 550 days of ApocryJas correspond to Irenaeus' report about Valentinian and Ophite traditions (AdvHaer I 3, 2; 30, 14).[23]

The location of ApocryJas is unclear. Since he returns to Jerusalem after the other disciples reject his revelation, one assumes that some place outside the city is intended. 1 ApocJas mentions a Mount Gaugelon, presumably also outside Jerusalem. Other examples of a Jerusalem locale are the temple in ApocPet and the Mount of Olives in PetPhil and PS. That may also be the intended location of ApocryJn. The versions differ in their information. In the long version, John leaves the temple for a deserted place; in the short version, a mountain is added. SJC, on the other hand, follows the tradition of a revelation on a mount in Galilee as does Book IV of PS and the ExcTheod.[24] The two non-Christian dialogues have the desert place, Zostr, and the mountain, NatArc. The mountain in NatArc is the resting place of the ark, Mount Seir. Mount Seir frequently appears as the depository of secret revelations in Jewish and hermetic writings.[25] Hence it is an appropriate locale for the revelation of gnosis. AcPet 12, on the other hand, is not tied to a traditional revelation site. It has used motifs from romance literature to tell the story of the dangers, hardship, and sea journeys faced by the apostles. The revelation itself occurs in a mysterious city in the middle of the ocean.[26]

---

[23]AscIs has the 545-day tradition, which J. Daniélou, *The Theology of Jewish Christianity* (Chicago: Regnery, 1964), 251–56, attributes to Jewish Christianity. Van Unnik points to other features which tie ApocryJas traditions to AscIs. Both have the expression "those who believe in the cross"; both describe the ascension; both share the idea that the righteous become like Jesus. However, ApocryJas has a system of three heavens, while AscIs has seven. Therefore, he rejects the idea that the two works are directly dependent upon each other: Van Unnik, "The Origin of the Newly Discovered 'Apocryphon Jacobi,'" *VigChr* 10 (1956), 155. On the various resurrection traditions in this period see W. Bauer, *Das Leben Jesu im Zeitalter der neutestamentlichen Apocryphen* (Tübingen: J. C. B. Mohr, 1909), 266.

[24]Bauer, *Das Leben*, 268.

[25]Cf. G. J. Reinik, "Das Land Seiris (sir) und das Volk des Serer in Judischen und Christlichen Traditionen," *JSJ* 6 (1975), 72–85.

[26]Readers brought up on Homer would hardly escape the aura of the *Odyssey* in this setting. Another Gnostic writing, *Exegesis on the Soul* (CG II, 6), quotes *Odyssey* passages about the dangers of sea voyages and Calypso's isle in its exhortation to vigilance against the lure of the material world (CG II 136, 16–35).

APPEARANCE OF THE REVEALER

The revealer's appearance can comprise three elements: cosmic signs, polymorphous shape and luminosity. AprocryJn and PS have adopted metaphors from the Old Testament language of divine epiphany (e.g., Is 24:18–23; 63:19–64:1) to describe signs which accompany the appearance. Such language also appears in the earthquakes and darkened skies of the Synoptic crucifixion accounts. When God visits his creation, cosmic disruption takes place. PS has taken over the more elaborate form of the tradition, which apocalyptic writers use to describe the destruction at the end of the world (PS I, 5f). Gnostic writers frequently use this mythic pattern of divine visitation and cosmic destruction in descriptions of the coming of revelation to the lower world both during the primeval history as a counter to the Creator God's attempts to suppress gnosis and as part of the final destruction of the world of darkness.[27] The revealer has to take on bodily form in order to prevent this reaction.[28] The reference to cosmic signs is much shorter in AprocryJn than in PS: "Behold, the heavens opened and the whole creation under heaven shone and the world was shaken, and I was afraid . . ." (1, 31–2, 1). Van Unnik points out that in Jewish apocalypses the opening of the heavens either lets the seer see or journey into heaven or—less frequently—lets something emerge from heaven like the *bath qol* in 2 Bar 22 or the dove in the baptism stories.[29] The descriptions of cosmic signs, then, draw on well-established metaphors of theophany, even though such language is not commonly applied to resurrection appearances in either canonical or Gnostic sources.

The second element in the description, the polymorphous appearance of the revealer, is also comparatively rare. It appears in ApocryJn, PS and Zostr. Zostr and ApocryJn combine the polymorphous description of the revealer with the characterization "child."

---

[27]See Perkins, "Rebellion Myth," 20–27.

[28]For example, ApocryJn CG II 30, 11–31, 25; TriProt CG XIII 41, 1–23; 43, 4–44, 28. TriProt contrasts the cosmic destruction of these first two descents with the coming of the embodied revealer in the third (CG XIII 49, 6–23).

[29]W. C. Van Unnik, "Die geoffenten Himmel in der Offenbarungsvision des Apocryphon des Johannes," *Apophoreta. Fest. E. Haenchen*, BZNW 10 (Berlin: Topelmann, 1964), 269–80.

Quispel tries to trace that combination back to ancient imagery of the god Aion.[30] Janssens refers to the double form of the revealer in GEve (Epiph. *Pan.* XXVI 3,1) and to the three angelic beings who instruct Adam in ApocAd, but she admits that neither explanation is entirely satisfactory. She comments that the author of ApocryJn probably understood the trimorphic manifestation as corresponding to the divine Father-Mother-Son triad.[31] This assessment of the theological intent of ApocryJn is probably correct. We can gain further light on the matter by turning to the form of the tradition in Zostr. There, pluriformity and appearing as a "child" are characteristic of various angelic beings who guide the seer (e.g., CG VIII 2, 6–14). Therefore, we must conclude that these motifs derive from an esoteric description of angelic guides. Like ApocryJn, Zostr has embedded this description in a theological reflection on the nature of the highest God and the neo-Platonic triad derived from him.[32] Its theological reinterpretation is more sophisticated philosphically than the simple identification presupposed in ApocryJn. PS—a late collection of Gnostic traditions and mythic fragments without the unity or reflection of earlier writings—solves the problem by dropping "child" as a characteritic and predicating the polymorphism of the light surrounding Jesus.

Unlike the previous two, the third element in the description of the revealer's appearance is so ubiquitous as to be the mark of Gnostic resurrection stories.[33] Second-century authors sometimes link the risen body of Jesus with an angel of light, thus making it halfway between the earthly form and that of the soul alone.[34] We have seen that the Gnostics used the transfiguration story as an argument for the spiritual nature of the Risen Christ. The luminous descriptions of the Risen Christ came to play an important role in the Gnostic argu-

---

[30]G. Quispel, "The Demiurge in the Apocryphon of John," *Nag Hammadi and Gnosis*, 1–33.

[31]Y. Janssens, "L'Apocryphon de Jean" *Museon* 83 (1970), 161f.

[32]CG VIII 2, 10–15. See the discussion of this theology in Robinson, "Three Steles," in Pearson, "Marsanes," and in Perkins, "Deceiving."

[33]So Robinson, "Gattung," 116.

[34]Origen, *Comm. Mat.* xi, 2; c. *Cels.* ii, 62.

[35]See Bauer, *Das Leben*, 258–60.

ment against orthodox doctrines of the bodily resurrection.[35] But, whatever its polemic use, the luminous revealer derives from Jewish descriptions of angelic messengers. In *Joseph and Aseneth* XIV, 3, an angel appears from the open heaven (compare ApocryJn) in indescribable light. Dn 10:5–6 attaches light metaphors to various parts of the body of the angel and says that his voice was like the roar of a crowd. That description reappears in 2 En 1, 4f. NatArc provides the closest parallel to this tradition. The angel appears like gold and wears a white garment. His power and appearance cannot be described (CG II 93, 13–16). Other descriptions simply refer to the revealer as a great angel of light who cannot be described. This restriction of visual imagery is typical of Gnostic writings. They never describe things in heaven like the divine throne even when they are utilizing such traditions. For the Gnostic, all such visual phenomena belong to the realm of the ignorant Creator God. ApocPaul contains an amusing example of Gnostic rejection of such mysticism in the encounter between Paul and the Jewish God, presumably seated on his throne, in the midst of his powers in the seventh heaven:

He opened the gate of the seventh heaven to us. I saw an old man . . . of light . . . was white . . . in the seventh heaven . . . light, brighter than the sun. The old man asked me, "Where are you going, blessed Paul, who was set apart from his mother's womb?" I looked at the Spirit. He nodded his head, saying to me, "Speak to him." I answered the old man, "I am going to the place from which I came." The old man responded, "Where are you from?" I replied, "I am going up from the world of the dead, that I may take captivity captive, that which was captive in the Babylonian captivity." The old man responded, "How will you be able to depart from me? Look and see these principalities (*arche*) and powers (*exousia*)." The Spirit answered, "Give him the sign which you have, and he will open for you." Then I gave him the sign. He turned his head down toward his creation and his powers (CG V 22, 23–23, 28; author's translation).

It is not difficult to see the irony of this passage when one compares it with the throne vision of Jewish seers epitomized in Dn 7:9f. Since Gnostics reject visual symbolism, their revelations are almost entirely auditory. The familiar dialogue with an angel who interprets what a seer sees in heaven is missing from their writings.[36]

THE REVEALER'S ADDRESS TO THE DISCIPLES

Almost all the dialogues have some description of the perplexity or mental agitation of the recipients. In Jewish apocalypses such distress usually focused on the fate of Israel and the sinfulness of humanity.[37] In Christian Gnostic writings, the departure of Jesus has left his disciples without a full understanding of the divine, of Jesus' fate, or of their own situation in a hostile world. These questions may be framed in a set list addressed to the revealer or given as the reason for the disciples' distress. Various dialogues show a pattern of items clustered around the revealer's address to the disciples:

ApocryJn	*NatArc*	*SJC*
questions	rebuke	questions
cosmic signs	I AM	appearance
appearance	purpose	(I AM and purpose occur later in in the dialogue)
rebuke	appearance	
I AM	I AM	
purpose	rebuke (?)	
commission		

Zostr #1	*Zostr #2*	*PetPhil*
questions	invoke angel	apperance
appearance	appearance	rebuke
rebuke	I AM	I AM

---

[36]Fallon, "Gnostic Apocalypses," 125.
[37]For example TLev ii; 2 En i, 3; 2 Bar i; 3 Bar i, 1; 4 Ezra iii, 1–3; v, 20–22; vi, 35–37.

| commission | rebuke | questions |
| | questions | |

PS
(purpose and questions, in a long introduction about the state of
the disciples)
appearance
I AM
questions

We conclude from these comparisons that the initial address
was felt to consist of three parts—rebuke, I AM statement identify-
ing the revealer, and statement of purpose. The statement of purpose
may be expanded to include commissioning the recipient as a preacher of gnosis, a motif commonly found in the concluding narrative.
Statements of purpose, sometimes coupled with reassurance to the
seer, are typical in Jewish apocalypses.[38] In Gnostic writings, the revealer comes to bring the required gnosis.[39]

The persistent element of rebuke is unusual in Jewish revelations. In 3 Bar I, 6f, the angel tells Baruch to "cease provoking
God." This rebuke is similar to the first of two rebukes in NatArc:
"Why are you crying up to God? Why do you act so boldly toward
the Holy Spirit?" (CG II 93, 4–6). In 3 Bar, the seer has hurled at
God a list of questions about the desolation of Israel.[40] Here, Norea
prays to be saved from the archons who are pursuing her. The second rebuke speaks directly to that issue: archons have no power over
the head of the Gnostic race (CG II 93, 22–32). But the first rebuke
and the 3 Bar passage claim that the seer is in some way provoking
or acting boldly toward God. The proper context for understanding
such language is to be found in Hellenistic Jewish speculation about
the proper boldness shown in the prayers of the great heroes of Isra-

---

[38]See Dn 8:18f; 10:10–12; 2 En i, 6–8; 3 Bar i, 3–6.

[39]NatArc CG II 93, 11–13; SJC CG III 93, 8–12; ApocryJn CG II 2, 16–25. ApocryJn incorporates a standard prophetic formula: "what is, what was, and what will
be," into its statement of purpose. See Van Unnik, "A Formula Describing Prophecy," *NTS* 9 (1962/63), 86–93.

[40]In 4 Ezra, the angel answers similar charges with riddles from the whirlwind of
Job rather than with direct rebuke—for example, iv, 1–11.

el, Abraham and Moses.[41] According to Philo (*Quis Haer.* i–xxix), such prayer requires courage, bold frankness in approaching God, a trusting relationship with him, and loudness. Even an anguished cry of reproach is acceptable as long as it is combined with *eulabia*, an attitude of humble recognition of divine sovereignty. The required trust and *eulabia* seem to be lacking in 3 Bar and NatArc; hence the rebuke. Presumably the revelations which follow are to instill such confidence and reverence in any readers who might be similarly afflicted. Thus we would trace the rebuke motif to Hellenistic speculation on appropriate prayer.

In other dialogues, the rebuke has a dogmatic function more like the second rebuke in NatArc. The seer should have known the truth which will now be the subject of the revelation (cf. ApocryJn CG II 2, 19–12; PetPhil CG VIII 134, 15–18; Zostr CG VIII 3, 31–4, 12). Thus the rebuke is no longer concerned with the proper attitude in prayer. Rather it shifts the blame for the necessity of this extra revelation to the recipients. God did not intend for them to be in such a state of ignorance.

Gnostic dialogues typically expand the revealer's greeting with an I AM statement. Other Gnostic writings have taken over the formula from Hellenistic aretalogies to frame a whole treatise (see *Thunder, Perfect Mind* and *Trimorphic Protennoia*). Shorter, hymnic I AM predications are embedded in other Gnostic narratives (see NatArc CG II 89, 14–17; OrigWld CG II 114, 9–15). A hymnic section concludes the long version of ApocryJn (CG II 30, 11–31, 25). Each of the three descriptions of the coming of revelation begins with a formulaic I AM:

> I am the richness of the Light.
> I am the remembrance of the pleroma . . .
> I came forth from those who belong to the light,
>   which is I, the remembrance of the Pronoia. . . .
> I am the Light which exists in the light.
> I am the remembrance of the Pronoia. . . .

---

[41]See H. Attridge, "Heard Because of His Reverence (Heb 5:7)," *JBL* 98 (1979), 90–93.

The I Am formulae in the appearance sections are shorter than these. They constitute recognition formulae.[42] NatArc contains two typical examples:

> I am Eleleth, Wisdom, the great angel who stands in the presence of the Holy Spirit (CG II 93, 8–13).
> I am Understanding, one of the four Light-givers (*phoster*), who stand in the presence of the Great Invisible Spirit (CG II 93, 19–21).

Compare SJC: "I am he who came from the boundless Light" (CG III 93, 8–12). Or ApocryJn: "I am the one who is with you forever. I am the Father. I am the Mother. I am the Son. I am the undefiled and incorruptible one" (CG II 2, 12–15). The latter opened with a reference to the recognition formula in Mt 28:20.[43] We find the simple "It is I" (Mk 6:50; Mt 14:27) used in PS I, 6 and in AcPet12 (CG VI 9, 14). 1 ApocJas uses "I am he who was within me" (CG V 31, 17f) to make a dogmatic point. The Risen Lord is identical with the inner nature of the earthly Jesus. Thus, the I AM self-presentation draws both on Hellenistic aretalogies and on recognition formulae from the New Testament. Since it is frequent in various forms of Gnostic writing and liturgy, the reader would immediately associate it with the heavenly revealer.

LISTS OF QUESTIONS

The formulaic listing of questions associated with the revealer's appearance is also a largely Gnostic development. The sorrowing seer addresses questions about Jerusalem's fate to God in 2 Bar III, 4–9 and 3 Bar I, 2. But the Gnostic lists are largely dogmatic in content and reflect Gnostic concern for the *teaching* of the Risen Jesus.[44]

---

[42]So R. Bullard, *The Hypostasis of the Archons*, PTS 10 (Berlin: Walter de Gruyter, 1970), 102.

[43]Janssens, "L'Apocryphon," 161f, points to the combination of this quotation with revelation on a mountain and rebuke of John's doubt as evidence that ApocryJn is drawing on the Matthean post-resurrection vision.

[44]Bauer, *Das Leben*, 268–70.

Such lists seem to have existed as Gnostic formulae independent of the revelation dialogue setting. The best known is preserved in ExcTheod 78,2:

> It is not the washing (baptism) alone that makes us free but the knowledge:
>> Who we were; what we have become; where we were; into what place we have been cast; where we are hastening; from what we are delivered; what is birth; what is rebirth.

A shorter version of this formula appears as the revealer's statement of purpose in ThCont: ". . . that you may understand: who you are, how you exist and how you will come to be" (CG II 138, 8–20).

In some of the longer writings lists of questions punctuate the text. We find at least seven sets in Zostr, the longest work in the collection.[45] GrPow contains two sets which are almost identical (CG VI 36, 28–37, 5; 43, 4–11). The first set in TestTr is dogmatic (CG IX 41, 22–42, 16) while the second is exegetical (CG IX 70, 24–30). Mar only contains one that we can identify (CG X 6, 18–29), but the work is so poorly preserved that there may have been others. Oral composition is normally episodic and fragmentary. Recital might break a work into sections between which there need not be complete continuity. The lists of questions seem to serve the purposes of such recital. They are formulaic and often introduce independent units, which could well have been the object of recital or commentary. Thus, it would be natural for a Gnostic writer to begin a revelation dialogue with a list of questions well-known from such a context. The lists in the dialogues usually make the transition to the points of teaching reflected in the content of the dialogue. They may provide an important clue as to how the materials included there were read.[46]

---

[45]CG VIII, 2, 21–3, 13; 7, 27–8, 7; 13, 7–24, associated with a whole appearance sequence; 22, 2–14; 45, 2–9; 96, 4–15; 128, 20–129, 1. Other lists may be lost in the lacunae.

[46]NatArc CG II 93, 33–94, 2; ApocryJn CG II 1, 21–29; SJC III 91, 4–9; PetPhil CG VIII 134, 20–135, 2; PS I, 6.

Concluding Commission

Commissioning of the recipients is a constant feature of the much briefer final narrative. These commissions combine features of Jewish apocalypses, where the seer is to make known what he has seen or is to assume a specific role,[47] with the mission charge of the Risen Jesus to his disciples.[48] Both 2 En and 2 Bar follow the commissioning with long accounts of sermons delivered by the seer upon his return. A similar pattern appears in two Gnostic revelations in which the seer is commissioned in heaven, *Paraphrase of Shem* (CG VII 40, 31–41, 20) and Melchizedek (CG IX 14. 9–15). The former is particularly close to 2 En, since Shem returns to earth and gives a paraphrase of the revelation as his teaching, much as in 2 En. Then, like Enoch, he ascends through the heavens at his death. Neither of these revelations is a dialogue. But their use of commissioning scenes for the primordial teacher of gnosis makes them close relatives of the dialogue type.

The conclusion of ApocryJn contains an elaborate and unusual curse against selling the revelation. Prohibitions against changing the words of the revelation are common enough in apocalypses.[49] Prohibitions against trafficking in revelations are rarer. AcPet 12 cautions the disciples to avoid the rich in their preaching. II Jeu xliii directs them to preserve the revelations and not give them to others in exchange for material goods.[50] The context for the prohibition in ApocryJn is probably the common slander that one's opponent was trafficking in revelation, magic or any other kind of wisdom. Irenaeus uses it against the Gnostics: "They do not teach openly but only those who pay a high fee" (AdvHaer I 4, 3). Including prohibitions against associating with the rich or selling the revelation in the commissioning scene is one way of answering the kind of charge that was

---

[47]For example, TLev v; 2 En xxxviii.

[48]See Bauer's survey of the patristic references to these scenes in *Das Leben*, 270–72.

[49]For example, 1 En civ, 10ff; Rev 22:18f. H. Koester, "One Jesus and Four Primitive Gospels," *Trajectories through Early Christianity* (Philadelphia: Fortress, 1971), 239 n. 131; Rudolph, "Dialog," 98 n. 23.

[50]J. Doresse thinks that this refers to other Gnostic sects: *Secret Books of the Egyptian Gnostics* (London: Hollis & Carter, 1960), 78.

directed against Gnostic teachers. They cannot be profiting from their revelations, since the Lord has expressly forbidden them to do so.

The narrative setting of the revelation dialogues, then, shows us a group seeking to establish its position among the various religious traditions of its environment. They use a variety of familiar metaphors and images from contemporary revelatory literature to invest their writings with the antiquity and authority of those traditions. But they also show developments unique to Gnosticism. The Gnostic reader would find them familiar: the luminous revealer, the I AM proclamation, the lists of questions. The majority of these dialogues seek to appropriate the authoritative tradition of Christianity by placing one or more of the disciples in the role of a legitimately commissioned Gnostic teacher. The variations in approach to this theme show that there was not one single Gnostic group or theology behind the revelation dialogues. Rather, we must assume that they come from a variety of settings and represent quite different solutions to the problem of religious tradition and authority.

CHAPTER FOUR

The Content of the Gnostic Revelation Dialogues

The setting of the revelation dialogues sought to legitimate gnosis by attaching it to primordial heroes like Norea or Zostrianos or to the apostolic heroes of the Christian tradition. The opening usually introduced the revealer as a heavenly being sent to address the perplexities of the recipients, who were still without gnosis. Having passed on the true teaching, the departing revealer commissioned them to preach the authoritative tradition to those worthy of receiving it. This restriction is a necessary condition of the Gnostic claim to represent the esoteric truth of larger religious traditions.

The contents of the revelation dialogues do not contain any particular items of Gnostic teaching that are not found elsewhere in non-dialogue writings. Form critical analysis of some of the materials contained in the dialogues suggests that the authors have adopted the modes of preaching and teaching typical of their communities. The Gnostic reader will hear the heavenly revealer speak in the same didactic and liturgical patterns to which his community life had accustomed him. Unlike philosophical dialogue, the revelation dialogue is not a vehicle for the theoretical elaboration and exploration of Gnostic teaching. These writings show little of the sophistication with which other Gnostics engaged contemporary philosophical and theological debate in the intellectual appropriation of their own traditions.[1] What the contents of these revelations do show us are the doctrines which Gnostics felt to be at issue between themselves and their opponents. They indicate those teachings that it was necessary to invest with all the authority of the guardians of the tradition.

FORMAL CONTENT OF THE GNOSTIC REVELATION DIALOGUES

Before examining the thematic content of the revelation dialogues, we will survey the forms of speech used. Chart Four shows that the types of discourse which occur in five or more examples are: Sophia myth, apocalyptic vision, hymnic or prayer language, sayings of Jesus, exegetical questions—usually about the New Testament—and doctrinal questions.

Although many studies of Gnostic creation myths have emphasized the role of Jewish traditions in formulating them,[2] ApocryJn is the only dialogue that interprets the Genesis story in light of Gnostic myth. NatArc prefaces the revelation to Norea with a midrashic account of the Urgeschichte that is closely linked to Genesis.[3] Its narrative account of Sabaoth shows the influence of Jewish apocalyptic, mystical and wisdom traditions.[4] These traditions are accepted answers to dogmatic questions, not objects of speculative or apologetic concern in their own right. ApocryJn, on the other hand, introduces an element of "reversal" into its dialogue on Genesis which—like the description of God in TestTr—suggests that its Gnostic interpretation of Genesis is part of a deliberate polemic.[5] In the introduction to ApocryJn, the seer's perplexity was precipitated by a Jewish charge that Jesus had taught his disciples to reject the traditions of their fa-

---

[1]See Perkins, "On the Origin of the World," and the discussion of topological theology in W. Schoedel, "Topological Theology and Some Monistic Tendencies in Gnosticism," *Essays on the Nag Hammadi Texts in Honour of Alexander Bohlig,* NHS III, ed. M. Krause (Leiden: E. J. Brill, 1972), 88–108.

[2]For example, F. Fallon, *The Enthronement of Sabaoth: Jewish Elements in Gnostic Creation Myths,* NHS X (Leiden: E. J. Brill, 1978), and G. MacRae, "The Jewish Background of the Gnostic Sophia Myth," *NovT* 12 (1970), 86–101.

[3]See R. Bullard, *Hypostasis,* 67–69.

[4]Fallon, *Enthronement,* 25–67, though some of the changes and inconsistencies that he uses as evidence of literary redaction seem to be the types of confusion that creep into oral traditions and may not indicate purposeful changes in the theology of the story.

[5]See above, pp. 16–17.

CHART FOUR
Formal Content of Gnostic Revelation Dialogues

	I,2	II,1	II,4	II,7	III,4	III,5	V,3	VI,1	VII,3	VIII,1	VIII,2	BG	PS
formulae for God above all		x			x		(x)			x			
theogony		x			x		(x)			(?)			x
Sophia myth		x	x		x		(x)			x	x	(?)	x
apocalyptic vision*	x					x			x[4]	x		x	x
hymn/prayer		x	x		x	x	x			x		x	x
liturg. formula/creed				(?)			x				x	x	
sermon/paraenesis	x			x		x				x			
wisdom about the cosmos+		x[2]		(?)		x							
Genesis citation		x	x		x								
sayings of Jesus	x			(?)					x		(x)		psalms
questions about:[1] Scripture	NT	OT	x	(?)	NT[3]	NT	(NT)	(NT)	NT	x	x	x	OT/NT
doctrine	x	x	x	x	x[3]	x	x			x	x	x	x
ironic/dumb ques.	(?)		x	x			x			x	x		x

* = visionary report; journey into or vision of heaven or of the fate of souls there.
+ = "pseudo-scientific" knowledge.
(?) = depends upon interpretation of a difficult or fragmentary text.
(x) = feature alluded to or barely mentioned.

[1] excluding the introductory lists discussed in the setting of the revelation dialogue.
[2] astrological lore; anatomical correlations between body, archons and elements.
[3] the relationship between the questions and the answers supplied from Eug is not always clear.
[4] takes the form of visions of the real events of the crucifixion; not the usual apocalyptic vision.

thers.[6] The questions and answers on Genesis may have been inserted from a separate source[7] as the author's response to that charge. Aside from ApocryJn and NatArc, the revelation dialogues take the story of origins from a Sophia myth that is regarded as established tradition. It is not an issue of controversy.[8]

Things are quite different with the New Testament. ApocPet has an unusual combination of visions and exegesis of the crucifixion account. Peter sees the crucifixion and then is told to look again to see what really happens (CG VII 72, 4—73, 18). Finally, he has a vision of the true, glorious nature of the Savior (81, 3–82, 3) that culminates in his commission as bearer of Gnostic tradition (82, 4–84, 6). Thus, ApocPet has taken over the format of apocalyptic vision to serve as New Testament interpretation. Peter's visions are interrupted by discourses on the various types of people and Church leaders whose true nature will be revealed at the parousia (e.g., 78, 7–79, 1). These discourses frequently allude to the Gospel of Matthew and other New Testament writings. Interpretation by allusion in a larger context is frequent in Gnostic writings. We also find *erotapokriseis* types of interpretation. Pagels and Koester suggest that DialSav used an exegetical source that interpreted the sayings of Jesus in a fashion similar to GTh.[9] ApocryJas seems to have used a collection of interpreted parables and kingdom sayings.[10] ThCont may have incorporated material from such a tradition of sayings interpretation.[11]

---

[6]CG II 1, 10–17.

[7]CG II 13, 17–27, "moving to and fro"; 22, 9–21, "serpent"; 22, 21–23, 4, "forgetfulness"; 27, 31–29, 11, the section on the imitation spirit, may represent an expansion of another such question.

[8]Irenaeus objects to Gnostic interpretation of the creation story in connection with his rejection of their doctrine of God (AdvHaer II 1–10). Many Christians might have been willing to accept the negative portrait of the Old Testament God in Gnostic writings, since they would have concurred with a severe judgment against the Jews. Some traditions explicitly excluded them from the mission charge of the risen Jesus; see Bauer, *Das Leben*, 271f. Jews and Christians continued to have somewhat hostile debates through the fifth century; see R. Wilken, *Judaism and the Early Christian Mind* (New Haven: Yale, 1971), 1–68.

[9]Pagels-Koester, "Dialogue," 67f.

[10]See below, pp. 100–103. The author has added extensive allusions to the farewell discourses of the Fourth Gospel.

[11]This material is embedded in sections that Turner, *Thomas the Contender*, 4, 109, 216–28, identifies as an *erotapokriseis* source.

Koschorke notes that their mode of appropriating other religious traditions is more universally characteristic of Gnostics than any specific mythological theme.[12] Synthetic accounts of gnosis like those in Irenaeus or in such Nag Hammadi writings as TriTrac are not complete without the transcendent Father, the origins of the pleroma, the story of the fall of a heavenly figure—usually Sophia[13]—and some account of the subsequent redemptive activity.[14] Among the revelation dialogues, only ApocryJn and SJC follow this pattern throughout. If the Genesis dialogue of ApocryJn represents an independent insertion, then the two even have a similar structure: (a) highest God and the aeons; (b) Sophia myth—broken by more material on the aeons in SJC;[15] (c) redemptive activity of the Savior on behalf of Sophia's seed;[16] (d) teaching on the destiny of the various types of souls. SJC simply lists the various locations in the pleroma for souls of different degrees of gnosis. ApocryJn has used another independent Gnostic catechesis that includes a two-spirit doctrine. Whichever spirit the soul follows determines its destiny.[17] This order is similar to Irenaeus' account of the Valentinians except that it lacks any account of Gnostic sacramental praxis. ApocryJn refers to an anointing with five seals as necessary for immortality but does not describe it.[18] Whenever SJC departs from its source for the description of God and the aeons, Eug, the narrative becomes confused. Many items of the mythic story, such as the boast of the chief ar-

---

[12]Koschorke, *Die Polemik*, 5.

[13]U. Wilkens, "Sophia," *TDNT* 7 (1971), 509, considers the wisdom myth the foundation of Gnostic systems. For systems centered on a male figure see the discussion of the Hymn of the Pearl and of Poimandres in Jonas, *The Gnostic Religion*, 112–73. TriTrac has taken a Sophia myth and adapted it to the male figure of the logos.

[14]Even Eug, which is concerned with the highest God and the aeons, includes references to the redemptive knowledge that will come through the activity of Sophia and the Immortal Man, e.g., CG III 71, 5–13. Its epistolatory conclusion, 90, 4–11, promises another teacher, but it is not clear whether that teacher is to be a Gnostic revealer or a revered Gnostic teacher like the author of Eug.

[15]See Perkins, "The Soteriology of the Sophia of Jesus Christ," *Proceedings of the Society of Biblical Literature Vol. I* (Cambridge: Society of Biblical Literature, 1971), 165–181.

[16]SJC BG 121, 14–122, 7; CG III 117, 1–118, 25; ApocryJn CG II 30, 11–31, 25.

[17]SJC CG III 117, 8–118, 3; ApocryJn CG II 25, 16–27, 30.

[18]CG II 31, 22–25.

chon, are only alluded to in passing.[19] Thus, SJC would hardly serve as a didactic summary of Gnostic teaching in the way that ApocryJn might.

Such passing allusions and short paraphrases are typical of the revelation dialogues. Both 1 ApocJas and Zostr mention all three stages of the Urgeschichte account. 1 ApocJas alludes to the teaching about the highest God and the aeons in a brief exchange between Jesus and James before the crucifixion. The Sophia myth appears as part of a liturgical formula to be recited by the ascending soul.[20] The fragmentary state of Zostr makes it impossible to define the character of its allusions to the emanation of the aeons and the Sophia myth.[21] PS contains extensive material about the aeons and Sophia's fall. Her repentance is the main theme of its exegesis of the psalms. But PS lacks the formulaic descriptions of the transcendent Father. Thus, only ApocryJn provides the systematic summary of Gnostic teaching that one might expect on the basis of Irenaeus' account of Valentinianism or the Sethian-Ophites.

The Sophia myth, on the other hand, occurs frequently. It is the basis of the revelation to Norea in NatArc and is paraphrased in PetPhil.[22] Various attempts have been made to resolve the versions of the myth into a simple original that was developed by later speculation.[23] MacRae has traced the influence of the fall of Eve and the fate

---

[19]CG III 107, 9–11.

[20]CG V 24, 19–25, highest god; 24, 25–25, 5, aeons. The author thus implies that Jesus taught James gnosis of the pleroma during his lifetime. Reference to the Sophia myth, 34, 1–15, occurs in a formula that AdvHaer I 21, 5 attributes to the Marcosians. Bohlig, *Koptisch-gnostische Apokalypsen aus Codex V von Nag Hammadi* (Sond. Wiss. Zeit. Martin-Luther Univ.: Halle Wittenberg, 1963), 32, points out that the two examples are probably independent of each other.

[21]For example, CG VIII 29, 1–38, 5 may have been a rather lengthy account of the aeons similar to that in ApocryJn. CG VIII 9, 6–11, 9 seems to be a short paraphrase of the Sophia myth.

[22]PetPhil CG VIII 135, 8–136, 15.

[23]For example, H.-M. Schenke, "Nag Hammadi Studien III: Die Spitze des dem Apokryphon Johannis und der Sophia Jesu Christi zugrundeliegenden Gnostischen Systems," *ZRGG* 14 (1962), 352–61; L. Schottroff, *Der Glaubende und die feindliche Welt* (Neukirchener-Vluyn: Neukirchener Verlag, 1970), 45–105, constructs an extensive typology of Gnostic Sophia myths. She thinks that SJC has elevated Sophia, while we see her dual role as a fundamental polarity in the Gnostic story.

of Wisdom from Jewish sources.[24] However, our consideration of the oral foundations of Gnostic composition makes us wary of such systematizing. All versions mix motifs of redemptive activity by Sophia or her consort with the redemption brought by the Gnostic Savior, usually Christ.[25] A set sequence of events may underlie the versions, with each teller rendering the story according to his own variations. What is called "myth" in most of the dialogues consists in a telling, paraphrase of, or allusion to the Sophia story. The features of the story are represented in the paraphrase of PetPhil and the two NatArc versions:

PetPhil	NatArc #1	NatArc #2
Mother creates an aeon without the Father	(boast of the lower god)	Mother creates without consort
Authades appears part left in chaos	power goes into chaos	Authades appears his boast leads to part going into chaos
lower heavens created they rejoice, but are ignorant praise from lower aeons makes Authades proud, envious creation of material	lower heavens created	lower heavens created
		Authades boasts
	visible world	Authades goes to chaos;
world, bodies as false images	after pattern of the invisible	his son, Sabaoth, is exalted

---

[24]MacRae, "Jewish Background." The combination of Eve's fall and the plight of divine wisdom in the world presupposed in MacRae's article suits the dual character fundamental to the Sophia figure.

[25]Perkins, "Soteriology," 172–77.

Valentinian speculation later straightened out the dual role of Sophia by dividing the figure into a higher and lower Sophia. Some Gnostic theologians revised the reason for her fall to fit their speculation on the nature of the Father. Her fault was an excessive desire for knowledge of the unknowable Father.[26] However, the revelation dialogues do not engage in such speculation. They seem content to paraphrase the myth in order to provide a basis for the redemptive activity of the Gnostic revealer.

We have already seen that apocalyptic traditions played a role in the presentation of the heavenly revealer. As part of the content of revelation dialogues, visions are usually associated with traditional topics. The visionary "sees" the heavenly regions or the fate of the souls in those regions. Since Gnostics reject the visual heavens of Jewish speculation as the creation of the lower god, there is little description of things in those heavens. ApocryJas makes a partial description of the disciples' attempt to follow the ascent of Jesus. It retains the traditional language about angels and trumpets.[27] But it, too, rejects visionary speculation, since the ascent is aborted before they attain the highest realm.[28] DialSav contrasts the vision, which shows the judgment of a soul, with the eternal vision of God. Jesus can show his disciples the former, but the latter is reserved for the person who has died.[29] GMary also contains a vision of the ascent of the soul, but lack of several pages makes it difficult to say how that vision was interpreted.[30] Zostr is the only revelation dialogue that makes the heavenly journey the mode of revelation. The seer's progress through the various aeons provides his initiation into knowledge of the highest God. PS contains both information about heavenly treasuries (PS I-III) and the fate of individual souls (PS IV). Apoc-Pet is unusual in that the seer's vision is a mode of interpreting ca-

---

[26]See Perkins, "Gnosis as Salvation."

[27]See M. Malinine et al., Epistula Iacobi Apocrypha (Zurich: Rascher, 1968), 81–84.

[28]See the discussion of ApocryJas below, pp. 151–152. The section may be intended as a rejection of Jewish throne mysticism. Malinine, Epistula, 85, suggests a parallel between this aborted trip and Sophia's attempt to grasp the inconceivable Father in Valentinian myth.

[29]CG III 132, 6–19; 134, 24–137, 3.

[30]BG 10, 1–17, 9. Perhaps attributing the vision to mind, which is between soul and spirit, is an indication of the lesser value of such experiences.

nonical Gospel traditions. Perhaps the devaluation of heavenly visions over against knowledge of the highest God led Gnostics to drop the visionary elements of Jewish apocalyptic traditions that they appropriated.

Apocalyptic visions often include wisdom material. The seer learns the secrets of the origins of the world, the disposition of its various elements and so forth.[31] Occasionally such wisdom about the cosmos surfaces in the Gnostic dialogues. Pagels and Koester have isolated a section of DialSav as a cosmological wisdom list.[32] But, as is the case with the vision of the soul, the authors use this list as a negative example. Without gnosis, all such knowledge is superfluous. The creation account in the long version of ApocryJn has incorporated sections of esoteric wisdom. Astrological speculation has been used in describing the archons.[33] The creation of man has been expanded with anatomical lore, which correlates various parts of the body with heavenly bodies and with the elements that compose it.[34] The question and answer on the rising of the sun in ThCont probably originated in such a context, though it has since been elaborately reinterpreted.[35]

Finally, some dialogues also contain extensive sections of homiletic and paraenetic material. Both ThCont and Zostr preach ascetic rejection of the world. ApocryJas contains a sermonic exhortation toward willingness to depart from the world.[36] The paraenetic sections of these writings probably represent the preaching traditions of their respective communities.

In general, then, the content of the revelation dialogue derives from the various didactic modes of discourse within Gnostic commu-

---

[31]Smith, "Wisdom and Apocalyptic," argues for the scribal origin of apocalyptic and hence its dependence on wisdom traditions.

[32]CG II 133, 16–134, 27. This section may have been tied to 127, 23–131, 15, which describes the creative activity of the logos.

[33]See A. J. Welburn, "The Identity of the Archons in the Apocryphon of John," VigChr 32 (1978), 241–54.

[34]CG II 15, 29–19, 10. The concluding reference to further information in a book of Zoroaster may simply be a topos of esoteric writing.

[35]CG II 139, 18–24.

[36]CG I 7, 10–35; 8, 10–10, 6; 11, 11–12, 7. Both ApocryJas and ThCont conclude with eschatological woes and blessings: ApocryJas CG I 11, 11–12, 17; ThCont CG II 142, 30–145, 16.

nities. Formulae describing the highest God, hymns, creeds, and other liturgical pieces may have been recited in common. Exegetical and doctrinal *erotapokriseis* material, especially set pieces on interpretation of Scripture and the fate of the soul, may have had a catechetical use. The paraenetic sermons must certainly have been directed at members of the community. They are not rhetorically designed to persuade the unconverted. Perhaps even the mythical paraphrases reflect homiletic or liturgical usage—usage we can document in the ApocryJas Sophia material. In all of these instances, the content is presented as traditional information, not as theoretical exploration by the author.

Topical Content of the Gnostic Revelation Dialogues

Our survey of the formal characteristics of the content has already introduced some of the content. Investigation of the topical concerns of these writings emphasizes the overriding concern with soteriology.

We have seen that the dialogues do not pursue a general outline of Gnostic teaching. The following topics appear five or more times: Sophia, the necessity of revealed gnosis, asceticism, ascent of the soul, New Testament interpretation, baptism. Other topics such as Genesis interpretation, the nature of the highest God, the crucifixion, and cosmic eschatology occur less frequently. They probably reflect the particular situation of their communities. The Sophia story is often the object of questions, while questions about the highest God and Genesis are comparatively rare. Only SJC, ApocryJn and Zostr ask about God. ApocryJn and SJC do so in the context of the common New Testament theme that Jesus as revealer has made him known.[37] The mystical tradition of Zostr is more concerned with how knowledge of God is possible.[38] The Genesis interpretation in Nat-Arc derives from a midrashic story that introduces the visionary, Norea. It is not the object of her perplexity or of direct statements by the revealer—whatever traditions of Jewish exegesis may have gone

---

[37]ApocryJn CG II 2, 25–3, 1; SJC CG III 96, 18–97, 16; 106, 5–8.
[38]For example, CG VIII 2, 13–24.

CHART FIVE
Topical Content of the Gnostic Revelation Dialogues

	I,2	II,1	II,4	II,7	III,4	III,5	V,3	VI,1	VII,3	VIII,1	VIII,2	BG	PS
URGESCHICHTE													
highest God	x	x	x		x		(x)			x			
Sophia	x	x	x		x	(x)	(x)			x			x
Adam/Noah	(x)	x	x										
SOTERIOLOGY													
revealed gnosis	x	x	x	x	x	x	x			x			x
asceticism	(x)	(?)		x	x	x	(?)	x		x			x
soul's ascent	(x)	(x)	(x)		x	x	x			x	(?)	x	x
TRUE DOCTRINE													
vs. OT/law	x	x					(x)		(x)				
interpretation of Scripture	NT	OT		(NT)	(NT)	NT			(NT)				OT/NT
Christ is Gnostic revealer	(x)	x			x		x						
crucifixion	x				x		x		x				
baptism	(x)		(x)	x	x	x			(x)			x	
ESCHATOLOGY													
vs. the powers					(x)	(x)							
judgment	(x)[1]	(x)[1]	x	x	(x)	(x)			(x)[1]		(x)		(x)[1]
eschatological blessings	(?)		x	x	x			x					

(?) = depends upon the interpretation of a difficult or fragmentary passage.

(x) = implied, barely mentioned or reinterpreted.

[1] post-mortem judgment of individual souls.

into the story of the enthronement of Sabaoth.[39] The Genesis section of ApocryJn, on the other hand, deliberately opposes Gnostic teaching to the usual interpretation of the Old Testament. This section may still be aimed at Judaism, though other Gnostic writings use the Old Testament or the Law to symbolize Christian opponents. Jews and Jerusalem commonly represent orthodox Christians in Valentinian exegesis.[40] It is often difficult to decide how such references are to be interpreted in a particular Gnostic writing. However, the primary exegetical interest of the revelation dialogues is the New Testament, particularly the teaching of Jesus. Irenaeus reflects this facet of Gnostic teaching in his repudiation of Gnostic interpretation of the parables.[41]

Since the Sophia myth was the main topic of interest, it is perhaps not surprising that soteriology is the main topical concern in the dialogue. The combination of motifs that we find here should warn us against accepting facile generalizations about "present salvation through knowledge" as the essence of Gnostic teaching.[42] Although revealed gnosis is clearly a necessary condition for salvation, it is never a sufficient condition. The catechism on the soul in ApocryJn warns that some, who are Gnostics, may apostatize.[43] ThCont, DialSav, AcPet12, Zostr, and PS all make asceticism a requirement for salvation. This requirement is indirectly alluded to in other writ-

---

[39]Fallon, *Enthronement*, 67, notes the ambiguity of the account of Sabaoth's enthronement in that there is no clear indication of its function in the narrative. He proceeds to argue that it was intended to validate revelation through Moses and the prophets, 67–88. But NatArc shows no concern with deriving gnosis from the Old Testament. Its Old Testament traditions are simply accepted as the story of the origins. The larger context of the Sabaoth account may be to represent a group—heterodox Jewish Christians?—within which the Gnostics are located rather than to validate the Old Testament. To that extent, Bullard's suggestion, *Hypostasis*, 110, that Sabaoth represents psychic Christians in a Valentinian division of humanity has some plausibility. However, Fallon's argument against direct Valentinian influence seems decisive: *Enthronement*, 77f.

[40]So Pagels, "The Demiurge and His Archons—A Gnostic View of the Bishop and Presbyters?" *HTR* 69 (1976), 301–24.

[41]For example, AdvHaer I 3, 1; 8, 1; II 10, 2. See Van Unnik, "A Document of Second Century Theological Discussion (A. H. I 10.3)," *VigChr* 31 (1977), 207f, 222–25.

[42]An unfortunate emphasis on Fallon's typology in "Gnostic Apocalypses."

[43]CG II 27, 21–30.

ings. The James tradition links renunciation of the world and martyrdom. SJC refers to the necessity for Gnostics to avoid the
"unclean rubbing" (*tribē*) that ties one to the flesh and makes one
forget one's divine origin.[44] Such preaching is much like the lengthy
condemnation of lust in ThCont.[45] The section on the imitation spirit
in ApocryJn presupposes a "two spirits" tradition. Souls who conquer the imitation spirit through the spirit of holiness are saved.[46]

These writings generally associate salvation with the post-mortem ascent of the soul. They have not interiorized the ascent so as to
perceive the stages of the journey as facets of the psychological transformation and divinization of the ascetic. Thus, Jonas refuses to consider Gnosticism a form of mysticism.[47] Zostr, as we shall see, may
even be opposing such mysticism as it had developed in Platonic circles. The dialogues insist that ascent of the soul represents the true
liberation from the bondage of this world.[48]

Although this journey is the main focus of Gnostic eschatology
in the dialogues, Gnostic writings do retain some examples of cosmic
judgment scenes that seem to be dependent upon those in Jewish
apocalypses.[49] NatArc is the only dialogue which contains the full
pattern of apocalyptic judgment in association with the coming of
the Gnostic revealer. Some of the language of such judgment scenes,
particularly the woes and blessings, has passed on into the paraenesis
of the ascetic tradition as in ThCont, AcPet12 and possibly Apocry-
Jas. Usually the individual souls face judgment after death as they either negotiate the passage out of the cosmos successfully or are
thrown back into it.[50] We find the eschatological overthrow of the

---

[44]CG III 93, 16–24; 108, 4–16.

[45]For example, CG II 139, 31–140, 5. In ParaShem, CG VII 4, 16–5, 21, "rubbing," leads to the generation of the lower world out of nature. Its imagery invokes the
old mythic pattern of the impregnation of the chaos monster.

[46]CG II 27, 7–22.

[47]Jonas, "Myth and Mysticism: A Study of Objectification and Interiorization in
Religious Thought," *JourRel* 49 (1969), 315–18, 329; also see E. R. Dodds, *Pagan and
Christian*, 27–29, and the discussion of this problem in my "Deceiving the Deity."

[48]Even when this ascent is expressed in terms of an apocalyptic eschatology as in
NatArc CG II 97, 1–20.

[49]See the chart in Fallon, "Gnostic Apocalypses," 148, 8.1–3, and Perkins,
"Apocalypse of Adam," 389–91; *idem*, "Rebellion Myth," 19–24.

[50]For example, ApocryJn CG II 26, 32–27, 30.

powers of evil historicized in some dialogues. It becomes a function of Gnostic preaching.[51] This historicization underlies the Gnostic teaching about "our conflict with the powers" in the introduction to NatArc (CG II 86, 20–25). It forms the key to the apostolic ministry in PetPhil:

> You are to fight with them like this, for the archons are fighting the inner man. You are to fight with them like this: come to a place and teach salvation with promise in the cosmos. Gird yourselves with the power of our Father and reveal your prayer and the Father himself will aid you.[52]

This passage is a collage of various New Testament passages commissioning the disciples. The explanation that the battle with the powers is with the inner man also appeared in the introduction to NatArc. It may represent the usual Gnostic interpretation of the apocalyptic language that had become part of its tradition.

Other doctrinal themes in the dialogues seem to be tied to the polemic setting of particular writings. Christian Gnostics require an interpretation of the crucifixion, since the powers of the lower world cannot gain control over the heavenly revealer. ApocPet presents such Gnostic teaching along with explicit reference to orthodox interpretation of the cross as a sin offering. No one, it says, is saved by belief in the name of a dead man. Those who think to have been made pure through his death are deceived.[53] The most common soteriological debate concerned the sacrament of baptism.[54] Many Gnostic groups had their own ritual substitutes such as the sealing and anointing of ApocryJn or the baptisms in the aeons of Zostr. ThCont and DialSav oppose orthodox reliance on baptismal forgiveness, since orthodox Christians used it to vindicate their rejection of the Gnostic ascetic praxis.

---

[51]For example, SJC CG III 119, 1–8. This may also be the proper interpretation of the conclusion to NatArc as Wilson, *Gnosis and the New Testament* (Philadelphia: Fortress, 1968), 125, suggests.

[52]CG VIII 137, 20–30. Author's translation from the *Facsimile Edition: Codex VIII*, (1976).

[53]CG VII 73, 32–74, 22. See the discussion in Koschorke, *Die Polemik*, 37–47.

[54]For a general survey of Gnostic baptismal polemic, see Koschorke, *Die Polemik*, 143–47.

Thus the predominant emphasis of the revelation dialogue is on soteriology, not on speculation about the cosmos or doctrine. It does not introduce new ramifications of Gnostic thought or theoretical refutation of opposing views. Most of its contents are familiar forms of Gnostic religious discourse. But the dialogue genre does provide the Gnostic believer with something not found in many of the non-dialogue forms of the same material. It provides an apologetic focus by which he or she can orient his or her convictions about salvation over against the authorities claimed by opposing religious traditions. Gnostic teaching comes from the authority of the great heroes of those traditions. We must now turn to detailed investigation of the polemic setting of the various revelation dialogues before returning to the general religious issues at stake in the Gnostic dialogue.

PART TWO

Traditions and Polemic in the Gnostic Dialogue

CHAPTER FIVE
The Gnostic Revealer

The range and severity of polemic varies widely from dialogue to dialogue as our survey of their contents has already suggested. The four dialogues in this group have little explicit polemic. Since we consider the claim to be the esoteric truth of the religious tradition within which one dwells essential to Gnosticism, we would suggest that these writings show Gnostic apologetic in situations where the religious authorities of the larger group have not yet mobilized against Gnostic preaching. Though some may have opposed the Gnostic message, the force of the larger tradition has not yet been brought to bear against the Gnostic option. Some brief observations derived from our surveys of the content of the dialogues support this suggestion. Neither of the works in which Christ is the Gnostic revealer, ApocryJn and SJC, presents controversy over specifically Christian issues. Both are close to the standard three-part summary of Gnostic teaching: God, aeons, Sophia myth. ApocryJn is the only revelation to a single disciple that lacks a hostile reaction to the communication of gnosis by other disciples. In SJC there is no hint of division among the disciples over their mission or the revelation given them. Neither writer feels the need to explain that the earthly Jesus really did teach gnosis. Nor do we find esoteric interpretations of the sayings or parables of Jesus. The simple presentation of the Risen Jesus as Gnostic revealer is sufficient.

The other two writings in the group, NatArc and Zostr, do not refer to Christianity at all in their presentation of salvation. Scholars are divided over their provenance. Are they secondarily Christianized examples of non-Christian Gnostic speculation? Or did the

Christian Gnostic authors feel no need to mention Christ, since they were concerned about events in the primordial time.[1] Both writings now contain superficial allusions to Christianity. The introductory letter to NatArc quotes Paul on the fight with the powers, and the concluding call to gnosis in Zostr seems to attack Christian baptism. Whatever the connection between the authors of these writings and Christianity may have been, they are certainly not interested in establishing Christ as the revealer of gnosis so as to exclude all others—a move that we see replacing the more fluid situation of revelation through Sophia and/or the Immortal Man in the soteriologies of ApocryJn and SJC.[2] Porphyry tells us that Zostr was read in those Gnostic circles against which Plotinus wrote his condemnation of Gnosticism (Enn II, 9).[3] Since Zostr lacks specifically Christian concerns, some interpreters suggest that it stems from a Platonizing pagan gnosis at Alexandria.[4] Its text is so fragmentary that a certain judgment is impossible. Christ could have appeared among its aeons. But whether from Christian or pagan circles, its primary concern seems to be with the kind of mystic Platonism that was common in both contexts. Plotinus' concern about the danger of Gnostic speculation among his own acquaintances shows that this Gnostic synthesis enjoyed some initial success. Plotinus marshals the resources of Platonic philosophy against this new speculation whose non-analytic approach to truth is opposed to the fundamental cognitive structure out of which Plotinus works.[5]

---

[1] See the discussion of the various views about NatArc in B. Layton, "The Hypostasis of the Archons," *HTR* 67 (1974), 363f. Layton opts for a Christian provenance for the writing.

[2] Perkins, "Soteriology," 170–172.

[3] Porphyry *Vit.* c. 16. See the discussion by A. D. Nock, "Gnosticism," *Essays on Religion and the Ancient World*, ed. Z. Stewart (Oxford: Oxford University, 1972), 943. A non-Gnostic tract in the collection, *Silvanus*, evidences an Alexandrian Christian philosophy which would be a likely milieu for the discussion of God and the use of mystic Platonism that we find in Zostr. On this type of Chritianity, see F. Wisse, "On Exegeting the 'Exegesis on the Soul,'" *Les Textes de Nag Hammadi*, 69, and J. Zandee, *The Teachings of Silvanus and Clement of Alexandria: A New Document of Alexandrian Theology* (Leiden: Ex Oriente Lux, 1977), 134–136.

[4] See the general discussion of J. Sieber, "An Introduction to the Tractate Zostrianos from Nag Hammadi," *NovT* 15 (1973), 233–37, and his introduction in *NHLE*, 368.

[5] See the discussion of Plotinus' objections in my "Deceiving the Deity."

In all four dialogues, then, the Gnostics are not on the defensive. They are free to make their case on their own terms. We know from Porphyry that Zostr was a foundational writing in Platonist Gnostic circles. The surviving manuscripts suggest that ApocryJn was equally important in its own context. The four surviving copies represent a long and a short recension. In addition, AdvHaer I 29 quotes a Gnostic writing very close to the opening section on God and the aeons. Irenaeus does not seem to be extracting his account directly from either known version of ApocryJn. He may have obtained it from Valentinians, who considered it a traditional foundation for their own speculation.[6] Thus, the foundational importance of ApocryJn seems assured. For SJC, we have a fragment of the Greek version,[7] and two Coptic copies which seem to be from a single recension. Two Coptic copies of Eug, the work SJC used for its account of the highest God and the aeons, also survive. These traditions, at least, would seem to have been of wide significance. Though NatArc only survives in a single version, close parallels between it and traditions that are expanded and interpreted in OrigWld suggest that it enjoyed some circulation.[8] However, as Layton points out, its terse and allusive style suggests that it was not intended to be an account of the fundamentals of gnosis.[9]

The diversity of materials within the Nag Hammadi collection has led scholars to question traditional patristic classification of Gnostic sects.[10] One cannot expect to hunt through patristic lists and find a sect behind each of these writings. Ancient religious groups were not overly concerned with doctrinal systematization. Orthopraxis, represented by adherence to a local group and custom, is what counts. This praxis and custom has always been an allusive fea-

---

[6]Perkins, "Irenaeus," 199f.

[7]See the edition of the Greek fragment by H. Attridge, "Poxy 1081 and the Sophia Jesu Christi," *Enchoria* 5 (1975), 1–5.

[8]See the parallels discussed in M. Tardieu, *Trois Mythes Gnostiques* (Paris: Etudes Augustinienes, 1974), and the detailed comparison of the Sabaoth accounts in Fallon, *Enthronement*, 10–24.

[9]Layton, "Hypostasis," 371.

[10]See the groundbreaking articles by F. Wisse, "The Nag Hammadi Library and the Heresiologists," *VigChr* 25 (1971), 205–23; "The Sethians and the Nag Hammadi Library," *Society of Biblical Literature One Hundred Eighth Annual Meeting Seminar Papers*, ed. L. McGaughy (Missoula: Society of Biblical Literature, 1972), 601–607.

ture in Greek religious life.[11] The names given to the aeons, the myths of Sophia, and the predictions of the coming of the immortal man or revealer have all led scholars to use the general designation "Sethian" for this tradition.[12] Other non-dialogue writings also belong to that all-encompassing category. The revelation of gnosis to a primordial ancestor of the Gnostics occurs in ApocAd, a testament from Adam to Seth, in GEgypt, a revelation Seth is said to have inscribed on pillars, and in ParaShem, in which the seer on a heavenly journey meets the sons of Seth in the aeons. This last is sometimes thought to be the *Paraphrase of Seth* referred to in Hippolytus, *Ref.* V, 19—possibly a Christianized version of related traditions.[13] The cosmologies of ParaShem and Zostr, the only dialogue with such a journey, are sufficiently different to make direct dependence of one on the other unlikely. Perhaps both drew inspiration from the Enoch literature which was widespread in this period. We find direct quotations from Enoch books in the Mani codex and the Turfan fragments.[14] Enoch journeys may have been part of the mystical literature of the circles which Zostr seeks to address. Like Enoch, Zostr returns from his heavenly journey to preach to men on earth—as does Shem.[15]

REJECTING THE TRADITIONS OF THE FATHERS

However, there is a crucial difference between Zostrianos and Jewish visionaries like Enoch. Zostr does not set an example of righteousness or piety according to the norms of a given tradition. Gnosis turns him from other traditions which he is said to have been preaching (CG VIII 1, 10–2, 5). Perhaps this reference is even to other forms of gnosis. This conflict with the older tradition is reflected in the charge of "rejecting the traditions of the fathers." John's Jewish adversary plunges the disciple into despair by leveling this charge

---

[11]Nock, *Essays*, 963.

[12]Fallon, *Enthronement*, 69.

[13]See J. C. Greenfield and M. E. Stone, "The Enochic Pentateuch and the Date of the Similitudes," *HTR* 70 (1977), 63f.

[14]See above, pp. 39–45.

[15]See J. L. Martyn, *History and Theology in the Fourth Gospel* (New York: Harper & Row, 1968), 61–68.

against Jesus in ApocryJn (CG II 1, 13–17). Jews commonly made this accusation against Christians. It occurs in Jn 7:12, 47, in Justin Martyr, *Dial* c. 1xix, and in the Talmud, *Sanh.* 43a.[15] In the *Acts of Philip*, the high priest Anamias[16] accuses Philip of trying to turn people from the traditions of their fathers.[17] Hegesipus preserves a similar charge against James for having gone astray after Jesus (Euseb. *H.E.* II 23, 4 and 10). The traditionalism of Late Antique society gave such charges a seriousness that we find quite unimaginable. Nevertheless, the Gnostics do not deny that their revelations involve such a departure. We have seen that the questions and answers in ApocryJn are formulated on the principle "not as Moses said." In his perplexity about God, Zostr is introduced praying according to the customs of his fathers. Finally, in desperation, he goes out to hand himself over to the beasts of the desert (CG VIII 3, 14–28). The angelic rebuke rejects those traditions by establishing Zostrianos as "father of your race" (=Gnostics) and reminding him that he has a different Father, Yalaos (CG VIII 4, 11–19). Thus, Zostr agrees that the revelation of gnosis implies rejection of ancestral religiosity. The vindication of such rejection is not exegetical as in ApocryJn but in the journey which will teach the seer the truth about God and about "his race."[18] Rejection of the fathers is not thematized in the setting of NatArc. But it does contain an unusual pericope in which the son of Ialdabaoth, Sabaoth, sees the evil in his father, repents and is given divine assistance. He does not become a member of the pleroma but is enthroned over the seventh heaven. There, Sophia's daughter, Life, tells him about the things in the Eighth.[19] If one accepts the suggestion that Sabaoth represents a splitting off of the good aspects of the Jewish God,[20] then one might almost say that the Father revolts against himself. Such revolts in Gnostic speculation are always in recognition of a higher God, the one to whom the Gnostics belong.

---

[16]Compare the name of the Pharisee in ApocryJn, CG II, Arimanias; BG, Almanios.

[17]AcPhil 19(14). See J. Blackstone, "A Short Note on the Apocryphon of John," *VigChr* 19 (1965), 163.

[18]Compare ParaShem CG VII 41, 29–31. ParaShem is closer to apocalyptic visions, since the seer sees what will happen to his race in the future.

[19]CG II 95, 13–96, 3.

[20]Fallon, *Enthronement*, 34.

Thus, we may suggest that Zostr, NatArc and ApocryJn represent different versions of the same apologetic argument. The Gnostics do reject traditions of the fathers, but they do so in reliance on the revelation of a higher deity. SJC, on the other hand, shows no trace of this polemic. Perhaps the debate there is an inner Gnostic one over Christian vs. non-Christian mediators of salvation.

THE NATURE OF THE ARCHONS

NatArc focuses on the Sophia story and the promise of future redemption for her seed. It opens with a Genesis midrash (CGII 87, 12–93, 2) that is followed by a revelation dialogue (93, 3–97, 10). The dialogue describes the origin of the archons and predicts their coming destruction. The Genesis material in the first part typically undercuts the values of the original stories. Such traditions may have originally been formulated to vindicate Gnostic withdrawal from the larger group of Jews or Jewish Christians.[21] We have seen that the Genesis dialogue in ApocryJn explicitly encourages such rejection of the tradition.

The epistolatory introduction interprets the conflict with the powers in Pauline terms. As is the case elsewhere, the language of apocalyptic destruction of the powers of evil has become attached to the effectiveness of Gnostic preaching. The most elaborate example of this tradition appears in PetPhil. Certain similarities between the two suggest that a common Gnostic tradition may have been used by both authors. Both open with the same questions: (1) What is the nature/deficiency of the archons? (2) What is the situation of the Gnostics in their struggle with the powers?[22] Both answer with an epitome of the Sophia myth.[23] Insofar as the versions agree, they follow a common story-line about boasting and rebellion in the lower world. However, the boasting stories in NatArc show certain peculiarities when contrasted with the common versions of the story. The chief archon boasts before his creation of the lower aeons as well as in the

---

[21]See Perkins, "Apocalypse of Adam," 394f; *idem*, "Rebellion Myth," 20f.
[22]See NatArc CG II 86, 26f; 93, 33–94, 2; 96, 15–17, 31; PetPhil CG VIII 134, 18–135, 2; 137, 18–25.
[23]See above, pp. 64–65.

traditional place where the boast is a response to the praise of his off-spring.[24] The second account in NatArc stands closer to Jewish hag-gadic traditions. There, the boastful Ialdabaoth is cast down to Tartaros by an angel. The restoration of cosmic order, which follows divine action against rebellion in Jewish stories, is here represented by the enthronement of Sabaoth.[25] ApocryJn has the more common version of the story.[26] Sophia, not Sabaoth, is the one who repents. Her plea initiates the process of restoration. Perhaps, NatArc has displaced the Sophia figure. The plea for help now comes from Norea. The first version begins *in medias res* without any account of the Mother's fall.[27] Replacing the repentance of Sophia by that of Sa-baoth would seem to represent a deliberate assessment of Jewish tra-ditions. Eleleth, one of the four Lights, who answers Norea's plea, appears in other versions. His voice, or that of all four angels, speaks from heaven and brings about the repentance of Sophia.[28] In GEgypt, Repentance creates the Gnostic seed.[29] Such parallels suggest that NatArc has displaced the Eleleth-Sophia theme to the beginning of the story and inserted the repentance of Sabaoth in its place. Howev-er, the repentant Sabaoth on his throne only rules the seven earthly heavens. Though he is told about it, he does not enter the Eighth. In other words, the vision of the heavenly throne chariot so prized by Jewish visionaries does stand at the height of this world, but it does not belong to the divine. This combination suggests that the tradition at issue is not the Old Testament per se but visions of apocalyptic seers on whose traditions the Gnostics drew for many of their stories. The partial truth in those visions derives from Sabaoth's repentance and his instruction in the realities of the world above him.

---

[24]NatArc CG II 86, 27–87, 11; 94, 19–95, 13. This double boast tradition is also preserved in OrigWld CG II 101, 2; 103, 4–32. If it is original with NatArc, then OrigWld must be dependent on some version of that work. If not, then both are de-pendent upon a common tradition. See the treatment of the double boast stories in my "Religious Polemic."

[25]Perkins, "Rebellion Myth," 16–24.

[26]ApocryJn CG II 13, 5–32.

[27]The theme of the boasting archon is so widespread that Gnostic authors often allude to it without further elaboration. See ApocryJn CG II 11, 15–22; 2 ApocJas CG V 56, 26–57, 1; GrSeth CG VII 53, 28–31, OrigWld CG II 107, 18–108, 5; 112, 25–113, 10.

[28]TriProt CG XIII 29, 13–40, 4.

[29]CG III 56, 22–59, 20.

Other modifications in the Genesis midrash show a similar approach. The restoration which concludes the first boast-rebellion scene requires that Pistis establish the lower archon's offspring according to the pattern of the world above (86, 27–87, 11). Notice that Ialdabaoth does not or cannot act according to a heavenly pattern. Contrary to the usual story, he does not set up his own heavens. This alteration fits in with other comments in the midrash. The powerlessness of the archons is continually emphasized. The story is punctuated by references to the heavenly reflection, "which appeared to them in the waters," that the archons would like to copy. Each reference is followed by statements indicating that the archons are powerless.[30] Gnostic stories usually mention the ignorance of the archons. This emphasis on their powerlessness is peculiar to NatArc. The revision of the story to show that, although he boasts, the chief archon cannot even set up his own heavens represents a dramatic confirmation of that powerlessness.

The Norea story and the associated revelation dialogue provide further evidence of the powerlessness of the archons. Any Gnostic reader will recognize that the prayer of Norea is similar to the one that he or she has been instructed to give on the heavenly ascent.[31] Comparing it with the liturgical formula for the ascent of the soul in 1 ApocJas we find the following pattern:

	NatArc	1ApocJas
(1) I am not from your race	II 92, 25	V 34, 1–10
(2) I am from above	92, 26	33, 15–24
(3) powers thrown into confusion	92, 32–93, 2	35, 5–35, 1[32]

---

[30]CG II 87, 15–20; 88, 1–3; 89, 5f; 90, 33.

[31]Another writing gives Norea's prayer upon ascent into the pleroma, *The Thought of Norea* (CG IX, 2); see Pearson, "Norea," 151f. Thus, the "bad girl" of Jewish haggadah has become a model for Gnostic piety.

[32]In NatArc the angelic revealer appears and disperses the powers; in 1 ApocJas, Jesus frees the soul by praying to the higher Sophia.

The apocalyptic conclusion to NatArc proclaims victory over the powers. When the Gnostic revealer comes, the Gnostics will trample the powers and ascend into the pleroma. We have noted that SJC interprets "trampling" as the apostolic preaching.[33] The introductory letter to NatArc supports a similar understanding of the victory over the powers. The eschatological promise may originally have been invoked as response to hostility experienced by members of the sect. They would be reassured that, like Norea, they are not of the race that belongs to the lower world.

The narrative divides humanity into three types. Fallon is probably correct in rejecting the suggestion that this division derives from Valentinianism.[34] There are those who follow the blind god, Ialdabaoth, who is ignorant, thinks he has gnosis and envies the Gnostics. Sabaoth protects another group, those whom he preserves in the ark.[35] But they reject Norea and leave her outside the ark where she is persecuted by the archons until Eleleth comes to rescue her. It seems that this second group represents the context within/against which NatArc is written, probably a form of esoteric Judaism.[36] Since there is no reference to active preaching on the part of the Gnostics, NatArc would seem to support a passive stance in the face of opposition. The Gnostics are to remain confident that their power and salvation even exceeds that of those who claim to have seen the divine chariot on which Sabaoth is seated.[37] The Gnostic will ascend above the realm of kingship into that of true divinity and the presence of the Father. The concluding judgment scene, then, functions as such scenes do in other sectarian communities. It assures the group of their own vindication and of cosmic ratification of the truth they possess.

---

[33]CG III 118, 15–119, 8.

[34]So Bullard, *Hypostasis*, 110; see Fallon, *Enthronement*, 67f.

[35]See Layton, "Hypostasis," *ad loc*.

[36]Unless the larger group is a Judaizing, mystic Christianity such as seems to have been represented by the Colossian heresy.

[37]We think that the rejection of symbols of kingship in NatArc derives from the association with this religious mysticism, and not from the political order as Fallon suggests in *Enthronement*, 80.

ZOSTRIANOS

We have already seen that the setting of Zostr is indebted to Enoch traditions, whose heavenly journeys probably appealed to this type of Gnostic. While one might expect a Platonist to internalize such a journey, Gnostics seem to lack the kind of metaphysical psychology required for a mysticism of that sort. Zostr is not mere speculation about heavenly regions, however. Its polemic edge is visible in the opening treatment of the traditions of the fathers. The Gnostic learns to reject those fathers and find new ones. This rejection is explicitly stated at the end of the journey. The seer is dismissed with the words: "Behold, Zostrianos, you have heard all these things of which the gods are ignorant and which are unattainable to messengers" (CG VIII 128, 15–18). In short, no other tradition mediates knowledge of the divine pleroma. Zostr then returns to the body to begin preaching gnosis. In order to do so, he must deceive the lower gods, who would otherwise oppose his preaching (130, 10–131, 25). Their opposition might even be said to underlie that experienced by the Gnostics. The general character of the statement indicates rejection of all other traditions, not just Judaism. A similar view appears in a longer section of TriTrac, where the truth of Christian gnosis is contrasted with the errors of pagan religions, philosophies, philosophical Judaism, Jewish interpretations of the Law, and finally the prophets.[38]

Zostr is in such a fragmentary state that it is not easy to discern its structure. The author seems to have compiled a variety of traditions. We have seen that he may have inserted blocks of Gnostic questions to organize and divide the sections.[39] The seven groups which survive indicate the major concerns of the author. They also show that, whatever the contacts between this writing and Plotinian circles, the author is still concerned with exteriorized journey language and with the eschatology of the various types of soul. This limitation characterizes all the Gnostic writings in this group and should caution us against interpreting them in terms of interiorized mysticism such as we find in Plotinus.[40]

---

[38]CG I 109, 5–114, 1.
[39]See above, pp. 55–56.
[40]See the discussion of this problem in my "Deceiving the Deity."

The surviving sets of questions focus on God and the differences in souls:

(1) *2, 24–3, 13:* The opening questions are a formal requirement of the dialogue genre. Here the seer is puzzled by a philosophical question typical of the period, the transcendence and unity of God. How does the One-Beyond-Existence emanate to produce the pleroma?

(2) *7, 27–8, 7:* The seer has received baptism in the aeons through which he has passed. He now asks their names and about the differences in human souls. A summary of the Sophia myth follows.

(3) *13, 14–24:* Zostr summons another angel to ask about the power of the different baptisms. An account of the waters proper to each member of the pleromatic hierarchy and of the purity of each level follows.

(4) *22, 2–13:* These questions apparently deal with the type of intellectual faculty required at each stage.[41] The powers of perfect mind, soul and pneuma, are described. Then follows an account of the types of soul and their places in the pleroma.

(5) *45, 3–9:* Zostr asks about the scattering of the different types of soul in the aeons and in matter. A long passage recounts their imprisonment and connection with various aeons and baptisms.

(6) *96, 4–15:* This set of questions is very fragmentary. It seems to have concerned the judges and punishment.

(?) Several pages are missing. We assume that they contained at least one set of questions introducing the context for the description of the harmonious existence of all the spheres of the cosmos.

(7) *128, 20–25:* These final questions return to the beginning: What is the truth about the highest God? The question is resolved when Zostr is brought up to the First-Appearing-Mind and joins those there in blessing the Hidden Aeon, Barbelo, and the invisible Spirit. This experience perfects the seer. He says: "I joined with all of them and blessed the Hidden Aeon, the virgin Barbelo, and the Invisible Spirit. I became all-perfect and received strength. I was written in glory, sealed, and received a perfect crown there" (129, 8–16).

---

[41]Compare GMary BG 10, 17–22. She asks which faculty sees the vision of the Savior.

He then descends to preach. On the way down, he meets the Gnostic race and leaves three tablets in the astral region for their later use.

Typically for Gnostic apocalypses, the visionary element is missing throughout. The seer learns or hears about different waters and types of soul in the heavenly region. He does not see them and then seek interpretation as a Jewish visionary would do. Nor does he withdraw into himself in silence and become unified with the One as in Plotinus' famous description:

> If, then, one of us, though unable to see himself, is possessed by that God and brings forth the vision to see (him), he brings forth himself and sees the embellished image of himself. But leaving the image behind—however beautiful it is—he becomes one with himself, no longer dividing the One, which is everything, and with that God, present in silence. He is with him as much as he is able and wishes to be. If he then returns to duality, being pure, he is near to him so that he can similarly be present with him again if he turns toward him. And there is this reward in turning around—he begins to perceive that he is "other" and turning within he has all; and abandoning perception, because he is afraid to be "other," he is one again. And if he desires to see something which is other, he puts himself outside.[42]

Thus we are again confronted with the "in between" character of Gnostic consciousness. The concrete visual imagery of Jewish throne mysticism is gone; so are the visions of the heavenly journey. They both belong to the transitory and material world. The Platonic strand in Gnosticism[43] has taught Gnostics to distinguish the world of "images," of matter, and mortality from the immortal, unchanging pleroma that has come forth from the highest God. Zostr has learned that lesson well and has applied Platonic language to its characterization of the levels of being and of the highest God.[44] But

---

[42]Enn. V 8. 31, 11; cp. VI 9. 9, 3.

[43]Layton, "Hypostasis," points out various signs of popular Platonism in NatArc.

[44]See the parallels to Plotinus' terminology discussed by Pearson in "Marsanes," by Robinson in "Three Steles," and by M. Tardieu, "Les Trois Steles de Seth," *RevScTh* 57 (1973), 545–75.

Gnostic descriptions of the origin and structure of the cosmos remain welded to narrative exteriorization. There seems to be no conceptualization of the inner life of the self that would make the transforming vision described by Plotinus a live religious option. Zostr seems to be an extensive compilation of Gnostic teaching on the destiny of the soul in relation to the pleroma and the highest God. Porphyry tells us that Gnostics used the book to support their claim that "Plato had not plumbed the depth of intelligible being." Since Porphyry also tells us that Plotinus' pupil, Amelius, wrote forty books against Zostr, we must assume that it enjoyed considerable popularity among Platonists.

Zostrianos is introduced as a person who had already attained ascetic perfection, "as much separation from the body as possible." He had also been preaching this doctrine (1, 5–2, 6). His desire to fathom the One-Beyond-Existence leads him to withdraw to the desert to be delivered from the body by the wild animals—an ascetic attitude familiar to late Roman man.[45] Epictetus issues a warning against suicide as a means of gaining release on the grounds that one must wait for the god.[46] The *medecin* Thessalos says that if his search for the secrets of astrological botany fails, he will commit suicide. Through priestly intercession, magical formulae, and a preparatory fast, he obtains a visionary interview with the god.[47] Zostr is appealing to the same topos when the seer goes to the desert to force a conclusion to his quest for the mysteries of the highest god. The ancient reader would have viewed him as a mystically inclined ascetic preacher. Zostr concludes with an example of this preaching cast in the characteristically Gnostic form of a call to awakening.[48] This short homily also contains clues as to the circumstances surrounding the writing. The elect are told to expect reproof and ill-treatment (130, 26–131, 1). It seems that opposition not only came from Platonists but from Christians as well. The Gnostics are warned not to be

---

[45]See P. Brown, *Making*, 79f; Dodds, *Pagan and Christian*, 27–33; W. Schoedel, "Jewish Wisdom and the Formation of the Christian Ascetic," *Aspects of Wisdom in Judaism and Early Christianity*, ed. R. Wilken (Notre Dame: Notre Dame, 1975), 188f.

[46]Epictetus, *Discourses*, 16–17; Schoedel, "Jewish Wisdom," 188.

[47]See A. J. Festugiere, "L'Experience Religieuse du Medecin Thessalos," *Hermetisme et Mystique Paienne* (Paris: Aubier-Montaigne, 1967), 157.

[48]See MacRae, "Sleep and Awakening."

"baptized with death." Though much of the doctrine in Zostr seems to be non-Christian,[49] this conclusion suggests that the author also had to deal with the problem of Gnostic converts to Christianity. He may also have hoped to win Christian Platonists to his teaching. However, neither Christian nor pagan Platonists would have found the radical dualism of the work with its emphasis on the unknowability of the highest God acceptable.[50] Notice that Zostr only ascends as far as the first-emanated Mind. He praises the highest God from there. He does not become identical with the highest triad as Plotinus might have spoken of an identificaton with the One. The following passage from Clement of Alexandria shows how Christian Platonists would have described the mystic ascent:

> . . . those Gnostic souls, who by the greatness of their vision even exceed the manner of life of each of the holy orders[51] among which the dwelling places of the gods are distributed and assigned. Considered holy among the holy, and carried completely beyond them, they attain places even better than the best, where they no longer receive the divine vision in mirrors through mirrors, but are feted with a vision that is perfectly clear and distinct, in which there is no satiety for living souls, who enjoy eternal bliss for unending ages, since they all are considered worthy of abiding in identity and transcendence. Such is the vision by direct apprehension of the pure in heart.[52]

Angelic orders of varying degrees of purity are all well known to us from Zostr. But Clement, like his pagan counterparts, assumes that the highest goal is direct vision and identity of the soul with the divine. Joining in divine praises one level below an unknowable God would hardly suffice.

---

[49]So J. Sieber, *NHLE*, 368.

[50]See the discussion of this passage and Clement of Alexandria's mystical doctrine in J. Daniélou, *Gospel Message and Hellenistic Culture* (Philadelphia: Westminster, 1973), 335–40.

[51]Compare Zostr on the purity of the various angelic realms.

[52]See Strom VII 3. 13, 1; 10. 57, 1–5, and the discussion in Daniélou, *Gospel Message*, 449f.

Thus, the polemic in Zostr is directed toward Platonist circles of the mid-third century. Zostr rejects both the Platonist and Christian versions of the ascent of the soul. The opening scene shows the reader that all the asceticism and prayer of the great Zostrianos was futile until he received heavenly revelation of gnosis. Plotinus accused such Gnostics of abandoning the traditions of their fathers and the true wisdom of Plato. He suggested that people who adopted such a view simply gave in to natural human arrogance and desire for superiority. But for Zostrianos the greatest ascetic practice and all the traditional prayers would have been futile, and he would have been devoured by the beasts, if saving gnosis had not come to show him the truth about God.

APOCRYPHON OF JOHN

Although the content of Zostr and NatArc did not deal with Christian themes, the final versions of both indicate contact between the Gnostics and Christianity. The remaining revelation dialogues are more explicitly Christian. The long and short versions of ApocryJn show some variation in the assimilation of Christian and Gnostic traditions. They differ in the degree to which Christ is identified with the redemptive activity that the Gnostic story assigns to other heavenly figures. We have observed that SJC Christianized accounts of salvation by Sophia and her consort, the Immortal Man, by adding statements about Christ's liberating activity as necessary not only for Gnostics but also for Sophia and her consort. ApocryJn is similar. Christ is included in the Gnostic theogony by being identified with the heavenly aeon Autogenes and anointed with the goodness of the invisible Spirit.[53] The invisible Spirit sets Christ over the pleroma and subjects the powers to him.[54] The primary figure in accounts of primordial revelation and salvation seems to have been the Epinoia of Light, Life, who is sent by the Father to help the power of the Mother that had been lost by her fall.[55] The short version emphasizes

[53]See S. Arai, "Zur Christologie des Apokryphon Johannis," *NTS* 15 (1968/69), 303–307.

[54]CG II 17, 15–30.

[55]BG 53, 4–10; 53, 18–54, 4.

the connection between Sophia's plea and the sending of the Spirit.[56] According to this version (see BG 71, 5–13), Sophia plays a role in sending Epinoia to humanity. The long version, on the other hand, drops the reference to Sophia's redemptive activity (CG II 27, 33–28, 5). In the short version, she is the one who awakens people and gives them knowledge.[57] The only Christianization of this activity comes in the Savior's statement that he is the one who caused them to eat of the tree.[58] In the long version, he actually gives a call of awakening from the tree.[59] The hymnic addition to the long version identifies Christ with the Pronoia who descends into the world to awaken people.[60] The parallel in the short version has the Mother descend into the world before Christ to raise up her seed (=Adam?).[61] She is also said to take on human form in her seed, while in the long version the revealer changes himself into her seed. Thus, the short version supposes that various heavenly figures have been responsible for the redemptive revelation of gnosis. The long version, on the other hand, brings all such activity under the auspices of Christ by equating his mission with the Epinoia/Pronoia figure.[62] A similar move may be reflected in the account of the Sethian-Ophites in AdvHaer I 30. There, Sophia is constantly active on behalf of her offspring, but she never descends into the world to aid them. The only descent is that of her brother Christ who comes to free her.[63] In both cases, the authors seem to be emphasizing the fact that all saving activity is tied to Christ. This shift may be a sign of increasing influence of orthodox Christian formulations in Gnostic circles. All revelation must now be traced to Christ.[64]

---

[56]BG 51, 1–17//CG III 23, 19–24, 3; BG 63, 16–64, 13//CG III 32, 9–22; Arai, "Christologie," 309 n. 3. Since Sophia is not at all involved in sending the spirit in the Codex III account, that version may be the earliest according to H.M. Schenke, "Nag Hamadi Studien III: Die Spitze," 357 n. 15.

[57]BG 55, 15–18; 57, 8–19; 60, 1–3; 60, 16–61, 7; 64, 1–13.

[58]BG 57, 20–58, 1; cp. CG II 22, 9, Arai, "Christologie," 318.

[59] CG II 23, 26–33.

[60]CG II 30, 11–31, 25; MacRae, "Sleep and Awakening," 502; Arai, "Christologie," 311f.

[61]BG 75, 10–76, 1.

[62]Arai, "Christologie," 312–315.

[63]AdvHaer I 30, 4–7.

[64]See D. Parrott, "Evidence of Religious Syncretism in the Gnostic Texts from Nag Hammadi," *Religious Syncretism in Antiquity*, 182–184.

Though it does identify Christ as the source of Gnostic revelation, ApocryJn is not yet involved in debating specific points of Christian teaching. We have seen that it is the most complete and the most catechetical in its presentation of gnosis. It follows a pattern of topics similar to that in Irenaeus' exposition of Valentinianism (AdvHaer I 1, 1–8, 6): (1) the One and the divine triad; (2) emanation of the Dyad and the first powers; (3) generation of the intelligible world; (4) Achamoth and the intermediary world (a Valentinian development to deal with the ambiguity of Sophia's role); (5) Ialdabaoth and the heavenly world; (6) man and the material world; (7) redemption. This descending order was probably characteristic of Gnostic catechesis.

We have already seen two charges against the Gnostics in the setting of ApocryJn. They turn from the traditions of their fathers, and they keep their revelations secret in order to command a high price for them. The first charge is commonplace in anti-Gnostic writings, but it is also one that the Gnostics might accept. As in Zostr, the true God sends the revealer to aid a humanity that cannot gain knowledge of him through the other religious and philosophical traditions. The apostle was puzzling over the identity of the Father who sent Jesus at the beginning of the revelation much as Zostrianos was anxious to know the mysteries of the highest God. Both go off to a deserted place to find the resolution of their perplexity. Since none of the ancestral traditions convey knowledge of this God, they will be rejected.

The second charge, trafficking in revelations, also appears in Irenaeus (AdvHaer I 4,3). ApocryJn must admit the secrecy of Gnostic teaching, but denies that Gnostics keep their revelations secret in order to make money from them. In fact, such dealings are forbidden by the revealer himself. Despite such indications of opposition, hostility is not as much of a preoccupation in ApocrynJn as it was in NatArc or even Zostr. NatArc pronounces eschatological judgment on those who oppose gnosis. Zostrianos' sermon issues a severe warning against them. ApocryJn takes a more irenic stand. The only souls that are eternally condemned are those that have been Gnostics and have apostatized.[65] When John tells the other disciples

---

[65] CG II 27, 21–30.

of his revelation, the hostile reaction so characteristic of other dialogues is missing. The reader would assume that they all accepted John's revelation as Christian teaching, though the reference to apostasy in the description of the types of souls shows that the author knows that rejection of gnosis is possible. Perhaps ApocryJn would not have evoked the kind of hositility from the Christian side that other Gnostic writings do because it does not attack peculiarly Christian doctrines. The traditions that are reversed are those of the Old Testament. Dialogues which evidence more hostility between the two groups take on sensitive Christian areas like the nature of salvation and the death of Christ. The main concern of ApocryJn is to show that Christ is identical with the Gnostic revealer and with the highest God. All true Christians are to be Gnostic Christians.

SOPHIA OF JESUS CHRIST

We have already seen that SJC is very similar to ApocryJn in the topics under discussion. The main exception is that concern for Genesis exegesis has faded from the picture. The eschatological promise that Gnostics will defeat the powers such as we found at the end of NatArc is attached to the victory of apostolic preaching. At the conclusion of SJC, all the apostles go off joyfully to preach gnosis. SJC employs the full imagery of resurrection scenes from the canonical Gospels to associate its Gnostic content with the apostolic mission.

Yet the content of the "Gospel of God" which the Gnostic apostles preach has little to do with Christianity per se. Its account of God and of the pleroma is almost a verbatim copy of another Gnostic tract, Eug.[66] As to salvation, it agrees with Eug that knowledge of God is essential for salvation. In Eug, saving knowledge makes a person immortal. The Gnostic knows the difference between the imperishable divine realm of the aeons and this perishable world. SJC concurs (see CG III 93, 22ff; 98, 6–9). SJC includes Christ in the system by using Johannine metaphors of Jesus as the revelation of the

---

[66]Parallel versions of Eug and SJC are conveniently printed in *NHLE*, 207–28; W. Foerster, *Gnosis 2. Coptic and Mandaic Sources* (London: Oxford, 1974), 24–39, has the Eug text followed by a list of the variants and additions from SJC.

true God. Those who can receive gnosis are "begotten not by unclean rubbing but by the first Father who sent him" (CG III 93, 18–22=Jn 1:13). No one has known God until the revealer has made him known (94, 9–14=Jn 1:18). Thus, Jesus summarizes his mission as having come to reveal the God who is above the universe (118, 15–26).

SJC uses a traditional theological argument to insert into Eug an explanation why the highest God emanated in the first place (96, 14–97, 11). The goodness and generosity of the highest God is the reason he produced the pleroma. He does not enjoy blessedness alone. Instead, he is glorified by the whole heavenly company of the immortals. This company includes the Gnostics. This argument is a traditional theological explanation of creation in Christian circles where it may have been derived from a similar argument in Philo.[67] For our purposes, the most interesting version of this argument appears in Irenaeus (AdvHaer III 25, 5f). Irenaeus attacks the Valentinian creation story as a failure to recognize the goodness of God as the beginning of creation. Creation, he insists, derives from divine goodness, not from ignorance or a fall (also see AdvHaer IV, 14). The Gnostic author has turned this traditional argument to his own purposes. He argues that the goodness of God is reflected in the emanation of the perfect pleroma down to its final form in the imperishable Gnostic race. Material creation has nothing to do with the goodness of the highest God.

Like ApocryJn, SJC presents Christ as the true revealer of gnosis. Its soteriology has grafted Christ onto the primordial salvific activity of Sophia and of her consort, the Immortal Man.[68] First, we are told that the Immortal Man will awaken humanity through an interpreter (101, 9–15). Later this awakener is identified as Christ (14, 21). The first block of soteriological material has a pattern that is repeated in the remaining sections:

(1) *Sophia acts (106, 24–107, 10):* She sends light to the world to subvert the ignorance of the Creator God.

---

[67]For example, Philo *Creat.* xxi; *Cher.* xxviii; Tertullian *Apol.* xvii, 1; Origen *de-Prin.* ii, 9–16; Athanasius *ResMort* xii.

[68]Compare the True Man promised as revealer at the end of NatArc. Contrary to Layton, "Hypostasis," 363, this figure refers to the primordial revealer figure, the consort of Sophia, and not to Christ.

(2) *Savior acts (107, 11–108, 4):* A first-person description of the Savior's role in freeing Sophia's drop follows.

(3) *Exhortation to gnosis (108, 5–15):* The section concludes with a second person exhortation to the disciples to be awakened and to trample the powers with their preaching.

The same pattern is repeated in the concluding section of the soteriology:

(1) *Sophia acts (CG III 114, 14–25; BG 118, 13–121, 13):* The Father creates the veil between the pleroma and the lower world. Light (=soul) comes to man from Sophia as a revelation of the higher world and of the gnosis that will be achieved with the future coming of the Immortal Man.[69]

(2) *Savior acts (BG 121, 13–122, 8; CG III 117, 1–118, 2):* Christ must free the Immortal Man and bring the gnosis necessary for the various types of soul to go to their places in the pleroma.

(3) *Exhortation to gnosis (118, 3–119, 7):* This exhortation is the commissioning of the disciples as Gnostic apostles.

SJC has identified Christ with the first light and with the revealer of gnosis. Neither the Mother nor the Immortal Man could succeed in freeing the fallen drop of Sophia. Schotroff suggests that the discrepancy between such claims on the part of Christ and the narrative references to Sophia's redemptive activity shows that later Gnostic thought moved to elevate Sophia above her fallen status.[70] Our investigation of ApocryJn suggests that the opposite process is involved. Intensification of the picture of Christ as the source of all Gnostic revelation leads to the demotion of other revelatory figures. Other features in SJC support this hypothesis. The descriptions of the Savior's activity in the soteriological material fit with I AM statements that SJC has inserted into the Eug material:

(1) I am from the Light. I am the one who knows it so that I can tell you the real nature of Truth (93, 8–13).

(2) No one knows the Ineffable One unless he wills to be revealed through the One-from-the-First-Light. I am the great Savior (94, 9–14).

---

[69]Again compare NatArc: the revelation to Norea included the promise of the future revelation of gnosis.

[70]*Der Glaubende,* 104f.

(3) I came from the Boundless One to tell you all things (96, 19f).

(4) I came from the Self-Begotten and the First Light to reveal all to you (106, 2–9). This last is an addition to a Eug statement about the glory of the kingdom of the Son of Man, which has never been revealed.

These additions also show that SJC emphasizes the role of Christ as revealer of gnosis. This emphasis seems to be at the expense of primordial revelatory activity by Sophia and her consort.

We have seen that SJC is not organized to be a complete, catechism-like presentation of gnosis in the way that ApocryJn is. The opening list of questions is purely formal. It is not dealt with in the elaborate account of the aeons which follows. However, the concluding statement of purpose—the revealer came to reveal the Unknown Father—does indicate the scope of these writings. The questions raised by the disciples during the dialogue also seem awkward, as they break into the text. But they do fall into the two categories mentioned in the final commission. They focus on the Father and the pleroma and on the disciples and their mission. We find:

(1) an acclamation: Jesus alone has gnosis (94, 1–14).

(2) requests for information about the Father of the aeons (95, 15–21; 96 14–17; 100, 7f; 106, 9–14; 107, 14–16).

(3) requests for information about something that has already been asked or revealed. These requests serve to emphasize the disciples' need to know the relevant material (105, 3–7//100, 17f; 112, 20//107, 14–16).

(4) the only exegetical question: Why does the Gospel call the revealer Son of Man (103, 22f)?

(5) questions about the gnosis of the disciples (98, 10f; 119, 9–12).

These questions seem to have been formulated with the setting and polemic in mind. None of them fit smoothly into the doctrinal exposition. Nor do they seem to derive from source material used by the author, as in the case of the Genesis and the soul material in ApocryJn. In connection with the setting of the work, the questions assure the reader that true apostolic preaching is the source of gnosis.

Thus, like ApocryJn, SJC presents Christ as the Gnostic revealer. Its emphasis on apostolic preaching and its incorporation of an established Gnostic treatise on God and the pleroma suggest that the audience of this writing may have been somewhat different. In ApocryJn, Christ reveals all the Gnostic doctrine necessary for a person to understand the basic tenets of the movement. Here, on the other hand, the soteriological information is so condensed that a person would require a fuller account of the Sophia myth to understand its allusions. The focus is on the revelation of the Father and the pleroma. I AM statements in the style of the Fourth Gospel have been adapted to show that Christ is the only one who can bring that knowledge. A traditional theological argument about the goodness of God as the reason for creation has been modified to show that that creation really refers to the emanation of heavenly aeons down to the immortal Gnostic race. These emphases suggest that the claim advanced in SJC is that true gnosis is only available in Christianity. Such preaching may have been directed at non-Christians who found the wisdom about God and the imperishable realm in Eug congenial. In order to be a true Gnostic, one must be a Christian Gnostic.

Three of the four writings in this category, then, have an evangelical stance. NatArc, on the other hand, seems to be directed inward, toward preserving a community under persecution.[71] Porphyry provides evidence for the popularity of Zostr. The manuscript tradition suggests that ApocryJn also enjoyed wide circulation. With two copies each of Eug and SJC, one would assume that its account of the Father and the aeons was equally widespread. In each case, the revelation dialogue associates gnosis or its revealer with the religious values of a specific community—an association explicitly drawn by the I AM identity formulae in SJC. For Zostr, gnosis is the only source of mystic perfection. For ApocryJn, the true teaching of Christ is gnosis. For SJC, the true revelation of God and the pleroma can only be found in Christian gnosis. As we know was the case with Zostr, it is likely that ApocryJn and SJC also formed part of the missionary propaganda of their respective communities.

---

[71]This inner directedness accounts for the terse and enigmatic style of the writing. The author is not going out of his way to be esoteric (pace Layton). In a small community with its own symbolic language, an author would not need to say more.

CHAPTER SIX

The True Ascetic: The Thomas Tradition

Our survey of the content of the revelation dialogues showed that the majority of them insist on some form of ascetic praxis.[1] Expressions like "bondage to femininity," dissolution of what has bound you," "look at light; flee darkness," and "do not be led astray" from the concluding homily in Zostr (CG VIII 131, 5–132, 5) typify Gnostic exhortation to become free of the desires and passions. SJC warns against becoming "subject to the fire of the flesh" (CG III 108, 8–14). Since Zostr was portrayed as an accomplished ascetic prior to receiving gnosis, the author could presume that his audience shared a common commitment to disciplining the body even if they were not Gnostics. None of these writings attacked others for insufficient ascetic praxis. The Thomas tradition, however, claims that orthodox Christianity fails because it thinks that salvation without rigorous asceticism is possible.

The anti-heresiological, Gnostic tract *TestTr* provides more explicit examples of the stance represented in this tradition. TestTr attacks both orthodox Christians and those Gnostics who permit marriage, which these ascetics claim was an invention of the evil archon to enslave humanity to passion (CG IX 19, 29–30, 17). Orthodox laxity is blamed on an unwarranted confidence in baptismal

---

[1]For further discussion of Gnostic asceticism, see Koschorke, *Die Polemik,* 123–27, and K. Rudolph, *Die Gnosis: Wesen und Geschichte einer spatantiker Religion* (Göttingen: Vandenhoeck & Ruprecht, 1978), 134.

forgiveness. True baptism is ascetic renunciation of the world (69, 7–30). The Thomas tradition shows a similar type of ascetic gnosis. Complete renunciation of the world and of enslaving passion is necessary for salvation. Scholars have long associated GTh with East Syrian ascetic traditions. ThCont and DialSav seem to represent the same tradition.

The reader can easily see from the analytic charts in Part One that both these dialogues are somewhat a-typical. Though both make it clear that the revealer is the Risen Lord prior to the ascension (ThCont CG II 138, 22; DialSav CG III 120, 4f), they lack the opening epiphany in response to the disciples' perplexity, which is so typical of revelation dialogues. ThCont contains part of that tradition in the revealer's opening statement of purpose: "I will reveal to you the things you have been pondering in your mind. Now, since you are called my twin and true companion, examine yourself so that you may know who you are, how you exist, and how you will come to be" (CG II 138, 6–10). Like GTh, both dialogues claim to be records of a secret conversation between Jesus and his disciples. But here the issue of praxis, not doctrine, takes center stage. How does the true Gnostic escape the snares of the world? However radical the wholesale condemnation of lust in ThCont may seem, such ascetic preaching could command a wide audience in antiquity. Even Porphyry felt obliged to explain his marriage.[2]

THOMAS THE CONTENDER

ThCont is introduced as a record of the secret sayings of Jesus. Most of the work, however, comprises an ascetic homily which condemns lust as the power that leads humanity to bestiality.[3] Baptism with water will not save a person. The only effective baptism is ascetic renunciation. Though the introduction's similarity to that in GTh might have led one to expect a sayings collection, this ascetic homily

---

[2] See R. Wilken, "Wisdom and Philosophy in Early Christianity," *Aspects of Wisdom,* 152f.

[3] CG II 138, 1–20; cf. GTh 1.

is the basic literary form behind the dialogue.[4] Thomas is called the Lord's "twin" throughout the apocryphal Thomas tradition. Jesus' assertion that it is not right for the "twin" to be without gnosis is identical with that in the apocryphal James material from Nag Hammadi that it is not right for the "brother" to be without gnosis.[5] In both cases, the special resemblance to Jesus justifies his giving the person a revelation apart from "the twelve."

The customary list of questions appears in the revealer's statement of purpose as we have just seen. Jesus also insists that he is the only source of gnosis, a motif that we have seen come into increasing prominence in Christian Gnostic dialogues like ApocryJn and SJC. When Thomas asks for that gnosis, a second introductory section begins. The apostle is again commissioned as preacher of gnosis. Jesus responds with a series of proverbial sayings modeled on Jn 3:12. They follow the pattern, "If you cannot understand 'x', the lesser or earthly thing, how can you expect to understand 'y', the greater or real truth?"[6] This pattern dictates the following exchange:

> Thomas said to the Lord, "Because of this, I beg you to tell me the things about which I am asking before your ascension. When I hear from you about what is hidden, then I will be able to speak about it. It is clear to me that the truth is difficult to do before men." The Savior answered, "If the things which are visible to you are hidden from you (pl), how will you be able to hear about what is invisible? (Compare Jn 3:12.) If the works of truth visible in the world are difficult for you to do, then how will you do those which pertain to the exalted Majesty and the invisible Pleroma? How will you be called 'workers' (*ergatēs*)? Because of this

---

[4]Turner, *Thomas the Contender*, 215–24, tries to isolate a sayings source behind the work and to argue that it represents a stage in the transformation of the sayings collection genre by the dialogue. The argument for an actual sayings source behind this work is not convincing.

[5]1 ApocJas CG V 24, 12–15; 2 ApocJas CG V 35, 15–23. So also Turner, *op. cit.*, 125.

[6]So Turner, *op. cit.*, 131. Turner misses the Johannine allusion behind the references to "workers" and tries to draw a parallel to 2 Cor 11:13.

you are 'disciples' and have not yet received the Majesty of perfection.'"[7]

The expression, "the truth is difficult to do before men," is a commonplace of esoteric tradition.[8] ThCont has reduced it to one of the "lesser things." This reduction suggests that even the Christians against whom the work is directed accept esoteric traditions—about the interpretation of Jesus' sayings and parables. The Johannine model for the passage requires that the reference to "workers" be to Jn 4:38 rather than to Mt 9:37f (= GTh 73). Heracleon interpreted that passage of John to mean that the disciples are just psychics (= "disciples" in this passage). He argued that the true "sowing" was not their preaching but the presence of the Gnostic seed in the world.[9] The same exegetical tradition seems to be behind this passage. The apostolic preaching of the author's opponents, even if it is derived from esoteric Thomas tradition, is presented as only psychic. It does not represent the perfection of gnosis.

The expression "know hidden things from the visible" may have originated in apocalyptic circles. In ApocPaul, it refers to knowledge of what is hidden in the various heavens.[10] We have seen that for Gnostics the secrets of the heavens become the secrets of the pleroma. Eug shows that the contrast visible/invisible was a standard part of the Gnostic cosmogony.[11] There knowledge of the "difference" is the key to immortality, since it represents knowledge of the ineffable Father and his aeons. ThCont, however, has no cosmogony. The Savior's opening presentation suggests that a person might have such cosmogonic knowledge and not have saving gnosis. He says: "For he who has not known himself has known nothing. But he who has known himself has already achieved knowledge of the Depth of the All."[12] The call to "know thyself" was commonly used in philo-

---

[7]CG II 138, 21–36; author's translation from the text in Turner, *Thomas the Contender.*

[8]Cp. ApocryJn BG 64, 18; 64, 3: "great things are difficult to reveal."

[9]See E. Pagels, *The Johannine Gospel in Gnostic Exegesis* (Nashville: Abingdon, 1973), 105f.

[10]ApocPaul CG V 19, 14.

[11]CG III 73, 8—74, 22.

[12]CG II 138, 16–18.

sophic circles for the turn from the body and the world of sense perception to recognition of the divine within. One attained likeness to God through recognizing this inner divinity. ThCont seems to be using a tradition of radical asceticism not only against non-ascetic Christianity but also against claims to cosmogonic wisdom.[13] Such esoteric knowledge is not sufficient. Without asceticism, one cannot be saved from entrapment in bestiality.

Turner tries to divide the content between two sources, a dialogue on perfection as freedom from passion (CG II 138, 4–142, 25) and an ascetic homily based on interpretation of the sayings of Jesus (142, 26-end).[14] The author of the revelation dialogue as we have it combined the two in order to use the homily as an example of the kind of preaching that the apostle was commissioned to give. We have seen that Zostr adds such an exemplary homily to the end of the dialogue as do non-dialogue revelations by Enoch, by Shem in ParaShem, and by Poimandres in the hermetic tradition. The exemplary homily, then, might be considered commonplace across a wide span of esoteric tradition. But the homily which Turner reconstructs consists only in a woe/blessing section. Such a woe/blessing pattern derives from apocalyptic judgment scenes.[15] Its content fits so well with the injunctions against desire, *epitumia,* throughout ThCont that we are inclined to see the whole dialogue as derived from a single ascetic homily. The author has introduced the homily as the "truth about the hidden things." Thus he continues the critique of earlier speculation implied in the introduction. There, Thomas' request for information about the "hidden things" is answered by condemnation of the body based on the irrational passion for intercourse which produces it (CG II 138, 36–139, 12). Such ascetic preaching was probably standard fare in the author's group. The revelation dialogue enables him to direct it against the competing wisdom of other Christians, who also accepted esoteric Thomas tradition but rejected such radical asceticism.

---

[13]See K. Koschorke, "Die Polemik der Gnostiker gegen das kirchliche Christentum Skizziert am Beispiel des Nag Hammadi Traktates *Testimonium Veritatis,*" *Gnosis and Gnosticism,* 46, n. 9.

[14]See Turner, *Thomas the Contender,* 14f, 105–110, 216–23.

[15]*Ibid.,* 136, 194.

The exhortation itself mixes Jewish, Christian and Platonic themes.[16] The order of presentation may have been a fixed topos. The paraenetic sections of ThCont present the following order of topics:

(1) *138, 39–139, 12:*[17] bestial nature of the perishable body.

(2) *139, 32–140, 6:* against the fire of lust which dominates the body.

(3) *140, 12–37:* the contrast between the wise man and the fool, who is led into bestiality by lust.

(4) *141, 6–18:*[18] destiny of those subject to the flesh.

(5) *141, 25–142, 2:*[19] fate of what is bestial.

(6) *142, 11–18; 142, 30–143, 7:* the punishments of the abyss.

(7) *143, 8–145, 16:* concluding woes and blessings.

Most of the woes are against the flesh. Some, however, have been reformulated to apply to the author's opponents. They are an opposing sect (143, 39–144, 1). Their doctrine and preaching lead others astray (144, 36–145, 16). The author may have added the parable of the grapevine (144, 19–36) either to encourage Gnostic efforts against their opponents or to justify Gnostic separation from them as "the weeds."

Redactional comments within the homiletic material provide the following picture of the author's opponents:

(1) They seem to be separate from the Gnostics.

(2) Though they are not now members of the same group, the two groups may have once been together, since the author seems to consider the opponents apostates. They have abandoned a truth which they once had. Clearly both groups are claiming to be Christians.

(3) They preach baptismal forgiveness. Perhaps they even claim that it makes radical asceticism unnecessary.

(4) They engage in their own preaching and seem to have been attempting to convert members of the author's group.

Much of the dialogue between Thomas and the Savior has been

---

[16]As Turner, *op. cit.*, points out in the notes to the various passages.

[17]CG II 138, 14–139, 2 may be editorial comment by the author.

[18]CG II 140, 10–13 is an editorial comment branding the opponents as apostates.

[19]CG II 141, 25–28 uses a standard rhetorical *topos* against the opponents: they are divided among themselves.

awkwardly inserted into the homiletic exposition to elaborate on the relationship between the Gnostics and their opponents. Gnostics must be encouraged to preach despite the aggressive hostility shown by the opposition.[20] The author quotes some of the arguments being used against the ascetics (142, 19–25). Arguing against the rejection of the body, the opponents claim that if the body were to be rejected, we never would have been born with one.[21] Secondly, they argue that true Christian asceticism is to be found in good works and the control of the tongue.[22] The opponents must also have argued that baptism cleanses the Christian from the dangerous *epithumia* that so troubles the ascetic.

The dialogue sections also emphasize the necessity of Christian revelation. The Gnostics present themselves as the true Christians. Thomas frequently makes statements of loyalty to the revelation of Christ. Such statements may have been traditional confessional formulae within the community. Thus we find:

(1) *139, 13–31:* This passage seems to be a parable about archers which the author has reinterpreted to mean that the Savior is calling the elect out of bestiality. It includes the formulaic expression, "You are our light. Enlighten us, Lord!"

(2) *140, 7–12:* The Gnostic must observe the teaching contained in this revelation. The formula here: "You are the one who is good for us."

(3) *140, 38–141, 5:* This exchange presents Gnostic polemic against their Christian opponents. The opponents have revelation—the introduction suggested their interest in esoteric traditions—but not knowledge. Their lack of ascetic praxis is leading them to destruction (140, 39f). Further, it is imperative for Gnostics to separate themselves from such Christians (141, 2–4).

---

[20] See CG II 138, 25f; 141, 1f, 19–25; 142, 21–26 and the editorial comments inserted into the final beatitudes.

[21] This argument suggests that the opponents are not Gnostic Christians. Gnostics would probably account for the "unnatural" state of having a body in terms of their creation myth. Turner, *Thomas the Contender*, 226f, notes that the anthropology and cosmology of this writing is much less explicitly Gnostic than that of other revelation dialogues. Perhaps the particular context of its polemic attack accounts for this difference. Or perhaps the difference is another indication that the author intends to exalt ascetic praxis over any kind of esoteric wisdom.

[22] Cp. Jas 3:2–12.

(4) *142, 3–9, 19–26:* The Gnostics are persuaded but still worried about the opposition. "It befits you, Lord, to speak and us to listen" (142, 8f). "We are persuaded" (142, 18–21). Thus, ThCont has adopted the revelation dialogue in order to counter the influence of a non-ascetic Christian preaching.[23] Apparently this preaching also relied upon esoteric traditions that might have seemed to some to be a short-cut to gnosis. Since many of the formal elements of the revelation dialogue are only mentioned in passing—for example the Savior as light, the post-resurrection setting, the commision to preach—or occur in an unusual position, such as having the list of questions included in the revealer's statement of purpose, one might assume that the revelation dialogue genre was well known. Both the author and the audience understood the passing allusions as establishing this dialogue with their authority. It seems that the author wishes to make it clear in no uncertain terms that the Gnostic revelation of the Risen Savior included radical asceticism as practiced by members of the sect.

Although asceticism frequently occurs in the soteriology of the revelation dialogue, it is not as radical as in ThCont. Zostr is an accomplished ascetic before he receives Gnostic insight into the mysteries of the heavens and the highest God, which constitutes salvation. Both ApocryJn and SJC contain some ascetic language and warnings against lust, but neither makes radical renunciation of the body a condition of salvation. The author's opponents might even have found such traditions congenial, though their argument about the body suggests that they would not have accepted a myth of its demonic origin such as we find in ApocryJn. Therefore, we must conclude that the opponents were probably orthodox Christians who also revered traditions that were said to have come from the Risen Jesus through Thomas. By the time ThCont is written, the ascetics seem to have withdrawn to their own sect, "resting among their own." But there is still enough interaction among the two groups to produce converts to one side or the other. One must admit, however,

---

[23]We would essentially agree with Turner's suggestion, *op. cit.,* 217–20, that ThCont is directed against ascetic, syncretistic Christians. It also seems to us that the author's group was under severe pressure from the preaching of that group. Perhaps the similarity of traditions held by the two groups accounts for the opponents' success.

that ThCont reads as though the opponents are having more success in winning converts for their version of Christianity than are the ascetics.

DIALOGUE OF THE SAVIOR

Like ThCont, DialSav contains very little of the usual revelation dialogue setting. We begin *in medias res* with Jesus instructing the disciples about the time of dissolution.[24] He himself is about to depart. Krause has noted parallels with the language of ThCont and GTh in the author's use of *monochos* and *copt*, "solitary and elect," to refer to members of the sect. DialSav is unusual in referring to Thomas as Jude rather than using the Jude-Thomas common in Gnostic writings.[26] Though Jude takes pride of place and speaks more than the others,[27] the revelation here is not just to him but to the twelve and the women, especially Mary Magdalene. Matthew, the scribe in ThCont, appears as the third favored disciple in the group.[28]

The opening scene has been partly modeled on the farewell discourses of the Fourth Gospel. Jesus is leaving his labors to return to rest. The disciples are enjoined not to fear, since he has opened the way. The Father is glorified through prayer. The disciples are taught how to address the Father.[29] They have believed the truth and learned to know him. DialSav draws on these traditions because it

---

[24]"Time of dissolution" refers to the ascent of the soul at death in C.H. I 24. That usage fits the eschatological context of DialSav.

[25]Krause, "Der Dialog," 28f: *monochoi*, "solitaries," DialSav CG III 120, 26: ThCont CG II 1141, 25ff; GTh 33; *copt*, "elect," DialSav CG III 120, 26; 131, 24; GTh 49; 75.

[26]Krause, "Der Dialog," 24.

[27]*Idem.* He is singled out for praise by Jesus. Perhaps he was the original recipient of the vision of the fate of the soul, since the author has introduced a shift from singular to plural; see Pagels and Koester, "Report," 67.

[28]Krause, "Der Dialog," 23, observes that Matthew also appears as a scribe along with Philip and Thomas in PS lxxi, 20ff. He is also named in 1 Jeu, SJC and GTh.

[29]Pagels and Koester, "Report," 66, point to other traditional New Testament language in the prayer that Jesus teaches the disciples: "believe in truth" 121, 2//2 Thess 2:12; "redeem your soul" 121, 22f//Jas 1:21; 1 Pt 1:9; through the sacrifice of Christ 121, 20//Eph 5:2, Heb 10:10–19; the armor of God 121, 10//1 Thess 5:8ff, Eph 6:11–17.

represents a Gnostic treatise on eschatology. The author does reject water baptism without gnosis (CG III 133, 16–134, 24), but his reason is not a conflict between baptism and ascetic praxis. DialSav downplays baptism because it only anticipates the real eschatological goal, the ascent of the soul after death.[30]

DialSav covers a broad range of topics. It contains some forty-seven questions and answers.[31] The author draws upon three types of traditional material: cosmological wisdom about creation, an apocalyptic vision of the fate of the soul, and sayings of Jesus, many of which have parallels in GTh.[32] Despite the difficulty of interpreting the fragmentary text, DialSav seems to have concluded with discipleship sayings in which the Lord predicts the mockery that his followers will face (147, 13–22). The answers in the earlier part of the work tend to be much longer than those in the final pages. Perhaps the former is using traditional blocks of material, while the latter is based on individual sayings.

The following outline seems to represent the present structure of the work:

I. *Jesus Proclaims His Departure* (120, 1–122, 1):

This section may stem from a post-resurrection discourse[33] into which the author has introduced thematic parallels to the Johannine farewell discourses. The conclusion of the prayer, which Jesus teaches to the disciples, refers to liberation from the body through ascetic discipline (121, 18–122, 1).

II. *The Time of Dissolution*
   (a) *122, 1–124, 21:*
   Jesus addresses his disciples about the time of dissolution—an

---

[30]See the discussion of baptism and the eschatology of DialSav in Pagels and Koester, 68–70.

[31]Krause, "Der Dialog," 16–18.

[32]Pagels and Koester, 67f, argue that the sayings with the most parallels to the Synoptic tradition are those which also parallel GTh. They even try to suggest a pattern in the eschatological sayings that would fit the order of the saying in GTh 2: seek, find, marvel, rule, rest. However, the fragmentary state of the text of DialCont makes this hypothesis difficult to sustain. Krause, "Der Dialog," 25–28, argues that the New Testament allusions are scattered and—unlike GTh—do not follow a Sticwort pattern.

[33]So also Pagels and Koester, 67.

expression used for the ascent of the soul. This section discusses the ascent past the cosmic powers. Thus, it represents a Gnostic interpretation of the way opened by Jesus. Our survey of the content of the revelation dialogues showed that information about or reference to the ascent of the soul occurred in all except ThCont, AcPet 12, and ApocPet. Its absence in those writings may simply derive from the very specific character of their polemic.

(b) *124, 21–127, 18:*

Several allusions to the New Testament contrast Gnostics who have light with the ignorant. The section presupposes an anthropology that separates mind, soul and body.

(c) *128, 11–129, 16:*

The anthropological question is discussed after an interruption by a section of cosmological wisdom.

III. *Cosmology* (127, 19–128, 11; 129, 16–131, 18):

Questions from Jude introduce both cosmological sections. The first concerns what was before heaven and earth; the second deals with the signs in the heavens. This material probably derives from a single wisdom source. The section begins with the text about the spirit moving over the water. Both NatArc (CG II 87, 12) and ApocryJn (CG II 13, 18ff) show that that passage characteristically introduced Gnostic Genesis exegesis. Perhaps DialSav even knew such traditions in the question/answer format that we find in ApocryJn. The second section gives a Wisdom interpretation of creation as the ordering activity of the Logos. Jude's act of worship may originally have stood at the end of the source.

IV. *Eschatological Questions* (131, 19–132, 19):

The opening claim that keeping the sayings of the Lord in the heart is necessary to enter life refers back to the previous eschatological section. There it was part of the process for overcoming the powers. When Matthew asks to know the pleroma, he is told that the kingdom of heaven is within (cp. GTh, 3, 49, 70, 113).

V. *Cosmology* (132, 19–33, 24):

This section, which is based on a cosmological list, probably continues the previous description of the sustaining power of the Logos. However, the author has introduced a Gnostic twist. A person can know all these things and still not be saved. He or she must have gnosis. We have seen the same anticosmological trend in ThCont. There, the person who knows the ALL is nothing without self-knowledge. In other words, without gnosis all speculative and esoteric wisdom is useless.

VI. *Vision of the Pit and Ascent of a Soul* (134, 24–138, 2):

This visionary fragment concludes the revelation about the time of dissolution. Like cosmological wisdom, such visions are not saving gnosis.[34] The disciples ask for a vision of the Father. Yet they have already been told that such a vision can only be had within. The scene concludes with the commissioning of the disciples, who are now said to have the Father within. Again note the allusions to the Johannine farewell discourses.

VII. *Concluding Questions and Answers on Eschatology* (138, 2–end):

The final section seems to have consisted of a series of short questions and answers on eschatology. These questions and answers were based on Gnostic interpretation of the sayings of Jesus. The Gnostics conquer the powers when they are stripped of the body (= the "works of femaleness"[35]) and are clothed in heavenly garments. The final pages seem to have developed the theme of the victory over the powers, which the Gnostic soul wins by its ascent.

Thus, DialSav has brought together a variety of Gnostic tradition on eschatology. The final section may even have derived from a set catechesis on the topic. Its rejection of cosmological speculation probably was designed to counter the claims of those writings to information about the destiny of various types of souls.[36] Wisdom about the secret governance of the cosmos by the Logos can only be valuable to those who have gnosis. The author and those whose wisdom he opposes probably share a common tradition of interpretation of sayings derived from the Thomas tradition. DialSav stresses the bearing of these sayings on eschatology. His interpretation of the

---

[34]*Ibid.*, 71. DialSav rejects all temporal visions.
[35]See the discussion in Krause, "Der Dialog," 29.
[36]See Collins, "Jewish Apocalypses," 25–28.

parable of the mustard seed is standard Gnostic exegesis.[37] The mustard seed is the sowing from the Mother, which was left in the world. The Father acts on behalf of the seed. The discipleship sayings in the final pages are interpreted to explain the mission of the Gnostics in this world, even though their true destiny lies in the other world.[38] The elect are to reveal the greatness of the Savior (140, 15–18). The interpretation of the sayings about the evil of the day (Mt 6:34b), the laborer worthy of his hire (Mt 10:10), and the likeness of disciple and teacher (Mt 10:25) presents the fate of the Gnostic in this world (139, 8–11). While he awaits a future reward, he can expect ridicule, but he is to take comfort in the fact that he shares the same task of revelation as the Lord.

Thus, DialSav seems to represent the eschatology of a group of Gnostics who preserved the Thomas tradition. One might even consider it the Syrian counterpart of the mystic tract from the Alexandrian school, Zostr. There is nothing in the eschatology of the work which would set it in conflict with ThCont, though it lacks the latter's emphasis on radical asceticism. Its predictions of ridicule are based on exegesis of the sayings of Jesus. The author does not have to lay the stress on preaching despite difficulty and opposition that we found in ThCont. Nor do these Gnostics emphasize their withdrawal to form a separate sect—though their eschatological teaching makes it clear enough that non-Gnostics cannot be saved.[39]

Linguistic parallels suggest that both ThCont and DialSav belong to the same area. The focus on Jude-Thomas as bearer of the esoteric sayings of Jesus suggests the region of East Syria in which the GTh tradition took shape. Both know of a larger context in which esoteric Jesus traditions and cosmological wisdom are combined. DialSav suggests that this Wisdom speculation may have been embodied in the tradition of heavenly journeys by the seer—even by the apostle Thomas? We know from Eug and SJC that some Gnostics made esoteric wisdom about the Father and the aeons the key to salvation, but both DialSav and ThCont reject that stance. Salvation is

---

[37]CG III 144, 6–12. See Pagels, *Johannine Gospel*, 105ff.

[38]Pagels and Koester, "Report," 71f.

[39]Non-Gnostics will wail, 127, 16; go to the pit, 135, 6–11; be forever condemned, 140, 14; see Krause, "Der Dialog," 32.

not possible without following the ascetic praxis of the Gnostic sect. If both ThCont and DialSav stem from the same group, the latter would seem to have been composed before the controversy over ascesis that embroiled ThCont and apparently led the Gnostics to form a separate sect. Perhaps ThCont would even be opposed to the gnosis of DialSav, though the latter gives no evidence of advancing the kind of arguments about the body and true Christian ascesis attributed to the opponents in ThCont. The ascetic strain in both works stands in line with the general tendencies of Christianity in the region. At least the moderate form which we find in DialSav might well appeal to syncretistic Christians of East Syria. The same commitment to withdrawal and ascetic conquest of the body might be a primary reason why these writings were preserved among the ascetics of the Egyptian desert, as the Pachomian documents from the bindings of some of the codices suggest was the case for this collection.

CHAPTER SEVEN

The Gnostic Apostle:
The Petrine Tradition

None of the revelation dialogues analyzed so far have dealt with issues peculiar to Christianity. ApocryJn and SJC identify Christ with the highest God and the heavenly revealer of gnosis, but they do not explain Christian accounts of his life and death in terms of that identification, though the allusions to the canonical resurrection appearances show that they were aware of such accounts. ThCont and DialSav both give evidence of a Gnostic tradition of interpreting the sayings of Jesus. This tradition is invoked to support particular ascetic and eschatological doctrines, but the opponents in both instances seem to share a commitment to the esoteric interpretation of Jesus' sayings. Hence, the existence of the tradition itself is not at issue. In fact, the relationship between the Gnostics and this larger group seems to have been quite fluid. ThCont gives evidence of arguments advanced against his sect's ascetic practice and suggests that the Gnostics have moved toward a stance of withdrawal. However, hard and fast doctrinal lines do not seem to be drawn. Quite a different situation emerges with the next group of dialogues. The Gnostic Petrine apocrypha show that the figure of Peter is emerging as a central symbol of orthodox opposition to Gnostic Christianity. His centrality is associated with the development of hierarchy and authority in orthodox communities.[1] But the Gnostics also expect to appropriate

---

[1] See Koschorke, *Die Polemik*, 15. Koschorke argues that the opponents are a Catholic Christian hierarchy which claims to be the only true exponent of right doctrine. He thinks that Gnostics are indifferent rather than openly hostile to Church office: *ibid.*, 67f.

the Peter figure for themselves. The real Petrine tradition, they claim, is Gnostic Christianity. The dialogues that we shall discuss in the next chapter do not share that expectation. There, Petrine tradition will be downplayed in favor of revelation to those whom "Jesus loves," often non-apostles like James, the brother of the Lord, and Mary Magdalene.

The content of the revelation dialogues that we have discussed so far could appeal to anyone interested in esoteric wisdom whether or not that person accepted the claim that Christ is the only source of the gnosis preserved in their pages. They presented fundamental doctrines of cosmology, eschatology, and ascesis. Some of the remaining dialogues, GMary and PS in particular, continue in that vein. But the rest are concerned with specifically Christian problems: the interpretation of the passion accounts, the true nature of the Savior, apostolic authority and the patterns of Church order.

Gnostic polemic against Christianity seems to have followed a fairly uniform pattern. This pattern is sketched out in the anti-heretical tractate GrSeth (VII 2) and seems to have been taken for granted in the polemic of the revelation dialogues:

(1) The Old Testament is rejected. All its heroes from Adam to the Baptist are mocked. They share the folly of the boastful archon who inspired the Old Testament (CG VII 62, 28–65, 1).

(2) Christ is identified with the Father or with the highest divine triad (as in ApocryJn). He is greater than Sophia or any of the other aeons and powers (49, 10–18).

(3) A Docetic Christology insures that Christ was not defiled by his presence in a body (51, 20–33). The archons did not succeed in harming him, since they merely crucified an image while the spiritual Christ laughed (55, 5–56, 9; 58, 13–59, 18).[2]

(4) The death of Christ had no saving significance (60, 15–35; cf. 49, 26f).

---

[2] The claim that the archons "merely crucify an image" parallels stories of their attempts to defile the heavenly Eve in the Gnostic Genesis stories. She escapes by leaving them an image (e.g., NatArc CG II 89, 19–30). Norea's answer to the powers who come after her, as they had her mother Eve, that she is not of their race (92, 20–26) represents standard Gnostic anthropology. Thus, Gnostic "Docetic Christology" is an extension of these more general principles to cover the particular case of the crucifixion.

(5) The orthodox are persecuting the Gnostics out of hatred. They—not the Gnostics—are the cause of division and disharmony in the community (59, 25–60, 6; 62, 14–25). Variations on these themes reappear in the anti-Christian polemic of the revelation dialogues and in other versions of Gnostic polemic. They are so standard that they hardly reflect an author's individual reflection.

Given the importance of Peter in orthodox circles, one might have expected the Gnostics to consistently paint a negative picture of the apostle such as we find in the rewriting of Peter's confession in GTh 13. We shall see such anti-Peter sentiment in the next chapter. However, there is also a Gnostic Petrine tradition which portrays Peter as the true Gnostic. Irenaeus seems to have known such traditions. He goes to some length to show on the basis of Acts that the apostles never taught Gnostic doctrine (AdvHaer III 12, 1–7).[3] The Gnostic Petrine tradition probably developed in the same area in which those of orthodox Christianity were taking shape as effective symbols for ecclesial and doctrinal organization. In addition to structural and doctrinal developments, canonical Scripture is also playing an increasing role in the consolidation of Christian belief.[4] In ApocryJn and SJC, it was sufficient to attribute Gnostic tradition to the risen Lord. In the Gnostic Thomas tradition, even the opponents shared a tradition of esoteric interpretation. But, for the writings to which we now turn, the situation is quite different. The canonical accounts of the passion are being used to shore up orthodox assertions about the saving death of Jesus. The Gnostic must defend his own views by reinterpreting those passion accounts. Canonical reports of the sayings of Jesus also begin to play an authoritative role. The Gnostics even redirect them at their orthodox opponents. Nor is it sufficient to limit instruction in gnosis to post-resurrection appear-

---

[3]See Perkins, "Peter in Gnostic Revelation," *Society of Biblical Literature Seminar Papers 2*, ed. G. MacRae (Missoula: Scholars Press, 1974), 8; H. M. Schenke, "Bemerkungen zur Apokalypse des Petrus," *Essays on the Nag Hammadi Texts*, 272–85, though we are not convinced by his argument that this is an attack on Simon Magus.

[4]The combination of canonical and episcopal authority was an important weapon in the orthodox struggle with Gnosticism, as H. Von Campenhausen, *The Formation of the Christian Bible* (Philadelphia: Fortress, 1972), 182–206, and *idem, Ecclesiastical Authority and Spiritual Power* (Stanford: Stanford University, 1969), 169–73, has pointed out.

ances. Instead, we are assured that Jesus gave such instruction to Peter or to all the apostles before his death.

APOCALYPSE OF PETER

Of the three Petrine apocrypha, ApocPet takes up the conflict between Gnostic and orthodox Christianity most directly. Visions of and reinterpretation of the passion frame predictions about the heresies into which the followers of Jesus will fall. Just as the archons worked through the Jews, so they are working through the orthodox opponents of gnosis.[5] The revelation to Peter takes place in the temple prior to the passion—and thus stands in the place of the Synoptic apocalypse.[6] The visionary reinterpretation of the crucifixion, which is about to take place, frames the prediction of heresy and persecution by orthodox authorities. The ecclesiological and Christological sections are linked together by the claim that the orthodox, who are oppressing the Gnostics, expect to gain salvation by "clinging to the name of a dead man" (CG VII 73, 32–74, 22). This profession of faith in salvation through the crucified and the comment that the opponents think that suffering will perfect the brotherhood (78, 32ff) suggest that orthodox preaching may have relied on Pauline theology.[7]

At the same time, the consistent discussion of New Testament Petrine traditions indicates that Pauline doctrine had been assimilated to ecclesiastical patterns of authority centered on Peter. The New Testament provides evidence of such a combination in 2 Pt. "Peter" warns against deviant readings of Paul (2 Pt 3:14–18). Thus, he may be said to have become the guardian of the Pauline doctrinal tradition. Some have suggested that this passage in 2 Pt represents orthodox use of a Petrine magisterium against Gnostic exegesis of Paul.[8]

---

[5]Koschorke, *Die Polemik*, 12f.

[6]*Ibid.*, 13. We disagree with Brashler's suggestion that ApocPet takes place in the heavenly temple after the resurrection. The Jerualem temple appears as part of the setting in other revelation dialogues in which the revelation is to a single apostle, for example in ApocryJn, where John leaves the temple to go to a desert place, and 1 ApocJas.

[7]Cf. Col 1:24; see Koschorke, *Die Polemik*, 39–42.

[8]See R. Brown and K. Donfried, eds., *Peter in the New Testament* (New York: Paulist, 1973), 156.

ApocPet contains one explicit quotation from 2 Pt and several possible allusions to the Petrine letters. These place the shoe on the other foot. Petrine authority is invoked against the combination of Pauline doctrine and Petrine ecclesiology being advanced by the author's opponents. Irenaeus shows us that such arguments often centered around Peter. He comments: "How could Peter have been in ignorance to whom the Lord gave the testimony that flesh and blood had not revealed this to him but heaven" (AdvHaer III 13, 2). ApocPet gives a Gnostic answer. The heavenly, luminous Christ revealed the truth about both his passion and the future of his Church to Peter. The apostle himself was not ignorant. Those who came after him distorted his teaching.

Jesus warns Peter that he will be reproved three times (72, 2ff)—a Gnostic interpretation of the denial prediction. The author has combined Jesus' prayer that Peter will turn and strengthen his brethren (Lk 22:31–33) with the story of Peter's name from Matthew 16. He may also intend an allusion to the exhortation to "stand firm" in 2 Pt 3:17. The Gnostics, who have been built on what is strong, are warned against words of unrighteousness and transgression of the Law (70, 13–72, 4) just as 2 Pt 3:17 warns Christians against being carried away by the error of lawless men. Finally the author quotes 2 Pt 2:17: the bishops and deacons are the "waterless canals."

We have seen that the Gnostics interpreted the transfiguration as proof that Jesus possessed a spiritual body that was the subject of resurrection, not his material body.[9] 2 Pt 1:16f refers to the Petrine testimony to the transfiguration. In ApocPet, the apostle sees light descend upon Jesus twice: "For I saw light greater than daylight. Then it came upon the Savior" (73, 24–26). The second vision even includes the acclamation of the angelic pleroma:

> I saw someone approaching us who resembled him, him who was the one laughing on the tree. He was filled with a Holy Spirit; he is the Savior. There was a great, ineffable light surrounding them and the multitude of ineffable and invisible angels praising them. And, when I looked at him, the one who gives praise was revealed. (81, 28–82, 16)

---

[9]See above, pp. 39, 50f.

The Savior explains the vision in terms of the threefold nature of the revealer:

> Be strong, for you are the one to whom these mysteries have been given, to know them through revelation. He whom they crucified is the first-born and the house of demons and the stone vessel in which those of Elohim dwell, of the cross which is under the Law. But the one who stands near him is the living Savior, the first in the one whom they seized and released, who stands and looks joyfully at those who attacked him while they are divided among themselves. Therefore, he laughed at their lack of perception, knowing that they are born blind. Since the body is the substitute, the one who can suffer will come. But what they released is my incorporeal body. I am the intellectual spirit, filled with the radiant light. The one whom you saw coming to me is our intellectual pleroma, which unites the perfect light with my Holy Spirit (82, 1–83, 15).[10]

This passage contains several allusions to Pauline preaching about the crucifixion. "First-born" probably refers to the "first-born of creation" in Col 1:15, 18. "Crucified under the Law" refers to Gal 3:13 or 4:14. The blind and ignorant archons who do not know whom they are crucifying recalls 1 Cor 2:8. Such a large number of allusions to Pauline material establishes that context for the preaching about Jesus in the Christian community from which ApocPet comes. The Gnostic claims that such "preaching the crucified" (e.g., 1 Cor 1:23; 2:2; Gal 3:1) is based on the deception of the demons by the fleshly Christ. Peter, on the other hand, is able to bear witness to the real, spiritual Christ. Our Gnostic author would say that Irenaeus was quite right to refer to what "heaven" and not the flesh had revealed to the apostle—too bad that the bishop refuses to accept that heavenly testimony.

Allusions to Matthew are scattered throughout ApocPet. They show that Matthean tradition played an important role in the devel-

---

[10]See the discussion of this passage in Koschorke, *Die Polemik,* 21–25.

opment of community traditions in ApocPet. Jesus praises the Gnostics as those who are built on what is strong so that they hear his word (70, 26–28), a combination of the reference to Peter as rock and the parable of the houses in Mt 7:24ff. Peter is told to become strong in accord with his name so that the Lord can make him the foundation (*arche*) of the Gnostic remnant (71, 16–19//Mt 16:18f). Gnostics use the Matthean "little ones" as their self-designation (78, 22; 79, 19; 80, 11). The author also uses Matthean language to condemn his opponents. His dualistic division between "immortal souls," whose origin is in heaven with the Father, the Gnostics, and "mortal souls," who are tied to matter and destined to perish with it, is bolstered by an appeal to Mt 7:18.[11] Mt. 15:29a is also said to point to the contrast between the immortal Gnostics and their opponents who are going to perish.[12] Those who lead the "little ones" astray are to be cast into outer darkness (78, 22–25//Mt 25:30). Church officials, like the Matthean Pharisees, neither enter nor allow others to do so (78, 26–28//Mt 23:13). Mt 23:6 chides the Pharisees for loving seats of honor in the synagogue (*protokathedriai*). ApocPet condemns those who call themselves bishops and deacons for thinking that their authority (*exousia*) comes from God. He says that they "bend under the judgment of those of the first seats" (79, 21–31).

In addition to such direct allusions to New Testament Peter traditions, several indirect allusions occur in the polemic sections. 1 Pt 5:1–3 invokes apostolic authority as witness to the sufferings of Christ. As witness and partaker of the glory that is to be revealed, Peter presents instructions to those who are to lead the flock after him. They must do so not by constraint but willingly, not for gain but generously; not domineering over their charges but setting examples. The opponents in ApocPet's description violate all of these injunctions. They have set up their own Law in opposition to Jesus. They traffic in his word and they impose a harsh fate on those immortal souls caught under them (77, 22–78, 31). GMary also contains an injunction from Jesus that the disciples are not to impose

---

[11]CG VII 75, 7–9. Mt 7:16 is cited to make the same point in 76, 4–8.

[12]CG VII 83, 26–29. The author must be referring to Mt. The parallels in Lk and GTh 41 lack the expression *kai perisseuthesetai*.

any law of their own.[13] We have seen that trafficking in revelation was a standard charge against one's opponents in this kind of religious polemic. ApocryJn has Jesus forbid it.[14] The final charge seems to refer to the saying about binding and loosing (Mt 16:18f), since it is followed by a promise that when he comes again, Jesus will forgive the Gnostics for those transgressions that they were forced into by the subjection to their adversaries.[15] The adversaries are even said to have taken the Gnostics prisoner (79, 21). Thus we see that Petrine authority is being used by the orthodox to sanction disciplinary action against Gnostic Christians. ApocPet does not tell us what kind of discipline was involved. Their official action may have had some success, since we are told that many who had accepted gnosis in the beginning have turned away (73, 18). At the same time, the Gnostics do not seem to have separated themselves from the larger group. When Peter expresses his fear of the multitude of "pseudo-Christians" who are misleading others,[16] he is told that the "little ones" are to be subject to such authorities for a time. Then the situation will be reversed and the "little ones" will rule over their opponents. Meanwhile, they are to take comfort from the fact that Peter himself has been commissioned to stand up to the hostile authorities who call themselves "bishops and deacons" (80, 31–81, 3).[17]

---

[13]Similar injunctions against the apostles imposing their own law appear in GMary BG 8, 31–9, 3; 18, 19f.

[14]Above, pp. 93–94. The injunction against being "merchants of the word" appears in a wisdom context in Silv (CG VII 117, 28–32), where one is enjoined not to speak about what one does not know. ApocPet has already accused his opponents of claiming to speak mysteries when they do not know the truth (76, 24–77, 21).

[15]Koschorke, *Die Polemik*, 17, 55–60, thinks that the charge that the opponents create a remnant in the name of a dead man, Hermes, refers to *Shepherd of Hermes* and indicates that ApocPet opposes orthodox penitential discipline.

[16]CG VII 80, 8–23. Similar expressions of fear upon learning of the crucifixion appear in 1 ApocJas (CG V 29, 4–8; 32, 13–22) and may be a stock feature of such accounts.

[17]Brashler, *NHLE*, 339, thinks that the sections refer to different groups of opponents. However, emphasizing divisions in the opposing school was a standard rhetorical tactic which Irenaeus uses in dividing the Gnostics up into sects. ApocPet makes the point that the opponents hold a variety of views and argue against each other as part of such an argument: CG VII 74, 22–75, 7. See Perkins, "Irenaeus," 196. Koschorke is correct in insisting upon a single group of opponents. He thinks that ApocPet is attacking orthodox authorities, whose hostility toward the "little ones" is keeping others from attaining gnosis: *op. cit.*, 15, 80–84.

The situation which provoked this revelation dialogue, then, seems to have been the way in which orthodox authorities were exercising authority against Gnostic teachers. The teaching at issue is clearly Christological. The orthodox "preach the name of a dead man" (75, 13f) and claim that one is saved through that name. Gnostic polemicists routinely use the expression "preaching a dead man" to refer to orthodox preaching about the death of Christ. GrSeth refers to its opponents as teaching a dead man (CG VIII 60, 20). In PetPhil, the ignorant powers think that Jesus is a dead man (CG VIII 136, 20). Irenaeus refers to Basilidean Gnostics who argue that those who "confess the crucified" are still in bondage to the powers of the world (AdvHaer I 24, 4). Arguments to show that the Savior did not suffer crucifixion are commonplace in Gnostic theology.[18] All the elements in the account of the crucifixion in ApocPet have parallels in other Gnostic accounts. One is required to distinguish between the fleshy part of the crucified and the "bodiless body" that was released. Similar distinctions between the fleshy, psychic and spiritual Savior occur in most other Gnostic explanations of the crucifixion.[19] The powers are deceived by a substitute which comes into being in the Savior's form (81, 21–23).[20] Thus they are tricked into crucifying what really belongs to them. Other accounts also have the Savior laugh at the deception[21] and have an inner part leave before the crucifixion.[22] ApocPet has turned Peter, the witness of the sufferings of Jesus, into the witness of the true meaning of those sufferings; they did not touch the heavenly revealer. His revelation is the source of the Gnostic community, a spiritual brotherhood that is identified with him. All the attempts of others to claim such a divine foundation are mere counterfeit. They are not united with the Savior.[23] The Gnostic Peter is the foundation of the true Church.

---

[18]See the survey in Koschorke, *Die Polemik*, 44–48.

[19]For example, Basilides, *Ref* VII 27, 9-12; Valentinians, *AdvHaer* I 7, 2; *ExcTheod* 61, 6f; Sethian-Ophites, *AdvHaer* I, 30, 13.

[20]Compare Basilides in Irenaeus, *AdvHaer* I 24, 4; GrSeth CG VII 55, 17–56, 14.

[21]*AdvHaer* I 24, 4; GrSeth CG VII 56, 15–33.

[22]*AdvHaer* I 24, 4; 1 ApocJas CG V 31, 14–26; TriProt CG XIII 50, 9–12; Cerinthus, *AdvHaer* I 26, 1; Valentinians, *AdvHaer* I 7, 2; *ExcTheod* 61, 6; Sethian-Ophites, *AdvHaer* I 30, 13.

[23]See the survey of Gnostic soteriology in Koschorke, *Die Polemik*, 47f, 60–62.

ApocPet shows how Gnostics in West Syria defended their own tradition against the lines of Church doctrine and authority that the orthodox were drawing around the figure of Peter. The dialogue concludes with a commissioning scene which combines the assurances of peace and courage from the Johannine discourses and the Matthean promise of Jesus' eternal presence with the Church. These Gnostics are making a sustained effort to counter the authority of the orthodox hierarchy by coopting its key symbol in support of Gnostic teaching. Only the Gnostic "little ones" stand in the tradition of the great apostle.

LETTER OF PETER TO PHILIP

ApocPet focused on Peter's individual authority. In PetPhil, on the other hand, Peter is the leader of a unified apostolic group. The epistolatory introduction emphasizes the unity of the apostles in their preaching mission. No single apostle is favored with the gnosis. All apostolic preaching is Gnostic and goes out under the direction of Peter (132, 10–133, 11). PetPhil begins with the standard dialogue setting. The disciples gather on the Mount of Olives; meet the risen Lord, and ask a standard set of Gnostic questions. As in NatArc and SJC, apostolic preaching is seen as the real conquest of the archons (137, 13–138, 3).[24] Though it follows the usual conventions of the revelation dialogue, PetPhil, like ApocPet, is careful to emphasize the fact that Jesus had already revealed gnosis during his lifetime. Jesus reminds the disciples twice that he has already taught them what is coming (135, 5–8; 138, 2f).

The revelation dialogue in PetPhil is part of a larger take-off on the introductory chapters of Acts. This rewriting provides clear evidence that the apostolic preaching has always been Gnostic. The second half of PetPhil includes a Gnostic Pentecost sermon in which Peter gives the typical Gnostic interpretation of the crucifixion (139, 9–140, 1).[25] The plot of PetPhil follows the Lukan scenario: after the

---

[24]See above, p. 94.

[25]K. Koschorke, "Eine gnostische Pfingstpredigt zur Auseinandersetzung zwischen gnostische und kirchliche Christentum am Beispiel der Epistula Petri ad Philippum (NHC VIII, 2)," *ZThK* 74 (1977), 323–43. Koschorke argues that the Pentecost

revelation by the Risen Jesus, the disciples return to the temple to preach and teach; they also heal great numbers (139, 4–8//Ac 1:8; 140, 7–11//Ac 2:43). They are filled with the Holy Spirit (140, 9).[26]

The Sophia myth (135, 10–136, 15), the Docetic account of the crucifixion (138, 18ff; 139, 11–30), and the description of the incarnation (136, 16–137, 3) all follow conventional Gnostic lines.[27] The disciples' main concern is how to act in the face of the opposition to their preaching, which is being mounted by the powers. Like Norea, the apostles prayed to summon the revealer Christ because they were in danger (134, 3–9). One would guess from this acount of the apostolic preaching and its struggle with the powers that Gnostic preaching had called forth hostility from orthodox Christians. Once again we see that the context of the Gnostic missionary effort is in Christian circles. These Gnostic missionaries are not going out to convert pagans.[28]

Further, the emphases in the narrative suggest that the primary counter-arguments to the Gnostic preaching were founded on appeals to canonical Scripture, particularly Acts, and to the unity of apostolic preaching. Concern to demonstrate the continuity of Gnostic teaching with Jesus' preaching and apostolic testimony leads the author to have all the disciples—not just their leader Peter—instructed in gnosis during the earthly ministry. His routine summaries of Gnostic doctrine are presented as the object of that teaching. This approach is quite different from other Gnostic writings which argue that Jesus taught the disciples in parables prior to the resurrection and only gave clear instruction in gnosis afterward (e.g., GrSeth CG VII 42, 20–31). A similar limitation is implied in ApocryJn. We are told that Jesus did not teach the disciples about the imperishable aeon during his lifetime (CG II 1, 29). The use of canonical Scripture against such traditions is reflected in Irenaeus' remark that the Gnostics reject the written Gospels in favor of their own oral traditions (AdvHaer III 2, 1f).

---

sermon rather than the revelation dialogue is the main focus of PetPhil. The dialogue takes what the Gnostics already know in order to present the teaching of Jesus as Gnostic.

[26]For other possible parallels to Lk, see Koschorke, *op. cit.*, 326f.

[27]*Ibid.*, 332 n. 23.

[28]*Ibid.*, 342f.

PetPhil's stress on apostolic unity is striking. Peter summons Philip to join the others by referring to Jesus' command that they come together and teach (137, 24). The apostles go off to preach after various revelations and then come back to Jerusalem for a final commissioning appearance in which Jesus imparts peace, benediction and eternal presence (140, 16–23). Only then do the disciples finally disperse into "four worlds" to preach (140, 23–27).[29] The emphasis on their unity looks like a response to increasing pressures from orthodox polemic against the diversity of Gnostic preaching. Irenaeus uses this stock rhetorical topos against them: he contrasts their diversity with the worldwide unity of the Church:

> The Church, which received this preaching and this faith, although it is scattered throughout the world, carefully preserves it as though occupying one house. . . . Just as the sun, that creature of God, is one and the same throughout the world, so also the preaching of the truth shines down everywhere and enlightens all men who are willing to come to a knowledge of the truth. . . . For faith, always being one and the same, neither does one able to speak about it at great length make any addition to it, nor does one who can say but little diminish it (AdvHaer I 10, 2).

PetPhil describes Gnostic preaching in such a way that it would fit these conditions of worldwide unity.

Thus, although he has only explicitly mentioned persecution and the rejection of Gnostic preaching, PetPhil has presented Gnostic answers to orthodox objections. The standard Gnostic doctrines are merely being summarized here as evidence of the teaching that the earthly and risen Jesus had given to all the disciples. The larger context of placing revelation dialogue within a Gnostic Acts shows the harmonious development and spread of apostolic preaching. The message sent out to the whole world was really that of Gnostic enlightenment. Peter's injunction not to obey "lawless men" (139,

---

[29]A late conclusion to PS has the apostles go off to preach in the four corners of the world; see C. Schmidt and V. MacDermot, *Pistis Sophia*, NHS IX (Leiden: E. J. Brill, 1978), 385.

28–30) may be aimed at orthodox authorities as is clearly the case in ApocPet. These authorities are equated with the hostile archons of the cosmos. But, despite such opposition, the Gnostics will continue to follow the directions given by the Lord in the beginning. Gnostic Christianity is to be spread throughout the world. This picture suggests that the anti-Gnostic polemic had had less of an impact on the group and its ideals than was the case in ApocPet.

ACTS OF PETER AND THE TWELVE APOSTLES

The Nag Hammadi collection contains one other Petrine writing, AcPet12. Though the genre of the whole is closest to that of apocryphal acts,[30] it does include a mysterious appearance of the Risen Lord and conversation with the disciples. The story is based on two allegories: Jesus as the foreign merchant selling pearls and Jesus as the physician healing souls.[31] Like PetPhil, the apostles are engaged in missionary activity at the beginning of the story. Their two encounters with Jesus lead to another commission to preach. AcPet12 does not defend any peculiarly Gnostic teachings. It could well have circulated in a syncretistic, encratite Christian milieu. Krause sees its emphasis on Christ as source of all revelation as an index of

---

[30]On the relationship between this work and the apocryphal acts tradition, see M. Krause, "Die Petrusakten in Codex VI von Nag Hammadi," *Essays on the Nag Hammadi Texts*, 54f. We cannot agree with Krause's claim that this work represents the lost beginning of the Acts of Peter found in the Berlin Codex, *op. cit.*, p. 56. First, AcPet12 comes to a formal conclusion in the commissioning scene, which would not suggest any further revelations. Such conclusions are characteristic of the revelation dialogue genre which is used in this text. Second, the rejection of association with the rich and powerful and the restriction of the miracle tradition are so a-typical of the apocryphal acts genre that they do not fit with what survives of the Acts of Peter in the Berlin Codex.

[31]Krause, "Petrusakten," 46–50, finds a variety of contradictions between the two stories. He postulates two sources: framework 1, 3–29; first source 1, 29–7, 23; transition 7, 23–8, 13; second source, 8, 13–12, 19. However, the contradictions that he mentions are so typical of oral story-telling that we would see the whole as a retelling of stories that circulated freely in the region. Any reader of Homer will hardly be surprised at such lapses, as uncertainty about whether the disciples heard the first exchange, 8, 20, implies that they did, but they were in the house, 2, 7f, or about the number of gates in the city. The earlier description mentions nine, but only one is mentioned when they arrive.

the Gnostic origins of the story.[32] He thinks that it is critical of Peter when it says: "Peter, it is fitting that you understand the parable I told you. Do you not understand that my name which you teach surpasses all riches?"[33] However, the style of that remark is typical of revelation discourse in the Fourth Gospel (Jn 14:8). It fits a pattern that we have also seen in ThCont, which indicates that the one who is speaking with Jesus should have understood some lesser thing if he wishes to understand the greater revelation Jesus is about to make. Therefore, we would not classify AcPet12 as anti-Petrine tradition on the basis of this remark. Rather, the passage functions like the explicit statements in PetPhil. It ties what Jesus is now telling the disciples with what he has told them during his lifetime. It also calls the reader's attention to the allegorical character of the story by establishing distinctions between outer and real truth. Such distinctions have been pointed out from the very beginning of the narrative. When Peter, who wants to know about the city to which the disciples have come, hails the merchant Jesus as brother and comrade, Jesus praises him for speaking correctly since they are both strangers in the city (2, 25–3, 11). Most of the symbolic interpretation focuses on the metaphors of pearl and physician. The free pearls, which the merchant has promised to the poor, turn out to be the powerful name of Jesus the physician.[34] AcPet12 is hardly unfavorable to Peter and the other disciples. They receive a revelation of Jesus which is not given to everyone (CG VI 8, 30–32). As a result of their journey to Lithargoel's city, they are able to bring back to the poor the treasure of spiritual healing which they could not have obtained for themselves. The Gnostic reader knows that these treasures are gnosis.

Several parallels to the PetPhil tradition suggest themselves. The location of the apostolic activity is a city in the midst of the sea, called "Habitation." Gnostics use the expression "dwelling place" to refer to life in this world (e.g., PetPhil CG VIII 134, 25). In PetPhil, the disciples ask why they are being held in this place. Here, the alle-

---

[32]"Petrusakten," 55.

[33]*Ibid.*, 54f. Krause also tries to argue that VI 11, 14–19 are directed against John.

[34]*Ibid.*, 50.

gory tells the Gnostic that he musst continue preaching the spiritual healing of Jesus. Similarly, AcPet12 symbolizes the unity of the disciples through the narrative rather than with explicit statements such as we found in PetPhil. AcPet12 opens with their agreement. Their hearts are united to do what the Lord has commanded (1, 9–12). They are to spread the word of God harmoniously (5, 10–14). But the apostles are also warned to expect storms and apostasies in Habitation (7, 23f). They twice express their willingness to perform the Lord's command (9, 26; 12, 14). As in the Thomas and James traditions, the proper greeting to Jesus is "brother"—a greeting which Peter is able to voice even when he does not know the true identity of the stranger before him (2, 35–3, 10). These similarities in the presentation of the apostolic ministry suggest that AcPet12 has a similar image of Peter as Gnostic apostle and represents a pro-Petrine Gnostic tradition.[35]

Like the apocryphal acts traditions in general, the teaching embodied in this story is not concerned with doctrinal issues but with proper Christian ascetic praxis. Unlike ThCont, the primary villain is not a body dominated by lust, but is wealth and material goods. When Jesus warns the disciples of the hardships they will have to encounter on the journey to his city, he preaches a homily on the necessity of renouncing material possessions. This homily is based on proverbial wisdom. The person who carries "x" (bread, costly garments, water, meat, green vegetables) is killed by "y" (black dogs, robbers, wolves, lions, bulls: CG VI 5, 19–6, 8). The disciples renounce all these things and are only concerned about food for a single day (10, 18f).[36]

The actual revelation dialogue occurs in the second half of the work after the disciples have successfully negotiated passage to the city of the mysterious merchant, Lithargoel. There, he reveals himself to them as Jesus Christ (8, 11–12, 9). The dialogue employs the misunderstanding type of question so common in Johannine dis-

---

[35]Although the content of AcPet12 is not particularly Gnostic, there are enough similarities to the concerns of PetPhil to lead us to assume that it is a Gnostic writing, against the view of Parrott, *NHLE*, 265. We also doubt that the author has carefully Christianized a Gnostic allegory in order to deceive readers as suggested by E. Segelberg, "Prayer among the Gnostics?" *Gnosis and Gnosticism*, 64.

[36]An encratite, Gnostic interpretation of Mt 6:25ff.

course to initiate the reader into the symbolic truth about Jesus that is presented by the narrative. Jesus commissions the disciples to go back to Habitation and heal the poor. They are to be physicians of the soul. Quite unlike the usual picture of the apostles in the apocryphal acts, the miracle tradition is downplayed.[37] Miraculous cures are only to initiate trust in the preaching of the apostles (11, 18–26). Other apocryphal acts tend to portray the apostles converting the rich and powerful. That too is rejected. People in the churches have been showing partiality toward the rich and have been leading others astray by their example (11, 27–12, 8). We saw in ApocPet that the charge of being "merchants of the word" was leveled against the author's orthodox opponents. In the first section of AcPet12, the rich merchants of Habitation reject Lithargoel's call about "pearls" when they look out and see that Jesus is not carrying a sack. As a result, Jesus does not reveal himself to them (3, 11–31). Jesus is the one who will give his pearls for nothing to anyone who will undertake the journey to his city (4, 30–5, 1). The apostles teach his name, which is of more value than any riches (10, 22–30). There is no indication in the story that we are to understand rich and poor as allegorical expressions. Therefore, it seems likely that the circles from which the story comes distinguish themselves from other Christians by their renunciation of wealth.

AcPet12, then, in using the authority of the apostolic tradition to defend an ascetic sect which finds itself beleaguered by rich and powerful Christians. It is not clear whether the author expects members of the sect to engage in wandering missionary activity like that depicted,[38] or whether the motifs of dangerous journey and preaching simply derive from the apocryphal acts genre. This allegorical tale may simply be an example of preaching within the community to keep members from being led astray by the teaching of rich Christians, people of influence, who no doubt also claimed to embody apostolic traditions.

---

[37] On the miracle traditions in the apocryphal acts, see P. Achtemeier, "Jesus and the Disciples as Miracle Workers in the Apocryphal New Testament," *Aspects of Religious Propaganda in Judaism and Early Christianity*, ed. E. Fiorenza (Notre Dame: Notre Dame, 1976), 164–75.

[38] Segelberg, "Prayer," 64.

The three accounts of Peter's apostolic authority that we find in the Nag Hammadi collection represent a wide spectrum of concerns and images that consolidated around the apostle as he came to be the central figure in the identity of Christian communities. Here, in AcPet12, we see the hero of the apocryphal acts tradition[39] being turned away from outward successes of physical miracles and association with the rich to a life of renunciation and spiritual healing. Both AcPet12 and PetPhil see Gnostic apostolic preaching as a sign of the willing unity with which the disciples follow the command of Jesus. PetPhil has more directly doctrinal concerns in that it wishes to revamp the canonical acts stories to show that from the very beginning apostolic preaching spread the message of Gnostic salvation throughout the world. Peter is the spokesman for the group and also the one who has Gnostic insight into the suffering of Jesus (CG VIII 138, 18–20). PetPhil presupposes the healing ministry of the disciples as described in Acts. His warning against subjection to the "lawless ones" (139, 28f) suggests some contact with the type of official hostility so central to ApocPet. Peter's doctrinal insight into the truth of the crucifixion parallels that in ApocPet. PetPhil seems to portray a Peter midway between the Peter of legend and story, whom we meet in AcPet12, and the Peter of Church office and ecclesiastical authority who dominates ApocPet. PetPhil shares with the latter the conviction that authorities who persecute the Gnostics are representatives of the archons. But ApocPet goes much further and takes on the major canonical warrants for such ecclesiastical authority. He reformulates those passages so as to drive a wedge between that authority and the teaching of Peter, the true apostle. Thus, he expects to show his readers that they have set up "their law and error" (CG VII 77, 25–29) against the express teaching both of Jesus and of his appointed foundation for the Church. Each of these Petrine writings presupposes that the Gnostics form a minority within the larger context of orthodox Christianity. But the relationship between the Gnostics and that larger world differs from case to case. This difference suggests that they stem from different communities. Another indication of different backgrounds is found in the fact that the

---

[39]We do not agree with Krause's view that the emphasis on Jesus as revealer is intended to demote the apostles from their status as heroes: "Petrusakten," 55.

sources upon which each has drawn for the image of Peter are different. ApocPet evidences a full-scale attempt by the orthodox authorities—apparently with some success—to bring the Gnostic movement under control. At issue are the Pauline tradition, the Petrine letters and the Matthean Gospel. PetPhil suggests a much less organized opposition to Gnostic preaching—though such ad hoc opposition might have hardened into what we find reflected in ApocPet. The Peter of Acts, head of the apostolic mission, is the Peter in question. Finally, AcPet12 is quite different. Opposition to ascetic rejection of material goods derives from the wealthy, who are perceived as having undue influence in the community. The apostolic tradition here seems to have been embodied in apocryphal rather than canonical tradition.

CHAPTER EIGHT

Those Whom Jesus Loves: The Non-Apostles

However bold the appropriation of the Peter symbol in some Gnostic communities, others did not follow that route. At least as frequently, Gnostics claim that their tradition gives them insight greater than that of the apostles (*AdvHaer* I 13, 6). The orthodox were quick to insist that Peter is the great defender of doctrinal orthodoxy. Hippolytus points to Peter as the one who resisted Simon Magus, whom the heresiologists consider the father of all Gnostic heresies (*Ref* VI 20, 2). Irenaeus counters Gnostic claims about the apostles with his own exegesis of Acts (*AdvHaer* III 12, 1–7). He wishes to prove on the basis of the canonical record of the teaching of Peter and the apostles that there is no basis for the claim that the "fountainheads of truth" taught Gnostic doctrine. Peter's Pentecost sermon—contrast PetPhil—proves that:

(1) the apostles did not teach another god or about the pleroma;

(2) they did not speak of the crucifixion as the separation of the fleshy Christ from a part that ascended; the Christ who dies is one;

(3) God fulfilled what had been predicted in the prophets about the suffering of Christ—contrast the rejection of prophetic witness in ApocPet.

Irenaeus then goes on to argue that the apostolic witness to the truth about Jesus occurred prior to the emergence of Gnostic teaching. Such a charge may have been known to ApocPet, since Christ twice tells Peter that he is not to give the revelation to "those of this generation" (CG VII 73, 18f; 83, 15–19). If the author has the question of the lateness of Gnostic revelation in mind, then the expression not only refers to the difference in origin of Gnostic and non-Gnostic souls but to the temporal emergence of gnosis. The James traditions explicitly acknowledge the fact that gnosis was not preached by the apostolic generation. Irenaeus reports a Gnostic argument that the apostles appear to accept the God of the Old Testament because they spoke like "Jews" (= psychics) with Jews and thus disguised their teaching.[1] He claims that such an argument is absurd. If the apostles were willing to risk persecution for preaching that the Jews had slain the Lord, they would certainly have condemned the Jewish God just as they condemned the pagan gods (AdvHaer III 12, 6). The Gnostic argument in question probably comes from Valentinian circles. Origen says that Heracleon appealed to Peter to support his claim that Jn 4:24 demands rejection of both pagan and Jewish worship.[2] Irenaeus turns to the Cornelius story to support his case. When Peter converts a Gentile, he converts him to the God of the Jews. The Gnostic would have to conclude that Peter himself was imperfect (AdvHaer III 12, 7). But the apostles cannot have been imperfect, since the Church throughout the world has its origin from the apostles, all of whom taught the same thing about God and his Son.

Irenaeus is perfectly right that at least some Gnostics did reach the conclusion that the disciples were deficient and did not possess true gnosis.[3] ApocryJas even suggests that this deficiency was tied to the issue of canonical Scripture. Such writings frequently demote Peter in favor of another person who has superior gnosis. Another disciple, Thomas, is superior in the Gnostic version of Peter's confession (GTh 13). In other writings, the disciples as a group are deficient. Then someone else, "whom Jesus loves," receives Gnostic teaching. Mary Magdalene and James the brother of the Lord are the two examples in the Nag Hammadi writings. All of the Gnostic traditions about Mary Magdalene set her in opposition to Peter. ApocryJas associates Peter and James in receiving a revelation. However, the conclusion of ApocryJas shows that Peter did not come to gnosis

---

[1] See Pagels, *Johannine Gospel*, 67f, 101.
[2] Heracleon, frag. 21.
[3] Pagels, *op. cit.*, 13.

even after that revelation. 1 ApocJas insists that the only true tradition about the teaching of Jesus comes through James. The apostles all rejected it. Thus, the superiority of the Gnostic understanding to that of the apostolic tradition is clearly being defended in these stories.

GOSPEL OF MARY

GMary launches a direct attack on the Petrine tradition. Peter is hostile to Mary because her gnosis is superior to his.[4] Though the beginning and some of the middle pages are missing, what remains follows a pattern similar to PetPhil, only here it is Mary who is the Gnostic leader. She is the one who must encourage the fearful disciples to embark on the preaching mission commanded by the Risen Lord. Like Peter in PetPhil, she must warn them that they are destined to suffer as Jesus did (9, 5–24). She demonstrates her own gnosis by recounting a revelation that Jesus had made to her (10, 1–6). As in ApocPet, the private revelation began with a vision of Jesus' true glory (10, 10–15; cp. CG VII 72, 22–26). The hostility that follows Mary's revelation establishes Peter as spokesman for orthodox objections to gnosis. First, the Lord revealed everything to the apostles in common—no private revelations are allowed. Second, the Gnostics are only able to convert senseless women (cf. AdvHaer I 6, 3). Peter objects that the Lord would never give a revelation to a woman that he had not given to all the apostles in common. GMary strikes another familiar note in the Gnostic/orthodox conflict when Jesus enjoins his disciples not to lay down any rules beyond those he has given (8, 21–9, 4). ApocPet has him speak of rejecting "their Law" (CG VII 77, 27). As in PetPhil, the work finally concludes when the apostles separate to go off on their preaching mission.

GMary contains two revelations. A dialogue between the Risen Jesus and his disciples, which may have been introduced with an appearance such as we find in the other revelation dialogues, begins the

---

[4]Compare ApocPet, CG VII 77, 2–16. People oppose the Gnostics and claim to know mysteries because they are envious of Gnostic salvation.

work. We are then told about the second, an earlier revelation that Jesus had made to Mary alone. Both revelations seem to have dealt with Gnostic eschatology. Thus, the content of this writing is closest to that of DialSav. We shall see that it even associates Mary with the interpretation of the sayings of Jesus just as DialSav does. As much as survives of the first revelation suggests that it dealt with the dissolution of all things into their origins. This question has introduced a discussion of the relationship between matter, passion and the body (7, 1–8, 11). The revelation to Mary described the ascent of the soul past the various powers to the highest aeon of silence. It may have been preceded by a discussion of the relationship between soul, mind and spirit, since Mary opens with a question about which faculty sees the vision (10, 1–17; pp. 11–14 are missing). In DialSav, Mary, along with Matthew and Jude, saw the vision of the pit and the ascent of the soul. There, her inclusion along with the disciples does not cause any comment. Here, on the other hand, it is a major source of dissension. She is called "the one whom the Savior loved more than the apostles because of her gnosis" (18, 10–16) and "more than the rest of women" (10, 1f). She clearly represents the Gnostic claim to a truth greater than that contained in the apostolic tradition.[5]

GMary is not the only place in which she symbolizes this claim to superior tradition. When Peter tries to have her excluded from the circle of disciples in GTh 114, Jesus counters by promising to make her male so that she too can enter life. GMary may know that tradition. While Mary is exhorting the disciples not to be afraid, she says, "Let us praise his greatness, for he has prepared us and made us into men" (9, 18–20). The final instructions to the apostles also reflect GTh traditions. Jesus says to them, "Beware, lest someone lead you astray by saying, 'Lo here! or Lo there! for the Son of Man is within. Follow him. Those who seek him will find him'" (8, 15–22). The first saying is closest to GTh 113 (also see 3 and 19). "Seeking and finding" occurs several times (2, 92, 94). Given the proximity of the two allusions, it is probable that GMary drew upon a variant of the GTh 113–114 tradition. Perhaps this sayings tradition also contained the prohibition of rules formula, "Do not give a law like a

---

[5]See Pagels, "Visions," 424f.

law-giver, lest you be bound by it" (9, 2f).[6] This injunction is repeated again at the end of the work (18, 15–24) as the apostles begin
their preaching (cp. ApocPet CG VII 77, 25–29). This sayings tradition is also responsible for the description of the apostles' mission as
"preaching the Gospel of the kingdom" (8, 21; 9, 8f). Thus, it seems
that the picture of Mary in GMary was formulated in association
with a Gnostic sayings tradition.

The particular community in which this tradition has been developed has some features in common with that in DialSav. The
opening discussion of the dissolution of all things into their roots
seems to have taught the necessity of rectifying the passions generated by association with nature (7, 10–8, 10). When she sees the vision
of the Savior, Mary is praised for *not wavering*. Not wavering or stability is a metaphor which Gnostics have derived from the tradition
of philosophic mysticism. It expresses the final state of the soul at
rest with the divine.[7] Mary's vision of the ascent of the soul follows
the liturgical model for such prayers of ascent. The soul conquers the
powers by proclaiming its superiority to them.[8] The actual list of
powers—darkness, desire, ignorance, trauma of death, kingdom of
the flesh, foolish wisdom of the flesh, and wrathful wisdom (16,
5–12)—suggests that the conquest of the passions was a major preoccupation of the group. They emphasized the transitory character of
all things, both those belonging to this world and those belonging to
what was traditionally considered the heavenly world. The soul says
to Ignorance, "I have recognized that the universe[9] is being dis-

---

[6]Following the suggestion for reading these lines made by G. MacRae, see H. M.
Schenke, "Bemerkungen zum Koptischen Papyrus Berolinensis 8502," *Fest. zum 150
Jahrigen Bestehen des Berliner Agyptischen Museums* (Berlin: Akademie Verlag,
1972), 322.

[7]See the study of this motif by M. Williams, "The Nature and Origin of the Gnostic Concept of Stability," unpublished dissertation, Harvard University, 1977.

[8]The author seems to have expanded an ascent prayer, which originally contained
two sets of answers to the powers and a prayer or a final proclamation of liberation
such as we saw behind Norea's prayer in NatArc, above, pp. 84–85. This new version
is formulated to suit Gnostic speculation about the structure of the planetary heavens.
The soul encounters four powers. The last is sevenfold, with its first three the same as
the earlier three. The second series is usually associated with desire.

[9]Although the Gnostic word *pterf* usually means the pleroma or the "totality of
divine stuff," cf. Layton, "Hypostasis," 389, and MacRae, *NHLE*, 473, it seems to be
translating the Greek *ta panta* in the sense of "universe" in this passage.

solved—both the things of earth and those of heaven" (15, 20–16, 1). However, this vision is seen by "mind," a power which the Lord tells Mary comes between soul and spirit. That limitation suggests that GMary is not presenting it as the culmination of Gnostic eschatology. Similarly, DialSav insisted that the vision of the fate of the soul was inferior to the eternal vision.

Not only has Mary received this special revelation from the Lord, but she is also the one who initiates the interpretation of the sayings of the Lord among the grieving apostles: "She turned their hearts to God, and they began to discuss the words of the Savior" (9, 22–24). This reference may well extend beyond the words of the post-resurrection dialogue to the words of the Lord in general, since GMary has clearly drawn on a wider sayings tradition. Mary seems to be presented as the initiator of the Gnostic tradition of interpreting the sayings of the Lord. Perhaps a similar connection lies behind the praise given her in DialSav, "woman who knows the All" (CG III 139, 12f).

Presumably the sect was not radically encratitic. The objections against Mary are not against femininity as such.[10] Rather, Andrew and Peter speak like orthodox officials. Their objections are typical of rhetorical objections to opponents in any context and are no indication of the sociological makeup of the various groups. Andrew protests that such teaching could not possibly have come from the Savior. Peter asserts that the Lord would not have revealed anything to a woman privately that he had not told all the apostles openly (17, 10–22). Both objections are common in anti-Gnostic polemic which insists that such strange teachings are in conflict with the apostolic tradition. Mary insists that she has not fabricated her revelation and

---

[10]We are skeptical of those who use this picture of Mary to claim that Gnostics upheld community leadership by women in opposition to the male dominated hierarchy of the orthodox Church; so Pagels, "What Became of God the Mother?" *Signs* 2 (1977), 300f. Mary is the hero here not because of an extraordinary role played by women in Gnostic communities, but because she is a figure closely associated with Jesus to whom esoteric tradition may be attached. Gnostic writings share a common presupposition of ancient ascetic writings: "Femininity is to be destroyed"; see Brown, *Making*, 87f, who rightly points out that the anti-feminism is not so much concerned with sex as with the whole pattern of family and social constraints that ties to women implied.

is not lying about the Savior. The negative overtones of the incident are intensified by the fact that the opening dialogue implies that all the disciples had received some Gnostic instruction from Jesus. As in the GTh sayings, Peter is taught gnosis by the Risen Lord but fails to achieve the proper understanding of it. Levi's defense is also typical rhetorical polemic. Peter is hot-tempered and contentious, but he can do no better than argue with women. Disciples have no business rejecting "one whom Jesus loves." They should get on with their preaching mission (18, 8–21).

Thus, the polemics in GMary are general. The orthodox object to the strange doctrine and the lack of respect for apostolic tradition among the Gnostics. Gnostics, in their turn, insist that apostolic tradition should be Gnostic. It is not, only because certain apostles like Peter and Andrew rejected the clear teaching of the Savior. That teaching is preserved in Gnostic Christianity.

PISTIS SOPHIA

The tradition of conflict between Peter and Mary is preserved in the late compilation of Gnostic traditions, PS. The text divides into two works, Books I-III and Book IV.[11] Book IV has a new introduction which places the revelation only a few days after the resurrection instead of the eleven years in Books I-III. Since Book IV is not close to the revelation dialogue genre, we will only be concerned with I-III. Our analysis of the setting of the revelation dialogue has already shown the similarity of this work to what we find in other dialogues. However, the opening questions are somewhat different. Instead of asking about Gnostic doctrines or about their own mission and relationship to the powers, the disciples ask about the purpose of a journey Jesus has just taken. This shift is reflected in the content, which includes fragmentary allusions to Gnostic myth, but which concentrates on describing the heavenly regions and mysteries. As in the other dialogues, the disciples are told to expect persecution.[12]

---

[11]So, first K. R. Köstlin, "Das gnostische System des Pistis Sophia," *TheolJahr* 13 (1854), 1–104, 137–96. See the general outline of its contents in MacDermot-Schmidt, *Pistis Sophia*, xiv-xviii.

[12]PS i, 7.

Jesus begins with a long description of how he has just readjusted the fates so that it will be easier for souls to get through. The disciples interrupt this exposition with questions about the action of fate on various types of soul. Mary Magdalene, who is described as the most spiritual of the disciples,[13] is the chief questioner.

Jesus takes the disciples on a heavenly journey. They meet Pistis Sophia, who must give thirteen repentances before she is readmitted to the pleroma. The references to her story contain fragments of a myth similar to ApocryJn.[14] Each of her hymns of repentance is followed by an exegesis based on Old Testament psalms, given by one of the disciples. Much of the dialogue centers on this—or occasionally New Testament—exegesis.[15] Other questions concern the various heavenly regions and the fate of souls who have received different mysteries. The primary interest of the Gnostic sect seems to be in the different heavenly regions and the corresponding fate of souls. Their fate depends upon the baptisms, mysteries and repentances which they have received. The ascetic cast of the preaching which Jesus tells the disciples to give is oriented toward the reception of such mysteries:

> When I have gone to the Light, preach to the whole world. Say to them, "Do not cease seeking day and night, and do not rest until you find the mysteries of the kingdom of Light." Say to them, "Renounce the whole world and all the matter within it, and all its cares, and all its sins, that is, all the relationships within it, so that you may be worthy of

---

[13]PS xcvi.

[14]Alv Kragerund, *Die Hymnen der Pistis Sophia* (Oslo: Universitetsforlagets Trynkningssentral, 1967), 203, lists the following: (a) fall from the pleroma; (b) Sophia's weeping and repentance in darkness; (c) her prayer and descent of help from above; (d) her exaltation into the aeons; (e) her final return to the pleroma. These elements of the traditions appear scattered about as fragments, not as part of a continuous narrative; cf. W. Till, "Of this well-articulated system of the Apocryphon of John with its fullness meaning, we find only sparse and scattered fragments, which have lost all sense," in "The Gnostic Apocryphon of John, *JEH* 3 (1952), 21f.

[15]G. Widengren, "Die Hymnen der Pistis Sophia," *Liber Amicorum: Studies in Honor of C. J. Bleeker*, Suppl. Numen XVIII (Leiden: E. J. Brill, 1969), 275–81, points out that the exegesis depends upon the prophecy-fulfillment scheme common in early Christianity (e.g., AdvHaer IV 33, 14), in which the Spirit of Christ speaks

the mysteries of Light and be saved from all the punishments within the judgments." Say to them, "Renounce complaining, that you may be worthy of the mysteries of Light and be saved from the fire of the Dog-face. . . . Say to them, "Renounce false witness so that you may be worthy of the mysteries of Light and escape and be saved from the rivers of fire of the Dog-face. . . ." (c. cii).

This long catalogue of vices and punishments includes warnings against erroneous teaching. The severest punishments are reserved for those who propagate such teaching or who turn away from gnosis:

Say to all who teach false doctrine and all who learn from them, "Woe to you! Unless you repent and give up your error, you will go to the punishments of the great dragon and the severe outer darkness. You will not be cast into the world forever but will be non-existent to the end." Say to those who abandon the teachings of the first Mystery, "Woe to you! Your punishment is more severe than all men. For you will remain in great frost, ice and hail in the midst of the dragon and outer darkness, and you will never be cast into the world from this time on, but will perish there. You will be consumed at the dissolution of the universe[16] and become non-existent forever" (c.cii).

A shorter catalogue of virtues that make one worthy of the mysteries and assurance that even the worst sinner can be saved if he or she repents follows this condemnation.

Like the journey tradition in Zostr, this elaborate picture of heavenly journeys owes some inspiration to the apocryphal Enoch literature. In ApocryJn, Christ (or the Epinoia of Light) speaks to

---

through the prophets. This view is quite different from that in a writing like ApocPet, which rejects the prophets (CG VII 71, 7–9). For an example of New Testament exegesis in PS, see c. xcvii: Mt 10:41 means that souls go to regions appropriate to the mysteries they have received.

[16]Literally, "the All," which apparently means "universe" here just as it does in GMary; see above, note 9.

Adam from the tree. Here, Christ speaks to Enoch from the tree of knowledge. The Enoch journeys have the seer see the tree of knowledge. He learns that in the last days the righteous will eat from it and gain the wisdom Adam and Eve did when they ate.[17] Here Christ gives Enoch the Gnostic books of Jeu—which also concern the various heavenly treasuries, mysteries and anointings bestowed by Christ.[18] Enoch is to deposit the books on Ararat to preserve them from the flood to be caused by the jealous archons until the time when Christ gives them to his disciples.[19] Gnosis, for this sect, consists in possession of secret mysteries about individual eschatology and in interpretation of scriptural passages. Even the myths are no longer a matter of speculation. Nor do these writings show interest in the kind of philosophical or theological speculation about the nature of the highest God and the soul's relationship to him that we find in many of the Nag Hammadi writings.

Since so much of PS seems to be traditional lore, one wonders if the stories of Mary and Peter that appear in the course of this lengthy work are not being treated in similar fashion. They reflect a tradition from the past known to the community rather than present realities of life among the Gnostics. GMary showed that she was considered a source of the esoteric interpretation of the sayings of Jesus. Here, she is a major participant in the dialogue. Peter sometimes demands that she stop talking so that he can have a chance (cc. xxxvi, cxlvi). The Lord allows Peter to speak but defends Mary for her gnosis. Elsewhere, Mary says that she could interpret what was said by the first Mystery but is afraid of Peter's threats. The first Mystery commands anyone with gnosis to give the interpretation (c. lxxii). Later the Lord tests Peter's mercifulness by demanding that he cut off a woman who has not done anything worthy of the mysteries after three baptisms (c. cxxii). Peter's refusal demonstrates his mercy. Mary is the one who interprets the incident. This story may

---

[17]Cf. c. xcix. See 1 En xxiv, 4–xxv, 6; xxxii, 3–6; 2 En viii, 3. The tree of life is also given the righteous in the last days in TLev xviii, 11 and Rev 2:7.

[18]There are occasional question and answer exchanges but none of the features of the revelation dialogue setting. See Schmidt-MacDermot, *The Books of Jeu and the Untitled Text in the Bruce Codex*, NHS XIII (Leiden: E. J. Brill, 1979).

[19]PS cxxxiv.

well be a variant of the tradition in GTh 114 where Peter sought to cut Mary off.

These passages witness to a well-established tradition about the conflict between the apostle Peter and the Gnostic Mary. Peter is always portrayed as the irascible opponent of gnosis who represents orthodox, anti-Gnostic polemic. He can only be silenced by direct command from the Savior or by the assertion of other disciples that he is going against the will of the Savior. His opposition to women is also a typical piece of polemic. It is common in both philosophical and heresiological debate to accuse one's opponents of only being able to convert women. In GMary, Levi rebukes Peter for picking a woman as an adversary rather than concentrate on the real opponents. The story of Peter's mercy in PS suggests that the polemic issue is no longer as strong as it was in GMary. Probably this group of Gnostic Christians had long since formed their own sect and developed their own ritual and organizational structures. They no longer seem to be involved with orthodox authorities, the conflict which called forth so much of the Gnostic Petrine tradition.

First Apocalypse of James

GTh 12 directs the disciples to another source of Gnostic authority—James, the brother of the Lord. Three writings are attributed to him in the Nag Hammadi collection, an apocryphal account of his martyrdom and two revelation dialogues.[20] Just as we saw was the case with the Thomas tradition, James' likeness to the Lord—though Gnostics always emphasize the fact that the two are not literally brothers—entitles him to receive gnosis. As in the Mary stories, the recipient of gnosis comes into conflict with the apostles, who refuse to accept the revelation. 1 ApocJas opens with a pre-passion dialogue between James and Jesus (cp. ApocPet). This exchange refers to Gnostic teaching about the highest God and the aeons. It is sufficient to show that Jesus did not limit Gnostic teaching to after the resurrection. A post-resurrection dialogue follows. There, Jesus reveals the truth about his passion, the ascent of the soul, and the chain

---

[20]Gnostic James traditions apparently combine all the James figures in the New Testament, see M. Malinine *et al.*, *Epistula*, xx-xxi.

of tradition by which the revelation is handed on. James asks about the place of Mary and the other women among the disciples and about the opposition that Gnostics will encounter (CG V 20, 13–42, 9). The final pages are fragmentary. It seems that James goes and rebukes the apostles and then begins preaching. A plot against his life results (42, 20–44, 8). As in GMary, GTh, and PS, the presence of women among the disciples serves as a surrogate for Gnostic possession of non-apostolic tradition. This claim is further spelled out in the instructions about how gnosis is to be transmitted until it is finally preached to the Gnostics (36, 13–38, 11).

The content of this dialogue seems to derive from short independent pieces of Gnostic teaching. An implied question about the Mother has been inserted into the account of Jesus' origins. James quotes a long Gnostic hymn in praise of Jesus' victory over the powers (28, 5–29, 3). When Jesus reassures James about the ascent of the soul, his instructions are almost identical with a liturgical formula that Irenaeus attributes to the Marcosians.[21] Many of the traditions preserved in this dialogue may derive from the liturgical usage of the community from which it comes.

The opening exchange between Jesus and James is cast as a farewell discourse similar to those in John. Jesus reveals that he is departing to fulfill his destiny and that he will return again to convict the archons (28, 13–30, 11; cp. Jn 16:4b–16). In response to a question, he confirms the fact that the structure of the heavens is based on the number twelve rather than seven as in the Old Testament. The upper ones in which the supreme deity dwells cannot be numbered (26, 2–27, 12). Such numerical considerations suggest contact with middle Platonism.[22] Jesus identifies himself with the highest God at the beginning of the dialogue (24, 19–26). His ascent through

---

[21]CG V 33, 21–35, 21//AdvHaer I 21, 5; see A. Bohlig and P. Labib, *Apokalypsen*, 30–33; Rudolph, "Dialog," 99. "Redemption" may have been the name of a sacrament in which the ascent of the soul was enacted (CG V 24, 11; 28, 9; 29, 12f; 33, 1; cf. AdvHaer I 13, 6).

[22]Compare the cosmological speculation in OrigWld (CG II 105, 10–16). Rejection of the biblical numbering of heavens implies a rejection of Genesis, since the latter is shown to have a false understanding of the cosmos. This rejection is based on its picture of the structure of the universe rather than on its picture of God or its failure to predict the Savior, two other common Gnostic charges.

the heavens is a victory over the hostile powers. It makes the ascent of Gnostic souls possible (30, 1–6). Jesus' identity with God is explained in philosophical terms. The author invokes middle Platonic speculation about the Dyad to explain how Jesus can be identical with that God. He also wishes to explain that contrary to much speculation—such as that in ApocryJn—the Female (Mother) was not part of the divine triad:

> Nothing existed except Him-who-is. He is unnameable and ineffable. I too am unnameable, from Him-who-is, just as I have been given many names—two from Him-who-is. And I, I am before you. Since you asked about Femaleness, Femaleness existed, but Femaleness was not first. It prepared powers and gods for itself, but it did not exist, when I came forth, since I am the image of Him-who-is, just as I have been given many homes—two from Him-who-is. I have brought forth the image of Him so that the sons of Him-who-is may know what is theirs and what is alien. (24, 19–25, 6)

Many features of this section are reminiscent of the Johannine farewell discourses: Jesus' identity with the highest God, his mission in making God known, his ascent, his return to convict the powers, his warning that the disciples will suffer because the powers are hostile to him, and Jesus' promise to return to the disciple. The reference to a comforter (= Paraclete?) is probably also based on that tradition.

The fragmentary condition of the concluding pages makes it difficult to reconstruct the account of Gnostic tradition. A contrast between the seed of Achamoth and the Gnostics is followed by an explanation of the "type" of the twelve (35, 19–36, 1). The twelve are tied to the twelve heavens of the Sophia, Achamoth, and thus given a lower status than that of the Gnostics, who are sons of the Father. (The explanation of the number of heavens in the opening part limited the number twelve to the lower heavens. Those in which the Father dwells cannot be numbered. These lower heavens may also be the "work of Femaleness" referred to in the passage above.) This arrangement implies that those Christians who depend upon the twelve for their tradition belong to the lower Sophia. They do not have any share in the knowledge of the Father brought by Jesus.

We are told how the Gnostics came to possess gnosis outside the tradition of the twelve. Revelation is to be kept hidden for a number of years. James only gives it to Addai. As far as one can make out, the time from the revelation until the manifestation of gnosis is several decades (thus agreeing with Irenaeus that gnosis did appear after the apostolic preaching). After James transmits gnosis to Addai, he is martyred right before the fall of Jerusalem. In the tenth year (after the revelation or after the martyrdom?), Addai writes the revelation down. It is then given to Levi. (Mary's defender in GMary now appears as a custodian of Gnostic tradition.) He transmits it to a Jerusalemite woman by whom he has two sons. Finally, the younger of the two begins preaching at age seventeen. It is his preaching which establishes the Gnostic seed. This is not the only allusion to the relative lateness of Gnostic preaching. Peter was told not to give his revelation to the "sons of this age." Norea—as might be expected of a primordial figure—learns that it will be three generations before the manifestation of her seed. But this chain of tradition is much more elaborately worked out. Gnosis is concealed throughout the apostolic age, and, according to its chronology, cannot have been preached before the beginning of the second century.

The conclusion also refers to a rebuke delivered to the twelve. Lacunae make it difficult to decide whether Jesus or James delivers the rebuke. Given the other examples of the disciple, who is the recipient of gnosis, trying to transmit it to the others, we assume that James was the subject. In ApocryJn, John appears to have succeeded. In GMary, controversy ensues, though the reader is intended to conclude that the disciples eventually capitulated and went out to preach gnosis. We shall see that ApocryJas has them explicitly reject gnosis. The rebuke probably refers to a similar reaction.

Of all the revelation dialogues, then, 1 ApocJas is the most explicit acknowledgment of the non-apostolic character of Gnostic traditions of cosmology, Christology and ascent of the soul. This teaching could not have been part of the original apostolic witness because it was not given to the twelve. It was carefully hidden from them, only to be delivered to the Gnostics, who would appear in a later generation.

THE APOCRYPHON OF JAMES

The other James dialogue, ApocryJas, lacks specifically Gnostic theologoumena.[23] Hornschuch points out that it shares many characteristics of the esoteric apostolic traditions referred to in Clement of Alexandria. He considers such traditions a "semi-gnosis," halfway between the orthodox concept of an apostolic tradition handed on to all the apostles and more radical Gnostic positions—like that of 1 ApocJas—which insist that Gnostic tradition is superior to apostolic.[24] We have seen that such a division is somewhat inadequate. Many revelation dialogues have tried to defend the apostolic character of their tradition by explaining how it came to be different from acknowledged apostolic preaching.

One of the peculiarities of this text in comparison with other Gnostic material is its evaluation of martyrdom. Of course, the apocryphal James traditions will deal with his martyrdom. 2 ApocryJas (CG V 4) is such an account.[25] Clement of Alexandria claims to have derived his doctrine of martyrdom from esoteric traditions (Strom IV 76, 1–88, 5).[26] But neither the other Gnostics nor Clement's tradition places the value on martyrdom that ApocryJas does.[27] ApocPet attacked opponents who thought that their sufferings contributed to building up the true Christian community (CG VII 78, 31–33). Predictions that the Gnostics will suffer persecution because the archons are hostile to them are common enough, but these sufferings are not interpreted in terms of martyrdom. The authors often allude to New Testament predictions (GMary BG 9, 10–12; PetPhil CG VIII 138, 15–28). 1 ApocJas has the Lord tell James about his martyrdom that (1) the powers are really seeking to attack Jesus (CG V 27, 18–26;

---

[23]Compare AcPet12. Malinine, *Epistula*, gives extensive notes suggesting Gnostic readings of ApocryJas.

[24]Hornschuch, "The Apostles as Bearers of Tradition," *New Testament Apocrypha* II, ed. Hennecke-Schneemelcher (Philadelphia: Westminster, 1965), 83f.

[25]See the text and commentary by W.-P. Funk, *Die Zweite Apokalypse des Jakobus aus Nag Hammadi Codex V*, TU 119 (Berlin: Akademie Verlag, 1976), 199–209.

[26]Hornschuch, "Apostles," 85.

[27]See W. H. C. Frend, *Martyrdom and Persecution in the Early Church* (New York: Doubleday, 1976), 259–63. Caught between Christians overly anxious for martyrdom and Gnostics who considered it of no value, Clement of Alexandria leans toward the latter.

29, 4–8); (2) suffering only affects the body (32, 13–22); (3) the Gnostic soul will escape using the ascent prayer taught by the Lord (33, 3–34, 20). ApocryJas departs from these traditions by placing a positive valuation on martyrdom in imitation of Christ. It makes the disciple beloved of the Father (CG I 4, 31–5, 20).

The connection with the death of Christ also brings with it a different assessment of the crucifixion. Like most other Gnostic accounts of the passion, 1 ApocJas had denied the reality of Jesus' suffering. The crucifixion was merely a "type" of the suffering of the lower Sophia, Achamoth (CG V 31, 23f; also PetPhil CG VIII 139, 21–25; AdvHaer I 8, 2). ApocPet coupled such interpretation with rejection of orthodox belief in the cross of Christ. Again, ApocryJas is quite different. The disciple is taught to remember the cross of Christ:

> "Therefore, despise death and concern yourself with life. Remember my cross and my death and you will live." But I responded, "Lord, do not mention the cross and death to us, for these are far from you." The Lord answered, "Amen, I say to you, no one will be saved unless he believes in my cross. But those who believed in my cross, theirs is the kingdom of God. Therefore, seek death as the dead seek life. For what they seek appears. What are they concerned about? When you seek death, it will show you election. For I say to you, no one will be saved if he is afraid of death, for the kingdom of death belongs to those who kill themselves. Become greater than I. Become equal to the Holy Spirit" (CG I 5, 31–6, 20).

Puech has even suggested that this passage reflects the kind of enthusiasm for martyrdom against which Clement directs his warnings.[28] The passage also seems to reprove James for doctrine explicitly taught in 1 ApocJas that sufferings are far from Jesus. There the Lord tells his sorrowing brother, "Never have I suffered in any way;

---

[28]H.-Ch. Puech, and G. Quispel, "Les écrits gnostiques du Codex Jung," *VigChr* 8 (1954), 1–51. Clement rejects the idea that the hope of reward is suitable motivation for martyrdom (Strom IV vii 46, 1–2; iv 14, 1).

nor have I been troubled" (CG V 31, 15–20). It is difficult to avoid the conclusion that the picture of martyrdom and of the death of Christ in ApocryJas comes from a different and more orthodox tradition than that behind the other two James apocrypha. Since this work is very much concerned with the interpretation of the New Testament, that exegetical tradition may be behind this unusual evaluation.

ApocryJas contains another ambiguous passage, 8, 35, which may also be a reference to 1 ApocJas tradition. The Lord says that he has already taught the response (*hypothesis*) which is to be made before the authorities (archons). 1 ApocJas gives the response of the soul to the archons as the key to salvation. How is that expression understood here? Most of the editors of the *editio princeps* took 8, 35 as a reference to earthly magistrates as in the Gospel sayings (Mk 13:9–11 par).[29] Quispel, however, pointed out that the author is probably referring to the formula recited as the soul ascends.[30] The Gnostics may well have had such an exegesis of the Gospel sayings about the response before the authorities. (Compare the combination of Gnostic eschatology and sayings interpretation in DialSav.) Perhaps ApocryJas wishes to suggest that such information was contained in the other apocryphon mentioned in its cover letter.

ApocryJas is framed by a letter from James to another Gnostic teacher (1, 1–35; 16, 12–30). The addressee is not to share the revelation with non-Gnostics, since the Lord did not wish to give it to all of the twelve (1, 24f; 16, 23ff). Such cover letters are a common literary device. Irenaeus addresses his *Adversus Haereses* to another teacher and warns him that there are things in it that not all can understand. His addressee is a minister to others. Irenaeus expects his writings to help this teacher to prevent Christians from being led astray. Perhaps ApocryJas is using a similar model as the basis for his cover letter.

The introduction, which sets the scene for the revelation dialogue, has other hints of anti-orthodox polemic. The appearance

---

[29] So Puech, Malinine and Zandee, *Epistula*, 60.

[30] *Loc cit.* See C. Colpe, "Die Himmelreise der Seele ausserhalb und innerhalb der Gnosis," *Le origini*, 438–44. Colpe argues that Gnosticism first brought the archaic motif of the heavenly journey of the soul into the service of a general eschatology and soteriology.

takes place eighteen months after the crucifixion. In some Gnostic traditions, that figure corresponds to the number of aeons (AdvHaer I 3, 2; 30, 13f). A similar period appears in Jewish-Christian tradition (*AscIs* IX, 16). The Lord singles out James and Peter for separate revelation. Tradition attributed to Clement of Alexandria refers to Gnostics who say that the Risen Lord gave gnosis to James, Peter and John (Eusebius H. E. II i, 4). The cover letter to ApocryJas has already informed the reader that James also received private Gnostic teaching from the Lord. The dialogue will go on to show the inferiority of Peter's understanding. (The dialogue itself refers to the special teaching given to James—8, 31–36.) Peter's questions consistently display misunderstanding. James will be the only one to return to Jerusalem where he receives a share with the Gnostic race (16, 10f). Perhaps Peter is included in the revelation to support the claim that the apostles did receive some true gnosis and thus to vindicate Gnostic interpretation of the New Testament which forms such an important part of this community's traditions. We have seen several references to Jesus' pre-resurrection transmission of gnosis. These references seem to be a Gnostic response to the increasing influence of the New Testament canon in orthodox circles. The opening of ApocryJas illustrates this influence in narrative form. When the Savior appears, the apostles are writing down their individual revelations (the "memoirs" of Justin's *Dial* ciii, 8 and cv, 5). The exchange between Jesus and the disciples over his impending return to where he came from and their own inability to follow him there reflects the Johannine farewell discourses (cf. Jn 13:3, 36; 14:3f; 16:5, 28). Later, an unidentified you (pl.) is rebuked for persecuting Jesus rather than accompanying him when he was eager to go (14, 20f//Jn 16:4b–5?).

The content of the revelation derives from at least two sources: (1) a sermonic section of blessings and woes which exhort the hearer to become a Gnostic; (2) Gnostic interpretation of the New Testament. The blessings and woes are scattered throughout the interpretation: 3, 8–38; 4, 4–22; 8, 28f; 9, 18–10, 6—now a condemnation of heretics; 11, 11–12, 17. The following passages give specific interpretations of the New Testament:

(1) *2, 29f:* Jn 13:36; 14:3f refer to "being full"—perhaps this interpretation is opposing Gnostic eschatology to Christian apocalyptic expectations.

(2) *3, 40–4, 1:* Jn 21:15f means leave reason and soul to become full of the Spirit. GMary also placed soul and reason below Spirit.

(3) *4, 28–30:* Mt 6:13, the Gnostic can expect persecution.

(4) *5, 3–5:* Jn 14:23, the Father's love is the reward for the martyr.

(5) *5, 35–38:* Mt 16:23 is alluded to in James' rejection of Jesus' suffering.

(6) *6, 19f:* Jn 14:11, "greater works," refers to the Gnostic who is made greater through possession of the Spirit.

(7) *6, 28—7, 10:* Mt 14:10ff (Jn 13:34), the beheading of John the Baptist, meant the end of prophecy. The time of parables has given way to Jesus' "open" speech (Jn 16:25, 29).

(8) *7, 22ff:* A growth parable composed of Mk 4:26; 12:20//Jn 12:24; Mt 3:10; 7:16ff; 12:33; Mk 11:14; Jn 15:2ff. The orthodox are a withered seed from which one obtains no fruit. The Gnostic rejects such useless plants.[31]

(9) *7, 36–8, 14:* Jn 17:5; Mk 4:10–12, the glorified Jesus can speak openly.

(10) *8, 5–10:* A list of parables, some of which will be interpreted later: *shepherds* (Mt 18:12–24//GTh 107; Jn 10); *seed*—this tradition seems to have combined the seed parables of sower, mustard seed, seed growing secretly and weeds (Mt 13:3–9//GTh 9; Mt 13:31–33//GTh 20; Mk 4:26–30//GTh 21-end; Mt 13:24ff//GTh 51); *building* (Mt 7:24–27); *virgins* (Mt 25:1–12); *worker's pay* (Mt 20:1–6); *woman and drachma* (Lk 15:8–10). Perhaps this list reflects a collection of parables which the Gnostics had interpreted as referring to their own situation. Irenaeus takes a strong stand against Gnostic parable exegesis (AdvHaer I 8, 1). He insists that all parable exegesis is subject to the rule (*hypothesis*) of faith. We have seen that in ApocryJas Jesus claims to have taught the *hypothesis* that the Gnostic is to give before the authorities (8, 35). Irenaeus argues against the Gnostic view that the parables do not concern the pleroma—or, in the case of the Gnostic *hypothesis*, the ascent of the soul into it. They detail the activity of God toward humanity.[32]

---

[31]Compare the exegesis of Mt 7:18 as explanation of the different reactions to Gnostic preaching in ApocPet CG VII 75, 7–9; 76, 4–8.

[32]He also argues against Gnostic parable exegesis in AdvHaer I 3, 1; II 10, 2. The

(11) *8, 10–26:* Mt 13:18–23, receive the kingdom through gnosis.

(12)   *9, 9f:* Jn 1:11f, Jesus is the great light. Compare a similar confessional formula in ThCont (CG II 139, 20).

(13) *9, 1–8:* Jn 1:11f, 14; 14:3f; 17:24, some will reject gnosis.

(14) *10, 1–5:* 1 Jn 3:9. (The passage is formally parallel to Lk 18:23–25.) The orthodox are rejected.

(15) *10, 7–21:* Jn 16:7, 20 (mourn/joy), the ascent of the revealer is final; there is no future coming (cp. 2, 29f). Jn 10:15, 25ff; 8:47; Mk 8:38, the revelation is limited to Gnostics.

(16) *10, 22:* Jn 14:3–28 refers to the Gnostics.

(17) *10, 30–34:* Jn 15:15; 17:20; 14:14f; 16:23 refer to the Gnostics.

(18) *10, 32–34:* 2 Thes 1:10; Mk 8:38f; Jn 14:19f; 16:22, the parousia or vision of Jesus is the ascent that he is about to make through the spheres.

(19) *11, 4–6:* 1 Jn 2:1f (Jn 14:16), Gnostics have the Paraclete. Also see the reference to the "Comforter" in 1 ApocJas (CG V 30, 24).

(20) *11, 7ff:* Jn 16:29f, against the orthodox claims to understand the teaching of Jesus. Compare ApocPet (CG VII 76, 24–34).

(21) *12, 18ff:* Mk 10:24–26, the "few" who are saved are the Gnostics.

(22) *12, 21ff:* Mk 4:26ff (GTh 12), self-knowledge (= gnosis) gains the kingdom.

(23) *13, 3–8:* Jn 14:2; Mt 7:27f, the heavenly dwelling prepared by the ascending Christ is the true foundation of the Church.[33]

The topical concerns of this exegetical tradition are more limited than a simple list of the passages might suggest. First, only Gnostics—not other Christians—enter the kingdom. Second, the Gnostics can expect persecution and rejection. Third, the eschatological teaching of the New Testament refers to the victorious ascent of Christ through the heavens, which has made it possible for the Gnostic to

---

hypothesis, for Irenaeus, is reflected in the traditional list of theological topics, "mysteries" suitable for reflection. See W. van Unnik, "A Document of Second Century Theological Discussion (Irenaeus A.H. I 10, 3)," *VigChr* 31 (1977), 207f, 222–25.

[33]Compare the ecclesiology of ApocPet, above, pp. 120–122.

do the same. Thus, our suggestion that the remark about the interpretation of the hypothesis before the rulers refers to an interpretation of the Gospel saying in terms of Gnostic eschatology is
supported by the exegesis. Possibly this *hypothesis* was a norm for
Gnostic interpretation of the parables listed in item #10, above.
When Irenaeus opposed the *hypothesis* of faith to Gnostic parable interpretation, he could well be referring to such a Gnostic technical
term. Finally, we find references to what seems to be a Gnostic topos: the end of prophecy came with Jesus' revelation of gnosis. The
overriding concern of all these passages is to show that gnosis is necessary for salvation. Non-Gnostic Christians will be rejected. It
seems likely that the author's opponents made their own case by appealing to the Gospels and the teaching of the Lord. ApocryJas uses
a tradition of Gospel exegesis that is very much dependent upon the
Johannine farewell discourses to answer orthodox objections and to
account for opposition.

Other elements of anti-orthodox polemic are embedded within
the narrative itself. We have seen that revelation dialogues can begin
with a rebuke of the seer, but it is much less common for that motif
to be continued throughout, since the heavenly revelation removes
the ignorance that precipitated the rebuke. ApocryJas, however, has
inserted material from the sermonic woe tradition in such a way as to
maintain a constant alteration of rebuke and encouragement. This alteration is not the result of some unreflective combination of sources.
Peter calls attention to it (13, 26–36). Jesus' response (cp. Jn 14:9)
implies that the disciples are still deficient in gnosis. No one with
true gnosis can be banished from the kingdom even if the Father
himself should wish to do so (14, 14–19). Compare the allusions to
binding by the opponents and Jesus' forgiveness of his "little ones" in
ApocPet (CG VII 77, 22–78, 31). One suspects that this exchange in
ApocryJas also refers to official disciplinary action taken against the
Gnostics. Perhaps they were being expelled (= put out of the kingdom) from the Christian communities to which they belonged.

ApocryJas has turned the Johannine discussion of the necessity
for Jesus' departure into an actual attempt by the disciples to prevent
him from going. They had forced him to stay and interpret the parables (8, 1–10; cp. PS vi, lxxxviii, xc, c). The author may hold—as
does GrPow (CG VI 40, 30ff)—that the parables belonged to a pre-

Gnostic stage of revelation. The disciples do not understand either the parables or the open speech of Jesus (7, 1–10//Mk 4:10–12; Jn 16:29ff). They do not follow Jesus (14, 22–25). ApocryJas suggests that Peter and James do not attain a vision of the highest heavens because the other disciples call them back (15, 23–33). Although they are said to believe the revelation given to Peter and James, the others become resentful of the Gnostic race. ApocPet also gave "resentment" as one reason for the persecution of the Gnostics (CG VII 76, 35–77, 16). James has to disperse them and return to Jerusalem alone. Thus, the dispersal of the apostles throughout the world is not a sign of unified preaching as it is in Irenaeus or even in Gnostic writings like PetPhil. Instead, it shows that the disciples failed to attain a share in the Gnostic race.

We have seen that Irenaeus associates the worldwide unity of doctrine with the apostolic tradition. We have also seen that Gnostic Petrine traditions make a similar claim. ApocryJas, on the other hand, seems at great pains to demonstrate the opposite. Not only is the concluding dispersion a sign of failure, but even the introduction to the work suggests disunity. Each disciple is writing his own combination of common and private revelation. The course of the dialogue shows them to be ignorant. By its conclusion they are so resentful that they cannot stay in Jerusalem. This scene may well reflect the tradition behind the rebuke of the disciples mentioned at the end of 1 ApocJas. They cannot receive the portion allotted to the Gnostic race. Since they are unable to stay in Jerusalem, they will not share the Gnostic Pentecost or have any claim to possession of the Paraclete. Unlike the Gnostics, they will not become "greater than Jesus."

The exchange between James and Jesus on prophecy (6, 28–7, 10) probably represents another area of controversy. AdvHaer I 13, 3–4 provides a clue. Irenaeus first accuses Marcus of prophesying through the use of a familiar spirit and then of seducing others into thinking that they can be prophets. Irenaeus is forced to admit that there are prophets (including women?) in the Church. Therefore, he argues that, unlike these Gnostics, Christians only prophesy when inspired by God. ApocryJas, on the other hand, interprets the be-

---

³⁴An interpretation of Jn 16:32?

heading of John as the end of all prophecy. A reference to the possession of the Spirit by Gnostics had led James to ask about prophecy. According to this passage, the Gnostic would answer Irenaeus by insisting that although Gnostics possess the Spirit, they do not demonstrate it in prophecy. A similar argument probably underlies the condemnation of the orthodox for seeking dreams suitable to their opinions in ApocPet (CG VII 75, 1–7).[35]

Some of the woe material has been edited to make it attack the orthodox directly. Often the same expressions were used against the Gnostics by orthodox heresiologists. The opponents are called "pretenders to the truth and falsifiers of knowledge" (9, 24–10, 6). Compare Irenaeus' references to "gnosis, falsely so-called." They are "sinners against the spirit" (Mk 3:28f) who should be preaching gnosis rather than attacking it. A judgment oracle is pronounced against the opponents patterned on Lk 18:25ff (10, 1–5): since the pure one cannot be defiled nor the man of light come into darkness, the orthodox have no hope of salvation.

The author uses a collage of New Testament allusions to mount an extended attack against the orthodox understanding of divine forgiveness (11, 11–12, 17). The orthodox do not have the Paraclete.[36] Unless a person has gnosis, he is like the man in Mt 12:43ff, just waiting to be seized by the archons. He will never attain the dwelling place prepared by Jesus (13, 3–8). Orthodox rites of forgiveness only deal with the body (baptism) and with the soul (word of forgiveness). They do not convey Spirit. Real liberation is only possible when one ascends beyond the powers as in the Gnostic rites for the ascent of the soul. Valentinian theologians have a more systematic version of this criticism of orthodox doctrine, but it follows similar lines.[37] Irenaeus uses a combination of Gal 5:19–22 and 1 Cor 6:9–11 to present the orthodox case (AdvHaer V 11, 1–2). He agrees that a person is only saved through the Spirit, but goes on to insist that spiritual conformity to an ethical vision, the "works of the Spirit," is necessary to attain eternal life. He consistently argues that the Spirit transforms

---

[35]This passage takes a stronger stance than ApocryJas, since it suggests that anyone who engages in dream interpretation as divination will be damned.

[36]Given the context, this passage probably refers to 1 Jn 2:1f rather than to Jn 14:16.

[37]See Pagels, *Johannine Gospel*, 61–65.

the flesh so that it becomes the locus of eternal life.[38] The Gnostics seem to have traditionally used the parable of the seven demons to support their view of redemption. The elect are removed beyond the demons while the orthodox are still subjected to their power.[39] The final woe section (13, 9–17) condemns those who do not receive the gnosis that Jesus was sent to reveal. They do not ascend to the "dwelling place" and hence are not redeemed.

In this context, the failed ascent of Peter and James is all the more striking.[40] The other disciples have prevented them from attaining higher knowledge, just as they had tried to prevent Jesus' departure. They will go on to disobey the Savior's command to "love those who are to come," that is, the Gnostics (a Gnostic interpretation of the Johannine love command?). They fail, thus, to love those for whose sake they have been saved (an allusion to Jn 17:20–23). It turns out that James is *the only one* who has received gnosis. He is the only one who follows the Lord's instructions to enlighten the "beloved, whom the Lord has made sons." All the other preaching outside this tradition is being carried out in ignorance and resentment. Even Peter, who had the best chance to gain gnosis, has apparently failed and been sent away from Jerusalem. This conclusion fits the emphasis on the exclusive transmission of gnosis that we found in 1 ApocJas. There is no possibility for true revelation or salvation to be attained outside this tradition.

Thus, far from being the non-Gnostic apocryphon that many have thought, ApocryJas represents a sustained and vigorous attack on orthodox attempts to eradicate Gnosticism. Not even the Father himself could exclude a Gnostic from the kingdom! The orthodox claims for the reliability of their apostolic tradition are portrayed as ignorant and malicious fraud. Though such preaching will never

---

[38]See the discussion of Gnostic pneumatology and Irenaeus' answer in H. D. Hauschild, *Gottes Geist und der Mensch*, Beitr. Ev. Theol. 63 (Munich: Chr. Kaiser, 1972), 48–55, 151–272.

[39]This tradition appears in Clement of Alexandria (Strom II cxv, 1–2). Clement argues against the apparent predestination of souls in Gnosticism, holding that if it were true, Gnostics would not even have to realize their own election, nor could the soul be a "house of demons."

[40]Contrast ApocPaul (CG V 2) where the apostle ascends through all ten heavens. The twelve are found in the ninth—an argument for the superior gnosis of a Pauline Gnostic sect?

keep the Gnostic from salvation, it may well hinder others from attaining the kingdom. ApocPet brought a similar change against the orthodox. The opponents' behavior is indeed—as they may have claimed—modeled on that of Jesus' disciples. These orthodox teachers take after those disciples who even with eighteen months of post-resurrection instruction are unable to understand the parables,[41] let alone the clear revelation that Jesus has given to them.

Not surprisingly, these writings have much in common with the Gnostic Petrine traditions. The two traditions have developed alternative formulations of the conflict between Gnostic and orthodox preaching and interpretation. GMary seemed to reflect the less organized opposition from orthodox Christians similar to what we found in PetPhil. The James tradition, on the other hand, is like ApocPet in that it seems to be responding to a more formalized opposition to Gnostic teaching. Perhaps it even reflects traditions and arguments used by Irenaeus. Its assessment of the orthodox position is not much different from that in ApocPet, though there is less explicit reflection on Gnostic subjection to Church authorities. Perhaps the disciplinary sanctions against Gnostics were not as severe as they had been in ApocPet. Or perhaps the Gnostics had come to form completely independent groups. Although other Gnostic doctrines are represented, the chief concern of all the writings in this group is eschatological. The Gnostic soul—and only the Gnostic soul—achieves salvation. This emphasis may reflect the polemic between orthodox and Gnostic Christians or it may simply be the main focus of the Gnostic sects in question. It certainly warns us against over-identifying Gnosticism either with myths about the origins of the cosmos or with a completely realized eschatology. The pressing soteriological question may have been intensified by the increasing prominence of canonical Scripture. With the words of the tradition apparently fixed in an unalterable text, it became harder to use the oral tradition of the sayings and their interpretation as support for one's views. Both the Petrine tradition and those traditions associated with non-disciples come to grips with the authority of canonical Scripture either by retelling its stories or by sustained argument

---

[41]The picture of the disciples as deficient after long instruction also appears in the introduction to PS. They are still deficient in gnosis after eleven years!

about the exegesis of the text. But the James tradition also seems to have given up some of the battle. It does not try to show that Gnostic teaching is the true apostolic preaching. Instead, every effort is made to show that the apostolic tradition itself is deficient. Unable to enlighten his disciples, Jesus turns to others, to "those whom he loves," the Gnostics. Only they are able to appreciate and to preserve the true meaning of his teaching.

SUMMARY

The Polemic Range of
the Revelation Dialogue

Our study of the revelation dialogues has shown that the Gnostics did not ignore the arguments directed against them.[1] Most of the dialogues defend the teaching or praxis of Gnostic groups against external pressure. With the possible exception of NatArc,[2] the polemic seems to involve competing claims of orthodox Christians. We have seen that other Gnostic writings presuppose the dialogue genre as an authoritative source of Gnostic teaching.[3] Gnostic authors, who used the genre to attack their opponents, invoke the authority of a well-established type of revelation. Before we turn to the religious and theological issues involved in this controversy, we would do well to survey the various contexts to which Gnostic polemic is addressed. Our investigation can be broken into three categories: conversion, repentance—that is, turning to asceticism—and defense of the tradition.

---

[1]This point has been emphasized forcefully by W. Schoedel, "Topological Theology and Some Monistic Tendencies in Gnosticism," *Essays on the Nag Hammadi Texts,* 106–108.

[2]Perhaps the similarities in Genesis exegesis between NatArc and ApocAd should lead us to trace NatArc to polemic between Gnostics and Jewish or Jewish-Christian baptismal sects. OrigWld shows that such traditions had become part of the collection of a Gnostic bibliophile by the end of the second century A.D.

[3]See above, pp. 20–21.

157

CONVERSION

Conversion of Christians, or possibly non-Christians, to Christian gnosis concerns those dialogues which present fairly extensive surveys of Gnostic teaching without direct attacks on peculiarly Christian doctrines. Their references to opposition and hostility are a topos of missionary preaching.

ApocryJn presents the most systematic exposition of gnosis. It seems to have been aimed at persuading fellow-Christians. There is no indication that the Gnostics formed a separate group. Nor do we find any suggestion that the other disciples had difficulty accepting John's revelation. ApocryJn states simply that Gnostic Christianity has the true message of the Risen Jesus. That message was not widely preached because the Lord had commanded the apostle to be careful not to give it to anyone not able to receive it. SJC seems to derive from a similar context. But, unlike ApocryJn, it presupposes readers who know some version of the Sophia myth and perhaps even the type of teaching about the highest God and the aeons that the author has taken from Eug. Therefore, it can hardly be emphasizing introductory catechesis. Either the work is aimed at non-Christian Gnostics to show them that their gnosis derives from the teachings of the Risen Jesus, or it is addressed to Christians who might be tempted to find esoteric wisdom in non-Christian sources. The I AM sayings of the revealer show that the author wishes to emphasize that esoteric wisdom can only be found in Christianity. No one else has the truth about the highest God, the aeons, or salvation.

External evidence allows us to associate Zostr with the mystical theology of Alexandrian Platonism. Such theology appears in both pagan and Christian circles. Over against both, Zostr contends that true understanding of the unknowable God can only be had through the Gnostic ascent of the soul.

ASCETIC PRAXIS

Other dialogues are primarily concerned with asceticism. If one follows the view that the Thomas traditions derive from Eastern Syria and the Petrine ones from Western Syria,[4] then we have examples from both areas. The ties between DialSav and the Thomas tradition suggest that its discussion of eschatology also belongs in the ascetic camp rather than among the conversion dialogues. This association may account for the dialogue's insistence on the relative worthlessness of cosmological and heavenly visions. ThCont evidences a more serious conflict between Gnostic ascetics and Christians who reject the ascetic claims about salvation.

The other-worldly, ascetic rejection of material wealth in AcPet12 may derive from Western Syria. Its picture of the wandering disciple as ideal Christian may have been influenced by traditions of discipleship behind the Matthean Gospel.[5] The Gnostics use their own apocryphal acts of Peter to counteract the growing influence of wealthy Christians in the community.[6]

DEFENSE OF THE GNOSTIC TRADITION

Defense of the tradition preoccupies our final group of writings. They are out to demonstrate the truth of a Gnostic tradition derived from the Savior and its associated Christology against the developing strength of orthodox tradition. This opposition insisted on the unity of tradition deriving from the apostles, on a non- or anti-Gnostic reading of the life of Jesus—probably associated with the development of the Gospel canon—and on the teaching authority of Church leaders.

---

[4]So H. Koester, "Gnomai Diaphoroi," *Trajectories Through Early Christianity*, 119–26.

[5]As in the reconstruction of the early Jesus movement by G. Theissen, which depends entirely upon such Matthean traditions, in his *Sociology of Early Palestinian Christianity* (Philadelphia: Fortress, 1978). See the objections of J. D. Kingsbury, "The Verb *Anakalouthein* as an Index of Matthew's View of His Community," *JBL* 97 (1978), 56–73. Kingsbury's characterization of Matthew's community as a well-off urban community fits in well with the type of Christianity of the "merchants" that is attacked in AcPet12.

[6]If NatArc derives from a baptismal sect, it might have been formulated to defend such a group against the charge of rejecting the tradition such as was explicitly raised in Zostr and ApocryJn. The episode of the enthronement of Sabaoth also suggests that the author considers throne visions of Jewish mystics secondary to true gnosis, though the writing itself contains very little information about the heavenly pleroma.

ApocPet shows that in Petrine areas, at least, this authority was bolstered by appeal to Matthean tradition. The Petrine Gnostics reject such orthodox claims. They claim that the authority of the apostle underlies Gnostic groups and, at least in PetPhil,[7] that Peter initiated a worldwide apostolic proclamation of gnosis. The orthodox have simply falsified the tradition.

GMary stands midway between these Petrine Gnostics and those of the James tradition who reject apostolic claims and insist that true gnosis comes from a non-disciple who was beloved of Jesus. In GMary, though Peter tries to resist the clear teaching and will of the Lord, he does finally submit and all the disciples go off to preach gnosis. The implication is that the author's orthodox opponents should follow the example of their hero.

The James tradition, on the other hand, simply denies the validity of apostolic tradition as a witness to Jesus. Peter and the other disciples to whom the orthodox appeal had the opportunity to receive gnosis. Jesus taught it both during his lifetime and after the resurrection. However, his disciples proved incapable of receiving it. Therefore, gnosis had to be preserved through a secret chain of transmission until the Gnostic race who could receive it appeared. 1 ApocJas seems to date this appearance in the second century A.D.

References to orthodox attempts to exclude Gnostics from the Christian community in ApocryJas suggest that orthodox hostility has solidified to the point of drawing definitive boundaries between orthodox and Gnostic Christians. Although ApocPet alluded to disciplinary action against the Gnostics, he does not suggest outright exclusion. The "little ones" are subject to the bishops and deacons for a time. Perhaps such a posture of subjection was a deliberate tactic on the part of Gnostics to avoid harsher measures. ApocPet's teaching that it is impossible to tell the difference between the immortal, Gnostic soul and the mortal ones in this age could well have provided the rationale for such a policy. Irenaeus also acknowledges the presence of Gnostics in the larger Christian community. He says that his predecessors have not been able to refute those heretics (Adv-Haer IV praef).

---

[7] It is not clear whether the concentration on Peter in ApocPet would have implied that gnosis is the universal apostolic preaching, as is stated in PetPhil, or not.

ApocryJas shows many points of contact with the anti-Gnostic polemic that we find in Irenaeus. The two groups could not yet have separated very far. For example, we find:

(1) an introductory preface directing the work to another teacher.

(2) concern for the unity and dispersion of apostolic tradition. ApocryJas has given that linchpin of the orthodox polemic an ironic twist. Apostolic dispersion is a sign of their failure to follow the Savior.

(3) the opponents are teachers of "false knowledge."

(4) the charge of fraudulent prophecy is denied. The orthodox may prophesy but Gnostic Christians know that the age of prophecy is over.

(5) the authority of the Gospel canon. That authority is modulated, since its authors are presented as writing their "memoirs" in a state of defective gnosis.

(6) concern for the interpretation of the New Testament—especially the parables and sayings. Presumably, Gnostic interpretation of Gospel traditions was considered the remedy for the defective gnosis of their authors.

(7) insistence on the fundamental connection between the Spirit and redemption.

Although none of these similarities is so close as to prove that the author of ApocryJas had Irenaeus' refutation before him, the combination suggests that the work is directed against an orthodoxy in which the type of argumentation used by Irenaeus was proving effective. Gnostics were being excluded from Christian communities. Perhaps some were even returning to the orthodox fold, as Irenaeus had hoped (AdvHaer V praef).

Despite the necessarily tentative character of such hypotheses, we may suggest that the revelation dialogue gained its initial prestige in Gnostic circles from its use in missionary propaganda such as we find in ApocryJn and SJC. We have seen that these are the dialogues which survive in multiple versions. Such widely used expositions of gnosis may then have generated more regional forms such as we find in other dialogues. Zostr takes on the mystical speculations of Alexandrian Platonists. The Thomas tradition and AcPet 12 defend Gnostic ascesis in their respective regions of Syria. Peter, Mary and

James all appear in various contexts as defenders of gnosis, the true Christianity, against the counter-arguments of Gnostic Christians.

Since neither ApocryJn nor SJC seems to have invented its dialogue format, we might hypothesize that it was familiar to them from accounts of the Gnostic Urgeshichte such as the exchange between the revealing angel and the ancestor of the Gnostic race in NatArc. Similar models may have come from apocryphal Enoch traditions, which also seem to have played a role in Gnostic speculations about heavenly journeys. However, the widespread diffusion and popularity of the genre does not seem to be associated with the content of primordial revelation and cosmological wisdom. Many of the later examples have no interest in this side of gnosis. They may even explicitly downgrade it, as seems to be the case in DialSav and ThCont. Thus, we conclude that the authority and popularity of the genre are dependent upon its use as a basic tool of Christian Gnostic propaganda. Gnosis contains the hermeneutic key to true Christianity because it derives from Jesus, the heavenly revealer.

PART THREE

Religious Issues
in the Gnostic Dialogue

CHAPTER NINE
Revelation and Its Source

With all the details of background, structure, exegesis and polemic context, it is easy to lose sight of what the dialogue was all about. Contemporary discussions of Gnosticism typically come at it from two different angles. The biblical scholars and Church historians use the tools of philology and historical criticism to find the place of Gnosticism within the broader spectrum of ancient religion and church history. From quite a different point of view, philosophers, psychologists, and creative artists look at Gnosticism as a manifestation of rebellious human spirit. The former seek to understand how the later orthodox consensus emerged out of the polymorphous collection of sectarian options that dominate the earliest Christian centuries. The latter see the Gnostic as the human spirit perennially able to manifest its own transcendence and freedom when all the traditional symbols of cosmic and psychic order break down.[1] Both tend to see gnosis as "on the way to" something else: orthodox Christianity, on the one hand; modern consciousness, on the other.

We have already begun to situate the revelation dialogues within the larger context of Christianity. Before we turn to a brief reflection on their connection with the debate over gnosis and modernity, we need a synthetic overview of what these dialogues have to say about the reality of God, world and self. We have seen that even within a single tradition, such as that associated with James, Gnos-

---

[1]See, for example, H. Jonas, "Gnosticism, Existentialism and Nihilism," *The Phenomenon of Life* (New York: Harper and Row, 1966), 211–34.

tics are capable of quite different assessments of the suffering of
Christ and of the martyr. Each of the topics in our survey could well
be expanded into a full-scale monograph on the Gnostic and patristic
evidence. Our purpose is more modest. We wish to survey what the
revelation dialogues have to say about the three major areas of con-
tention that have appeared in our study: the nature of God, of salvation, and of authority. Contrasts with their Gnostic opponents will
help us to outline the peculiarities of the Gnostic argument, but for
the most part we are concerned with the religious vision of these
Gnostic writings. In assessing this vision, we have to weigh two types
of evidence: direct statements of Gnostic doctrine and the probable
intent of Gnostic stories. In addition, one may call on the impact of
the liturgical and formulaic traditions contained in the writings. We
must admit from the outset that the latter are more subject than the
former to the larger hermeneutic of religious phenomena held by a
given interpreter.

TRANSCENDENCE, DUALISM AND REVELATION

The dialogues which begin with a description of the highest, unknowable Father show that the language of negative theology was
stock-in-trade.[2] The introduction to Zostr makes a point that one
also finds in the more analytical Gnostic treatises: the true God has
not been known by other religions or philosophers.[3] Although he is
already an accomplished philosopher-ascetic whose mind is not
trammeled by the material body, Zostr has still not been able to attain knowledge of the highest God, the Existence-which-does-not-
exist.[4] The author insists that no one else, either gods or their messengers, has known what is revealed in gnosis (CG VIII 128, 15–18).

---

[2]For example, ApocryJn CG II 2, 33–4, 20; SJC CG III 94, 5–95, 18. On negative
theology in Gnostic descriptions of the transcendent, see H. A. Wolfson, "Negative
Attributes in the Church Fathers and the Gnostic Basilides," *HTR* 50 (1957), 145–56;
Rudolph, *Gnosis,* 70–72; Daniélou, *Gospel Message,* 324–40. Daniélou sees use of the
term *anousios* and stress on the radical unknowability of God as peculiarly Gnostic
developments.
[3]As in the opening of Eug CG III 70, 3—71, 1.
[4]CG VIII 1, 10—3, 28.

ApocryJn opened by pointing out that the earthly Jesus did not really reveal the Father who sent him or the heavenly pleroma to which he was going (CG II 1, 20–29).[5] SJC's source for its treatment of God and the pleroma, Eug, was also insistent that no other philosophy had known the truth about God-who-is or about the cosmos that is ordered under him.[6] These assertions are not simply apologetic ploys, since they appear at greater length in Gnostic theoretical treatises as well.

To a degree unparalleled by their pagan or Christian counterparts, Gnostic thinkers emphasized the radical transcendence and unknowability of the highest God.[7] Such radical transcendence is founded on a discontinuity between God and the cosmos in which human beings find themselves. No chain of being links this God with the cosmic divinities. Middle Platonists and Christians who followed their lead did agree that knowledge of God is difficult. Plato (Tim 28C) was invoked to support their claim.[8] Not all people would even be capable of such knowledge of God. Both Platonist and Christian would agree against the Gnostic, however, that humanity can attain a natural knowledge of God through the soul which turns inward on itself.[9] Both Jewish and Christian apologists turned language about the transcendence of God to their own purposes. It was said to show the necessity for revelation to counter the errors of paganism and to make knowledge of God available to all.[10] The apologists would even go beyond their Middle Platonic teachers and insist that the mind

---

[5]This passage is probably an allusion to Gnostic interpretation of the Johannine discourses on the departure of Jesus.

[6]This introduction is retained in SJC, though the latter places much less emphasis on the necessity of knowledge of God for salvation. SJC's focus is on the Savior's liberation of humanity from enslaving powers.

[7]Daniélou, *Gospel Message*, 336–338.

[8]Tim 28C is quoted in Justin II *Apol* x, 6; Clement *Protrep* VI 68, 1. Middle Platonists use the same passage; see Proclus *In Tim* 93b; Apuleius *Plat* I 5; Celsus in *c. Cel* vii 42.

[9]Clement of Alexandria, for example, considers knowledge of God's existence a natural concept, *physike ennoia,* infused at creation: *Strom* VII 2, 8, 2; *Protrep* VI 68, 2f.

[10]Knowledge of God was considered difficult prior to the coming of Christ; so Clement, *Protrep* VI 68, 1. See Daniélou, *Gospel Message,* 324–47.

needs divine assistance to see the vision of God.[11] Daniélou detects three different approaches to divine transcendence:

(1) For Jewish apologetic traditions, the transcendence of God means that he is not measured by any created thing. Though he is incomprehensible to the created mind, his existence can be known.

(2) For the Platonist, transcendence means that God is greater than any concept the mind can form on the basis of the sensible world. But if the mind can shake itself free of that world, it can grasp the divine. (Zostr is clearly pictured as such a mystic and as proof that it does not deliver the required knowledge.)

(3) For the Gnostic, both God's essence and his existence are unknown. Only gnosis overcomes the situation.[12] We have already seen that the Gnostics carried this doctrine of radical transcendence into their assessment of the claims of apocalyptic and mystic visionaries. These Gnostics reject the stable vision of God which the philosophic mind claims to attain. Instead, Zostrianos joins the highest powers in giving praise to the unknown God.[13] Schoedel suggests that the language of negative theology in Gnostic writings be interpreted as "numinous language."[14] Gnostics are not interested in making precise philosophical or theological statements about God. Nor are they using the language for apologetic purposes to demand that pagans convert—though they would agree that pagan religions do not attain the truth about God. For the Gnostic, this language is primarily a language of worship, a way of magnifying the being of God.

Rudolph has pointed out that the Gnostics could never have articulated such an extreme doctrine of the transcendence of God if they had not had a tradition of esoteric revelation which made that same divine reality accessible.[15] The structure of the Gnostic cosmos

---

[11]For example, Justin *Dial* iv, 1.

[12]Daniélou, *Gospel Message,* 335f. Some Valentinians interpret the Sophia myth in such a way as to attribute her fall to the attempt to know the unknowable Father. At the same time, they emphasize the constant activity of Christ as Logos or of the divine Pronoia in this cosmos. However, that activity is never such as to make saving knowledge of God possible; see my "Gnosis as Salvation."

[13]See above, pp. 87–90.

[14]Schoedel, "Topological Theology," 91.

[15]Rudolph, *Gnosis,* 72.

would seem to make such contact unbelievable. Not only are we faced with the peculiar Gnostic dualism that sets man and God together in opposition to a cosmos which separates them,[16] but the multiplication of aeons in Gnostic systems has vastly increased our distance from the source of being. The poetic effect of descending through the ranks of aeons as in ApocryJn or SJC or of journeying through heaven after heaven as in Zostr removes the divine as far as possible from the world as we know it. 1 ApocJas takes the Bible to task for having only seven instead of seventy-two lower heavens and none of the innumerable regions belonging to the highest God. This emphasis on transcendence contrasts strongly with the common second-century view of the divine. People assumed that access to divine power was relatively easy. Relationships with gods followed the patterns of those between people.[17] In the third century Christianity would cash in on the distance from the divine created by the combination of monotheism and the philosophic language of transcendence. Divine power would be localized in individuals, church offices, canonical Scripture, and sacraments. The ascetic movement thrived on this new view of divine power. An educated pagan like Plotinus, who was not at all interested in the gods of mythology, would nevertheless protest Gnostic attempts to cut away the divine underside of this cosmos. He accuses them of stripping the world of its beauty and order, the very beauty through which the philosophic soul might begin its contemplative ascent upward to the One.

THE PASSIVITY OF GOD

If this rupture between the transcendent divine and the cosmos might seem strange to pagans, the philosophic passivity of the Gnostic God is quite antithetical to the biblical stories of divine activity. The philosophic requirements of self-sufficiency and impassivity are met by this deity who has no relation to changing, material creation. No Gnostic would accept Justin's dictum that Christians do not offer sacrifices not because they are atheists but because they worship the

---

[16]Jonas, "Delimitation of the Gnostic Phenomenon," *Le origini,* 94.
[17]Brown, *Making,* 9f, 65–69.

Creator (= demiurge) of the universe (= the All).[18] Gnostic stories identify the demiurge of philosphic speculation with the Creator of Genesis, who is arrogant, jealous and hostile to humanity. He is a God who has tried in every way possible to keep us from knowing the true God and Father of the All (= the Gnostic pleroma, rather than the material cosmos as in Justin).

The sheer distance from us and the featureless passivity of the true God contributes to the general mood of pessimism often associated with the Gnostic picture of life in this world. Though this God might be said to form the symbolic opposite of the world in the Gnostic scheme, he is never directly involved in the salvation of Gnostic souls. Prayers and requests are passed up to him through all the levels of the pleroma. His action takes the form of a permission for some lower member of the pleroma to act. The following passage from ApocryJn is typical: "When the Mother wanted to get back the power which she had given to the First Archon, she prayed to the Mother-Father of the All, the very merciful One. He sent five Lights by holy decree down to the place of the chief archon's angels" (CG II 19, 15–21). The distance between them and God might occasionally have felt problematic to Gnostics who were persecuted and were not confident of divine activity on their behalf. NatArc has inserted editorial comments into its account of the origins of humanity and the lower world to assure its readers that, although the hostile powers did not know it, they were doing everything in accord with the will of the Father and under the secret direction of Wisdom.[19]

However great the distance between this world and the divine and however bleak the human situation, Gnostic salvation happens almost by magic. There is no direct conflict between the agents of salvation and the demonic powers such as one finds in creation myths in which the monster of chaos must be defeated before cosmic and social order can be established, or such as one finds in the myths of Jewish and Christian apocalyptic in which the satanic dragon

---

[18]I *Apol* xiii, 1.
[19]NatArc CG II 87, 20–23; 83, 10f; 88, 10f; 88, 33–89, 3; 96, 11–14.

must be defeated before a cosmos patterned upon the eternal divine order of righteousness will come into being.[20] Gnostic revealers are specialists in covert operations. They get into the cosmos disguised as mortals. Revelation and the power of the luminous beings from the light world are automatically victorious over darkness.

NatArc presents a vivid narrative example of a person who asks how this victory works out for a person who might feel abandoned in the cosmos. The issue of the power/powerlessness of the archons dominates the present version of the story. What is the power of gnosis against that of the archons? We are assured that the envy and jealousy of the powers, the intracosmic gods and demons, shows that they are inferior to the Gnostic. The archons in most Gnostic stories—especially the Chief Archon—behave very much as people saw the "great ones" of the world behaving every day. In the Gnostic stories, those who are afflicted by the archons never escape by their own power. They are always plucked from the situation by angelic revealers. In that regard, their rescue is no different from the common stereotype of divine action such as we find in Apuleius' *Golden Ass* or the miraculous rescue of the apostles from prison in Acts. Brown has pointed out that many ancient stories about intervention by the gods belong to this class. So do accounts of private revelations that they give to individuals. They have nothing to do with a despair over reason that causes people to look for divine revelations. Rather such stories show people that an individual with the right combination of aggressive push and luck gains assistance from the divine sources of power just as he might expect to do from earthly ones.[21] And, often enough, as is the case with Lucius, the rewards of such luck ran along the same lines: tangible benefits such as a prosperous life here on earth and immortality after death. The Gnostic is assured of the latter, but his or her God is exalted above all such material concerns just as the One of the philosophers is.

---

[20]For example, see the material collected in A. Y. Collins, *The Combat Myth in the Book of Revelation* (Missoula: Scholars Press, 1976), 57–100.

[21]Brown, *Making*, 63f.

REVELATION AS SALVATION

What is peculiar about the Gnostic divine protector, then, is its resolutely a-cosmic character. Salvation cannot take any form except the revelation of a higher destiny and of a God beyond those conceived in earlier religious and philosophic traditions. The distance which makes it impossible for the Gnostic God to have any relationship with the cosmos demands such a component in salvation. God is not reflected anywhere in the cosmos. At best, the powers have copied an image of the heavenly Man when they created man, and the Creator God has ordered the heavens as a perverse model of the pleroma. The same lack of relationship to anything cosmic also means that the Gnostic God is superior to any other source of divine power. The Gnostic is promised an association bordering on identity with that realm. Thus, he or she may not feel as oppressed by the cosmic distances as is sometimes supposed. The Gnostic's own status is as exalted as that of the deity. The failure has been the intracosmic gods that other people claim as patrons. They act like tyrannical kings and overlords. But the Gnostic is not to worry about them, since he or she does not belong to their world. People in the third century began to identify the true self with a divine that was thought to be as far above the soul as the soul is superior to the body. The usual assumption was that a person's status in the worldly hierarchy reflected that of his personal divine protector. The Gnostic has the "good luck" to discover a divine-in-self that is superior to this hierarchical ordering.

Pagan opponents like Plotinus were quick to recognize that Gnostic claims violated the proper hierarchical structures of cosmic order. When viewed against the general acceptance of the divine ordering of society, the Gnostic stories are quite remarkable. Man's place is clearly exalted above the demiurge and the intracosmic gods. The angels sent by the Father had duped the powers into endowing humanity with the power taken from the Mother. This power makes the soul superior to the lower gods who created the body and its soul, as ApocryJn says:

> Immediately, the rest of the powers became envious, for he had come into being through all of them, and they had giv-

en their power to the man, yet his intelligence was greater than that of those who created him, and greater than the First Archon. When they realized that he was Light and thought better than they and was free from wickedness, they took him and threw him into the lowest part of all matter (CG II 19, 33–20, 9).

Thus, humanity is clearly above the Creator in the Gnostic scale of being.[22]

This relocation is only possible because the intracosmic deities, even the visible divinities in the stars, have been demoted. Artimedorus' work on dream interpretation distinguishes gods seen by the senses from those known only by the intellect. Visions of sensible gods, as well as of heroes and demons, are inauspicious, since they signify fears, dangers and crises.[23] The Gnostics treat the demiurge—philosophically an "invisible god"—as such a demonic, visible one. He and all the powers derived from him are quite different from the invisible aeons of the Gnostic pleroma.[24] Later, Gnostic gems would provide a variety of representations of the part animal, part human shapes of the demons we read about in Gnostic stories.[25] According to these stories the superior part of mankind derives from above, while his body is the attempt made by the archons to capture the image of the heavenly Man in material form.[26] Since there is such a distinction between the true, divine inner self and the material body, the Gnostic would argue that it is impossible to use the latter as an index of humanity's place in the larger hierarchy of being. This concern is

---

[22]Rudolph, *Gnosis,* 100; Jonas, *Gnosis und spatantiker Geist,* I (Göttingen: Vandenhoeck & Ruprecht, 1934), 383.

[23]Artimedorus *Onir* ii, 37. Later he equates dreams about the gods with those about masters (iv, 69). Thus, the translation of the order of intracosmic gods into that of society was commonly accepted.

[24]Since Gnostics have no visual imagery associated with the pleroma, heavenly revelations of the conventional sort have to belong to a lower order.

[25]See the pictures in Rudolph, *Gnosis,* 27 nos. 3–7.

[26]For example the short version of ApocryJn (BG 48, 10–49, 5). The long version (CG II 15, 1–10) modifies the story so that it is closer to Genesis. The Creator tells the archons that man is created "according to the likeness of the heavenly Man and according to our likeness." NatArc (CG II 87, 29–33) emphasizes the twofold nature of man.

another way of negating the common philosophic conviction that the created order reflects the divine.

Since the revelation is the only way to find the unknown Father, and in so doing to recognize one's true identity, many of the traditional modes of contact with divine power are devalued. We have seen that Gnostics were accused of rejecting the traditions of the Fathers. Jonas has observed that of all the religious movements in antiquity, the Gnostics seem to be the least restrained by tradition.[27] To some people, gnosis may even have seemed to be organized *impietas!* Gnostic writings often present their teaching as new, as something that cannot be derived from any earlier tradition. In NatArc, for example, there is no chain of gnosis from primordial times to the present. Norea is told that her seed will not appear for three generations. Then the coming of gnosis will overthrow the cosmic powers. The Gnostic rejection of tradition may have been part of the liberating effect of rejecting cosmic hierarchy as the principle of order. Yet it may also have had a fatal flaw. People demanded the traditional. Christians were careful to forge their own tradition out of their Jewish heritage even while they sought to dissociate themselves from all that pagans felt offensive in Judaism.[28] But any such appeal to tradition would run counter to what the Gnostic had found to be a liberating new insight into the human situation. He had discovered that, in his deepest self, man is tied to a transcendent God who is not at all bound up with this world and its symbols of order. In some writings, like SJC, that proclamation appears in the apocalyptic image of the victory over the powers of the universe. Everything that had been devised to keep humanity from this insight has failed. The Gnostic may exultantly "trample the powers."

It would seem that this spiritual explosion, which SJC associates with Jesus' revelation of the true God and of the Gnostic's place in the pleroma, must have been partially precipitated by Jewish and/or Christian preaching of one God over against the many gods of paganism. Daniélou has shown that the language of divine transcendence in Jewish and Christian circles derives from such apologetic.[29]

---

[27]Jonas, "Delimitation," 100.

[28]J. Pelikan, *The Emergence of the Catholic Tradition* (Chicago: University of Chicago, 1971), 14f.

[29]Daniélou, *Gospel Message*, 324f.

Perhaps Christian preaching precipitated or at least intensified the Gnostic turn against the Jewish God. Christian apologists often explain Christian revelation by saying that the revelation of God in the Old Testament is only partial. Prior to the emergence of a fixed Christian canon, even Christians have to "correct" the Old Testament revelation in light of that of Christ in order to have any true knowledge of God. Gnostic claims about the Old Testament revelation do not sound quite as radical in this pre-canonical situation.

The best the Gnostic can do to overcome the offense of his nontraditional religion is to appeal to the primordial character of the gnosis, which is now manifested in the teaching of the revealer. We have seen that the Gnostic stories of origins contain references to earlier descents of Sophia—or even of Christ himself—in primordial times. Hippolytus accused the Valentinians of depending upon private visions (Ref. VI 42). Irenaeus makes a similar charge against the Marcosians (AdvHaer I 14, 1). These accusations have no foundation in the revelation dialogues, which are generally critical of the demand for such visionary revelations.[30] Unlike Christianity which was developing its martyr and ascetic heroes, Gnostics have no contemporary heroes. Theirs are all figures from the primordial times or from the apostolic generation. There is no evidence that they sought to recreate the visions from the past. The Gnostic enters into that past by retelling its stories. The variety of liturgical fragments embedded in the revelation dialogues, the summaries of the myths and the lists of divine attributes all suggest that the tradition was appropriated by public recital. Just as the highest experience for the seer Zostr was entering into the praises of God, so the Gnostic could join in telling the praises of the unknown Father. Such recital might even border on identification with what is proclaimed. Oral identification of that sort is a typical mode of religious experience in an oral culture. There is no indication the Gnostics pursued a mode of religious awareness that exalted the individual over the group. One's divine identity is found through participation in the group. Gnostic concern for such participatory identity is clearly reflected in its ecclesiology.

---

[30]There is no evidence for the repeated assertions by Pagels that the visionary traditions in the revelation dialogues show that Gnostics held individual vision and creativity to be the final religious authority even against their own tradition; see her "Visions," 427f; *Gnostic Gospels,* 36–51.

There is no differentiation in the Gnostic picture of the Church. What is emphasized over and over again is the heavenly solidarity of the Gnostic race. John receives the revelation for his "fellow spirits," the immovable race (ApocryJn CG II 31, 30f); Norea receives it for her seed, the undominated race (NatArc CG II 97, 4). Gnostics are the immortals in the midst of mortal humanity (SJC CG III 93, 23f; ApocPet CG VII 73, 9–14; 77, 15–19). Their real origin is in a heavenly aeon (SJC CG III 108, 15–18; DialSav III 139, 16–20; Zostr VIII 29, 16–21). There are no differentiations or distinctions possible in these metaphors.

In the context of oral religious experience, revelation does not carry with it the same distance that its association with a fixed written text might imply. It is perceived as a call, an address being made directly to the believer. Such address is always different in each context in which it is spoken. This variability is the real source of the charge that each Gnostic interpreted the Scriptures as he chose (Tertullian, *De Praes* xlii, 1). The development of canonical authority along with the dictates of legal training in dealing with texts led heresiologists like Tertullian to conceive revelation in the text rather than in the oral address. But such a conception has clearly not penetrated Gnostic spirituality and hermeneutics. The call is immediate. Addressed by the revelation, the hearer responded with his or her own proclamation either in the divine praises or in formulaic celebration of his or her new identity with the divine. Orthodox writers can only regard such liturgical praxis as idolatrous. Thus, Hippolytus accuses Valentinus of claiming to be the Logos on the basis of such a liturgical acclamation (Ref VI 42, 2).[31]

---

[31]This is a liturgical rather than a dogmatic proclamation of Gnostic identity with the divine—a point that Pagels consistently misses; see *Gnostic Gospels*, 9, 44. Gnostic insight does not seem to be developed in solitary interior quest as Pagels also suggests in *Gnostic Gospels*, 154–69, where most of the texts she refers to either deal with the cosmogonic foundation of Gnostic truth as in GTr or with liturgical praxis in the oral mode, not in that of the silent visionary mystic like the Middle Platonists. Many of the I AM statements in Gnostic writings derive from liturgical recital, as is the case of the hymn which identifies the saving activity of Christ with the divine Pronoia in ApocryJn (CG II 30, 11—31, 25).

CHAPTER TEN

Salvation and the Image of Christ

Gnostics do not relocate humanity in the universal hierarchy simply out of a desire to protest oppressive structures in a distant, imperial society. Although patristic writers have made much of Gnostic cosmology and speculation about the aeons, our Gnostic sources make it clear that such speculation is secondary to the question of salvation.[1] The heresiologists may even have used the cosmological material to disguise the fundamental claims about soteriology made by their Gnostic opponents. By using that imagery to show that the Gnostics proceed from a different foundation, they avoid the embarrassment of having to admit that the Gnostics claim to offer the true interpretation of exactly the same tradition to which the orthodox appealed.[2] It is particularly important to remember the inchoate state of Christian doctrines of anthropology, Christology and soteriology in the second and early third centuries. It is much less easy to draw distinctions between orthodox and heretical interpretations from within that context than it is for modern Church his-

---

[1]For example, Pelikan, *Emergence*, 89; A. Grillmeier, *Christ in Christian Tradition I*, rev. ed. (Atlanta: John Knox, 1975), 81–83: Gnosticism is primarily a soteriological anthropology.

[2]See the discussion in Koschorke, *Die Polemik*, 207–211. This point is made very forcefully by Pagels, *Gnostic Gospels*, 7f, 27–43, 131–45.

torians who look back with the aid of later clarifications.[3] Pelikan has pointed out that soteriology never was dogmatically defined.[4] We encounter quite different views of soteriology in the Gnostic dialogues. ApocPet castigates the orthodox for thinking that they are saved/purified through clinging to the name of a dead man (CG VII 74, 13–15). On the other hand, ApocryJas insists that no one who does not believe in the cross of Jesus will be saved (CG I 6, 3–6). Though none of the apologists would go so far as to deny the significance of the death of Christ, they, too, are quite diverse in their presentation of salvation. Irenaeus sees Christ's death as a necessary part of his recapitulation of the experience of a disobedient humanity (AdvHaer V 16, 3). But the death of Christ is not central to the soteriology of all authors. Pelikan has pointed to the proper locus of such doctrine when he points out that the saving power of the suffering and death of Christ was more explicitly celebrated in the liturgy than conceptually elaborated in theology.[5] The reference to purification in ApocPet also suggests that the orthodox were affirming their belief in the cross in a liturgical setting.

Daniélou points out that the apologists rarely focus on the incarnation and passion of Jesus. Instead, they are interested in the role of the divine Logos as Creator and sustainer of the world. Thus, their preaching revolves around two poles: the doctrine of God, monotheism, and eschatology. Justin moves directly from belief in the Creator God to the promise of immortality for those who are worthy of reigning and dwelling with him, free from suffering and corruption (I *Apol* xiii, 1). Passages in which he deals with the incarnation and passion of Jesus are much less typical (e.g., I *Apol* xiii, 3).[6] These observations show us that the sequence one true God, creation, eschatology that we find in ApocryJn fits in with the larger context of Christian apologetic preaching. One might even say that

---

[3]This is the weakness of Grillmeier's presentation of the Gnostic position. Even Pelikan's more historical approach occasionally evaluates phenomena of the second and third centuries in terms of the later synthesis. Thus, while appreciating the strengths of the Gnostic position in its time, he comments that the Church would have to reject it: *Emergence*, 97; contrast Pagels, *op. cit.*, 6–12, 19–21.

[4]*Emergence*, 142

[5]*Ibid.*, 146; also Daniélou, *Gospel Message*, 22f.

[6]Daniélou, *op. cit.*, 20–23, 39, 77f.

the only difference between the Gnostic and orthodox apologist is that the former has taken the vehemence which the latter unleashed against paganism and its gods[7] and applied it to the Creator God of the Old Testament, who is now pictured as the father of all such demons. There are a few references to paganism in Nag Hammadi texts. They are included in the account of all previous religions and philosophies in TriTrac as inferior to Judaism (CG I 109, 5–22). However, Gnostics have remarkably little to say about paganism. Its deities seem to be subsumed under the lesser demons. Gnostic attention is focused on the God of the Jews and the orthodox Christians, who, Gnostics argue, is not the true God at all. Though this hostile stance is often traced to the esoteric Judaism from which many of the Gnostic exegetical traditions derived, it might well have originated among Gentile Christians who shared the general pagan dislike for those things in Christianity, which derived from Judaism.[8] As the orthodox came to use Old Testament traditions and symbols to establish Church order—the setting up of "laws" contrary to the will of Jesus that we saw referred to in ApocPet and GMary—the Gnostics retaliated with all the vehemence of their rejection of the Creator God.[9]

If we look at the soteriological metaphors of the period, we find that one of the most pervasive is that of Christ's victory over the demonic powers of death, a victory manifested in the resurrection. Humanity has been enslaved and held captive by the demonic powers (often = pagan gods) until Christ.[10] Thus, the language of victory over the powers that we found in Gnostic writings like SJC fits into the more general context of early Christian soteriological preaching. Daniélou suggests that the preoccupation with this theme in the apologists stems from the struggle with paganism.[11] The Christian

---

[7]*Ibid.*, 31–37. Daniélou comments that denunciation of idolatry as demonic fraud is absolutely primary in the apologists.

[8]Pelikan, *Emergence*, 14.

[9]See the discussion of the use of Jewish symbols to bolster Church hierarchy in Pagels, "The Demiurge and His Archons—A Gnostic View of the Bishop and Presbyters," *HTR* 69 (1976), 301–24. Also see Pelikan, *Emergence*, 25, who points out that the "re-Judaization" of Christianity was concerned with hierarchical and ethical matters, not with theological speculation.

[10]Pelikan, *Emergence*, 149–53; Daniélou, *Gospel Message*, 183–92.

[11]Daniélou, *Gospel Message*, 183.

may also be said to triumph over the powers through the victory that Christ works in him or her. Orthodox Christians saw this victory represented in the martyrs.[12] We have seen that Gnostics locate the Christian's share in the victory in the preaching of Gnosis as the Savior had done (e.g., SJC CG III 119, 1-9; PetPhil VIII 137, 20-25). ApocPet also associates the victory with the Docetic account of the crucifixion. The powers are crucifying what they think is the Savior, while the living Jesus is standing aside and laughing at them (CG VII 81, 15-24). Patristic authors could never go this far and deny that Christ died, but they do agree that those who crucified him were deceived in thinking that they had gained power over him. Origen even speaks of Christ laughing with scorn at the ignorance of those who accepted the Son handed over to them (*Comm Matt* xiii, 9). Thus, Gnostic preaching shares broad lines of thought with other Christian preaching. These similarities show how a Gnostic soteriology might find a sympathetic audience in larger Christian circles.

THE EXALTATION OF HUMANITY AND GNOSTIC ANTHROPOLOGY

We have seen that the real debate between the Gnostics and the Christians centered around the Creator God. Christians worship the Creator; Gnostics insist that he is not the true God but the chief archon—though he is the only one with any connection to the world of divine reality. The peculiarity of Gnostic anthropology was to exalt humanity over the Creator of the cosmos, over the God who had created it. This superiority was not simply a feature of the heavenly Man in whose image humanity was created. It was applied to Adam, to humanity as creature, as we saw in ApocryJn.[13] The Gnostics do not possess a philosophically differentiated doctrine of the self, which they might use to distinguish the various aspects of inner reality. Spirit, inner self, spark, seed, and even soul may appear as designations for that part of the divine world whose inner presence exalts

---

[12]Origen, *Comm Matt* XII 25; *Exhort ad Martyr.* XL 1.

[13]Rudolph, *Gnosis*, 100f; Jonas, *Gnosis* I, 383, sees the basic question of all Gnostic systems as the metaphysical status of humanity in the order of being.

a person over the Creator.[14] Both Christians and Gnostics centered much of their soteriological reflection around the role of the divine Spirit. Interpretation of Genesis 1:27 and 2:7 plays an important role in this reflection. Alexandrian theologians were concerned with the relationship between God's having made man in his image and his having breathed living spirit into him. To what extent could God be said to have breathed in his own divine spirit? Is the image referred to man's body or his soul?[15] The Christian exegete was confronted with the problem of relating this first "inspiration" to the redemptive activity of the Holy Spirit. Irenaeus, in his concern to counter Gnostic rejection of material creation, identified the image of God with the body. This image, he claimed, is inseparable from the soul breathed into the body. The real likeness to God, however, only comes when the Spirit given by Christ enables humanity to reach the incorruption, which the earlier formation by God had made it capable of. Further, he goes on to argue against the Gnostics, incorruption extends to the body, which is transformed by the Spirit.[16] Clement of Alexandria takes the more common view that the rational faculty of man represents his link to the divine Logos and thus the image of God that is referred to in Genesis (*Strom* VI 14–16). He uses Pauline texts to conclude that this rational soul is opposed by a bodily spirit which is responsible for leading men astray. Thus, the Holy Spirit is necessary if one is to achieve perfection, since it can rule the rational faculty and bestow knowledge of God. Clement is careful to explain that the Spirit acts on the soul through its power. It does not bestow some new substance on humanity.[17]

A common charge against the Gnostics is that they claimed that there were substantially different types of soul, and that only the spiritual type would be saved. This substantialist interpretation seems to be common among the heresiologists. We have seen that

---

[14]Rudolph, *Gnosis*, 97f; Perkins, "Gnosis as Salvation"; Daniélou, *Gospel Message*, 411.

[15]See the summary in Hauschild, *Gottes Geist*, 256–63.

[16]AdvHaer V 6, 1; III 22, 1; V 12, 2; see the discussion of Irenaeus' teaching in Daniélou, *Gospel Message*, 398–404.

[17]See Pelikan, *Emergence*, 47; Hauschild, *Gottes Geist*, 17–44; Daniélou, *Gospel Message*, 411–413.

Clement accused them of a doctrine of predestination that would even render gnosis unnecessary.[18] Recently, interpreters have begun to question this assessment of the Gnostic evidence. The doctrine of types of soul can appear as a designation for different types of people or as a description of the varied inner realities of the same human person in a single Gnostic treatise.[19] Like Clement, Gnostics know a doctrine of two spirits at work within the individual. ApocryJn describes the war a Gnostic must wage against the *antimimnon*, "imitation," spirit in order to be liberated from the body and from the powers of this world.[20] Theodotus speaks of a material soul at war with the psychic one.[21] Both the material and the psychic soul derive from the creative activity of the demiurge. The spiritual seed of the heavenly Sophia, on the other hand, comes from outside.

The problem of determinism in Gnostic anthropology arises when Gnostic thinkers try to give an account of why people fail to respond to their preaching. The passage on the various types of soul in ApocryJn distinguishes between people who accept gnosis and the spirit of life immediately and those who do not. The souls of the former become stronger than the antimimnon spirit. These souls dwell on the immortality that they are to receive. Souls which do not turn to gnosis right away have a longer struggle. They must go through further incarnations in order to be saved. Those who accept gnosis and later reject it cannot be saved at all. The division of souls is not tied to the anthropogony of the Genesis section. ApocryJn's description of the pleroma does include two places for humanity. The Gnostics, the seed of Seth, go to the third of the four great lights. Those

---

[18]In connection with the "house of demons" parable, see above, pp. 153–154.

[19]See the discussion of the so-called Valentinian theology of "natures" by E. Pagels, *Johannine Gospel*, 93–113. General descriptions of Valentinian theology may be found in Daniélou, *Gospel Message*, 396–98; Hauschild, *Gottes Geist*, 151–82; Rudolph, *Gnosis*, 99. OrigWld has three classes of men as different images of Adam (CG II 170, 6–9) and as belonging to one and the same person (165, 28–35). The threefold Valentinian distinction, material, psychic and spiritual, appears in the context of wisdom preaching as an indication of types of people in Silv (CG VII 90, 10—94, 32). See the discussion by Schoedel, "Formation," 169–99.

[20]ApocryJn CG II 26, 8—27, 21. Hauschild, *Gottes Geist*, 238–47, details the parallels between ApocryJn and the two spirits traditions in Judaism. The antimimnon spirit may have originated in esoteric Enoch traditions about the origins of post-flood sin.

[21]ExcTheod 50, 1–2.

who only come to gnosis later or who are deficient in it go to the fourth (CG II 9, 14–24). SJC has a similar two-part destiny for those the apostles are to convert (BG 118, 8–24; CG III 118, 1f). SJC does not give any indication that the souls need the assistance of the Spirit beyond mentioning signs that they are to bring the Savior. ApocryJn is more explicit. Souls require assistance from the Spirit of Life—the same Spirit that awakened and assisted Adam. Thus, the Spirit which makes created man superior to his Creator is not sufficient on its own to bring him to his destiny and to free him from the imprisonments of hostile archons.[22]

Hard and fast distinctions between types of soul according to substance, *kat'ousian*, emerge in those situations in which the Gnostic community finds itself under pressure from the larger group. These distinctions function as an explanation for the rejection faced by the Gnostic. We see this development clearly in ApocPet. The Gnostics have immortal souls; other Christians have merely mortal ones. As a result, other Christians envy the Gnostics whose destiny they can never share.[23] Such intensified dualism does not represent Gnostic anthropology generally. The elevation of humanity above the Creator and the cosmos assures its transcosmic destiny. Metaphors of the true human soul as part of the light lost by the Mother would seem to require that all are eventually to reach that destiny. But, when severe conflict between Gnostics and non-Gnostics makes it apparent that not all of humanity will accept this teaching, then other explanations are forged. For example, ThCont never explicitly describes types of souls. However, its paraenesis implies that the non-ascetics only have bestial souls and are destined for dissolution like all the rest of material creation (CG II 139, 24—140, 37). Conflict, apologetic, and paraenesis generate the dualistic expressions in Gnostic writing. They do not derive from a systematic reflection on Gnostic anthropology. In general, Gnostics seem to have shared with Christians at large the conviction that, however it becomes available,

---

[22] Also Hauschild, *op. cit.*, 231–35.

[23] CG VII 75, 26—76, 22; 76, 35—77, 16. Tensions between communities are typically expressed in myths in which the members of the foreign community are given less than human status; see E. Voeglin, *Anamnesis* (Notre Dame: Notre Dame, 1978), 24.

some assistance from the divine Spirit is required for salvation.[24] In many respects, then, Gnostics come very close to the soteriological language of their orthodox counterparts.

THE GNOSTIC AND THE SAVIOR

ApocryJn used the two spirits tradition to explain how humanity had been held in bondage until the coming of the Savior. The primary mission of the Savior is to issue the call that awakens humanity to awareness of its bondage and its true identity. The revelation is the focus of Gnostic preaching. But the Savior must also break up the order of the lower cosmos to make salvation possible. PS said that he had rearranged the fates. ApocryJn associates him with the required divine assistance:

> I am the Pronoia of the pure light.
> I am the Thought of the virgin Spirit,
> the one who raises you to the honored place.
> Arise and remember that you are the one who has heard,
> and rest with your root, which is I, the merciful.
> Guard youself against the angels of poverty, and the demons of chaos, and all who grasp you, and you will awaken from the heavy sleep and from captivity in the inside of Amente.
> I raised him up and sealed him with the light of the water with five seals so that death would not have power over him from that time on (CG II 31, 11–25).

Similarly Zostrianos receives various purifications and anointings on his journey through the heavens. When he returns to preach gnosis he warns against empty baptism, calls his audience to strengthen their souls (apparently a reference to ascetic victory over the passions), and promises aid from the Father: "The gentle Father has sent you the Savior and given you strength" (CG VIII 131, 14–16).

---

[24]Thus it is a mistake to suppose that Gnosticism declined from the liberating effect of gnosis of one's origin and destiny into a sacramental cult as M. Krause does, "Die Sakramente in der Exegese uber die Seele," *Les Textes de Nag Hammadi*, 47.

Other examples have the Savior open a way through the heavens and reveal the formula necessary for the soul to ascend. But, lest one assume that that formula is some kind of post mortem magic, 1 ApocJas has the final prayer in the ascent uttered not by the Gnostic but by the Savior himself (CG V 35, 18–25). This assistance is necessary because the Gnostic does not have the same perfection as the Savior. The Savior has been able to come into this world and not be defiled by its powers and by matter. James recites a hymn in celebration of this purity (V 28, 7–20). He then points out that the Gnostic does not have such purity. He has been in bondage to the powers and has been clothed in what belongs to them. Thus, even though 1 ApocJas contains one of the strongest statements of identity between God and the Gnostic of any dialogue, salvation is still impossible without the activity of the Savior. Jesus tells James that when he is able to cast off the bondage of the flesh, he will no longer be James, but will reach Him-who-is (27, 1–12). This identity is true knowledge of God. It is an even more exalted destiny than the places in the pleroma allotted Gnostic souls in ApocryJn or SJC. It goes further than Zostrianos, who reaches the highest triad but not the unknown Father himself. But however they conceptualize the final destiny of Gnostics, all of these writings stress the reality of bondage in the lower world. Zostrianos tries the mystic route of philosopher-ascetic but cannot find God. ApocryJn treats the Genesis story as a series of countermoves to divine aid which progressively sink humanity further and further into the bondage of matter. Finally, the prison even goes beyond the material body. The antimimnon spirit shuts off true knowledge of God in humanity's innermost being. After his praise of the undefiled Savior, James delivers an equally moving account of humanity's own defilement and imprisonment. It will require aid even on the final ascent.

The distinction between the Gnostic and the undefiled Savior that is introduced in 1 ApocJas presents a problem that will come to preoccupy theologians in later centuries. What is the relationship between Jesus and the humanity he came to save? Both Gnostic and orthodox Christians begin with the presupposition of the sinlessness of Jesus. However, when sin is associated with defilement by bodily and psychic (the passions) reality, then the Savior cannot be caught in the same trap as humanity. So Gnostics minimalize the connection between the Savior and the body required for his presence in this world. Some even go so far as to argue that he never took the final step of assuming a mortal body at all. He merely used the psychic one. He does not have to assume the former, since he has not descended to save what is material (cf. AdvHaer I 6, 1). Though people today are uncomforatble with the picture of an impassible Savior that resulted from this division,[25] it corresponds to a widespread ascetic ideal in Gnostic, Christian and philosophical circles. The perfected soul reflects the *apatheia* of god.

We have seen that ApocPet seeks to differentiate Gnostic souls from those of non-Gnostics ontologically. It explains the crucifixion in terms of the tripartite nature of the Savior. The fleshy part is crucified. The "living Jesus," the psychic body of other accounts, leaves and stands by laughing. The innermost reality of the Savior is the noetic spirit which is identified with the Holy Spirit and with the pleromatic light. 1 ApocJas used a simpler two-part distinction to divorce the Savior from suffering. There is the body and the true Savior, the image of God, that dwelt within that body. The latter was untouched by the events of the crucifixion. ApocPet apparently applies the distinction between the three parts of the Savior to souls much as 1 ApocJas applies the body/inner reality division to the suffering of the martyr. After describing the envy of non-Gnostics, ApocPet comments: ". . . if the immortal soul receives power in an intellectual spirit" (CG VII 77, 16–22). Earlier, the Gnostics are referred to as "men of like essence" (71, 14f) to the exalted Son of Man. Finally, Peter is instructed that the revelation is to be given only to those who are "from an immortal substance" (83, 24). TriTrac knows a related tradition. After giving the Valentinian tripartite division of humanity, the author refers to those who not only plotted against the Lord but are envious of the Church. This is the same combination that we find in ApocPet. Those who plot against Jesus are correlated with orthodox officials who are trying to wipe out Petrine gnosis. TriTrac goes on to warn that those who persevere in their hostility will be condemned. Psychic Christians can repent, receive instruction, and finally be included in the Gnostic pleroma—though at a less exalted

---

[25]Pelikan, *Emergence*, 89–92.

level. The elect, on the other hand, share "body and essence" with the Savior (CG I 122, 1–123, 24). Thus, it seems that such claims of identity in essence between the Savior and the elect emerge in contexts in which the Gnostics find themselves pressed to defend their own particularity over against orthodox Christianity. Otherwise, the Gnostic does not have to consider the reality of the Savior identical with his own. In fact, the Gnostic account of human bondage tends in the opposite direction. The Savior cannot be caught in the situation from which he must provide liberation.

We have seen that second-century theologians did not articulate a consistent account of the relationship between the death of Christ and salvation. Therefore, the explanation offered by Gnostic authors might well have been felt sufficient even by some Christians. The usual Gnostic explanation of the crucifixion is to see it as a "type" of the cosmic situation of humanity. Either it reveals the "passion" of the fallen Sophia, which stands at the origin of the cosmos (AdvHaer I 8, 2), or it reflects the consequences for humanity, its entrapment in "smallness," the body (PetPhil CG VIII 135, 8—136, 15; 138, 19f).[26] In short, it demonstrates the reason for Gnostic redemption but is not itself a factor in that redemption. There was no other way for the Savior to make contact with his own without knowledge of the cosmic powers than by taking on a body. In the martyrdom stories of James and in the Acts-type material of GMary and PetPhil, Jesus' suffering also stands as a warning to Gnostic preachers of what they can expect.

ASCETIC CONSEQUENCES

The correlate of the distinction between the Savior and the material body for most Gnostics is the ascetic call to renounce the body and its desires. Such renunciation is embodied in the ascent formula that we find in GMary. The martyr is told that he must become a "stranger to the flesh" like Jesus (1 ApocJas CG V 25, 2–6; 32, 16–22).[27] We have seen that it formed part of the call to gnosis in

---

[26]Cf. Koschorke, *Die Polemik*, 194f.
[27]*Ibid.*, 196.

ApocryJn and Zostr. SJC includes it in the commission that Jesus gives to the disciples:

> You were sent by the Son, who was sent that you might receive light and remove yourselves from the forgetfulness of the powers, so that the unclean rubbing that is from the dreadful fire, which came on their fleshy part, might not appear again because of you. Trample on their providence (CG III 108, 5–16).

ApocryJn describes the souls of the Gnostics looking forward to their ascent into the pleroma as:

> Those on whom the Spirit of Life comes and dwells with power will be saved. They will become perfect and worthy of great things. They will purify themselves in that place from all wickedness and concern with evil. They will not be concerned with anything except incorruption alone, since they will care about the place without wrath or envy or jealousy or desire and greed for everything. They are not seized by anything except the substance (*hypostasis*) of the flesh itself; this they bear while looking forward to the time when they will be visited by the receivers. These are the ones who show that they are worthy of incorruptible eternal life and the calling. They bear everything; they endure everything that they may complete the good (fight?) and inherit eternal life (CG II 25, 23–26, 7).

A similar benign but necessary ascesis seems to be implied in Dial-Sav. The Gnostics are told that they will rule the archons and that they will be able to put on light and enter the pleroma when they remove envy (CG III 138, 15–20). When Mary asks to know all the things that exist, she is told to oppose enjoyment of the world and its wealth instead (cp. the opposition to wealth in AcPet12). One must seek life. Perfection and victory belong to the person who has understood the saying about the struggle with his eyes. This exchange reflects the general stance of DialSav in which all the esoteric wisdom in the world is valueless without gnosis—here the true interpretation of the discipleship sayings of Jesus. Hippolytus also quotes a Gnostic teacher who opposes the Gnostic turn within oneself to the quest for cosmological knowledge (Ref VIII 15, 1–2).

ThCont is our chief example of the rejection of cosmological wisdom for an ascetic conquest of desire and of the flesh. Self-knowledge is knowledge of the "depths of the All" (CG II 138, 17f). We have already seen that ThCont warns against any concessions to the body and its desires. The ascetics are promised: "When you come forth from the sufferings and passions of the body, you will receive rest from the Good One and will reign with the King, joined with him and he with you, from now on, forever and ever. Amen" (CG II 145, 12–16). Zostr was also concerned with asceticism. The seer had already straightened out his intellectual soul through the power of the Holy Spirit, and he had separated himself from bodily darkness, desire, and the psychic chaos of the perceptible world (CG VIII 1, 10–18). But non-Gnostic ascetics could make the same claim, so the author has set out to show that even at such heights knowledge of the true God cannot be attained except through the special revelation and purification of gnosis.

For the Gnostic, complete realization of his or her salvation only comes when he or she is released from this cosmos and returns to the place in the pleroma from which the Gnostic race originated or to unity with the divine. However certain a Gnostic may be of immortality, this present life does not represent a time of indifference to bodily reality, or, more precisely, of indifference to the passions, which are its psychic correlate. The Gnostic must strive to realize the same separation in this life that he hopes to attain when he is finally freed from the bondage of cosmic reality. One can hardly accuse the Gnostic of underestimating the difficulty of this task. The creation of man in ApocryJn, for example, involved the layering on of chain after chain in the material and psychic world. One might even suggest that the Gnostic would have to have great confidence in the ultimate source of his liberation and in the superiority of his destiny to even attempt to untangle the webs of desire, envy and jealousy that surround the human person. Or, as Pelikan has suggested, the Gnostic story of the descent of the spirit preserves a more authentic account of human alienation than much of the moralistic preaching by which the Gnostics' orthodox counterparts sought to render people free from suffering and worthy to "reign with the King."[28]

---

[28]Pelikan, *op. cit.*, 97.

CHAPTER ELEVEN
Canon, Community and Authority

The pluralism of second-century Christianity shows that Gnostic expressions of salvation are closer to those of orthodox Christians than they now—with the hindsight of later Christological controversies—appear to be. A shift in the overall religious life of the empire began in the third century. Religious boundaries were consolidated. Access to the divine was more limited so that people appear who claim to mediate access to divine reality. Christian martyrs and ascetics are often the focus of such claims.[1] Pagans were more cautious than Christians about such individuals, but the image of the philosopher-saint takes on great importance in neo-Platonic circles. We have seen that Zostr cast his hero in that mold.[2] By the middle of the third century, Christian communities have become settled entities in the cities and towns. For many members, Christianity is now their traditional religion. Christian groups begin to crystalize divine power in the hierarchical structures of a community in which both intrapersonal relationships and relationship to the divine were simplified in comparison with those in the surrounding society. The Christian knew that he or she had a personal identity as one freed from demonic and astrological powers. He or she also had a clear definition of who counted as "neighbor" and what duties were owed to that neighbor. This definition broke with the complex family and patronage relationships of the larger society. Studies of tombs in Phrygia, for example, show that very few pagan tombs include non-family. On

---

[1]Brown, *Making*, 56–59, 91–95.
[2]*Ibid.*, 59–62.

191

the other hand, many Christian tombs include such people. Christianity, in effect, allowed people to "create an identity" through their choice of neighbors;[3] they were not "stuck with" the traditional web of relationships. The condition for these Christian certainties was an unalloyed allegiance to the leaders and symbols of the Christian community.

Though their picture of the transcendence of God certainly cut off access to divine power through intracosmic deities such as was common in paganism, Gnostics continue the more general second-century view that the divine is available to all—at least all Gnostics. This conviction intensified their resistance to all forms of mediation as they were becoming dominant in Christian circles: Sacred Scripture, salvation through sacraments—though many Gnostics followed sacramental practices, and veneration of martyrs, which Gnostics explicitly reject, as well as the increasing hierarchical organization of Christian community.[4]

Even though Gnostic and Christian ascetics seem to differ very little in language and practice, Gnostics never set up individuals as heroes of the divine. Certainly the Gnostic could agree with his third-century Christian counterpart that the move to the desert symbolized rejection of all the strains, tensions and obligations of the small face-to-face world in which people lived.[5] The Gnostic had before him an image of the chief archon and his underlings as motivated by all the sins that beset such associations: boasting, envy, jealousy, anger, irrational violence, and constant concern over who might outdo or become superior to oneself. We have seen that ApocryJn characterizes the true Gnostic soul as one which concentrates on its immortality and is not bogged down in such passions and conflict. The Syrian ascetic of the Thomas tradition escaped such passions and pressures by withdrawing, by becoming a "solitary one." No one who did not wipe out the passion of lust which drives men

---

[3]*Ibid.*, 73–78. See the discussion of the development of an idea of "inspired" office out of that of charismatic teacher in Von Campenhausen, *Ecclesiastical Authority*, 193–212.

[4]This rejection underlies most Gnostic criticism of Church leaders: see Pagels, "Visions," 429. Though she misses the larger social context of the shift, she also has an informative account of the ecclesiastical debate, *Gnostic Gospels*, 53–72, 117–45.

[5]Brown, *Making*, 83–95.

into family and social relationships could expect salvation. Those same family and social relationships could, of course, also embroil one in religious observances that represented submission to the ignorant Creator and his minions. We have seen that ApocPet has to promise the Gnostics forgiveness for things they have been forced to do as a result of their subjection to the orthodox.

The Gnostics responsible for the preservation of the Nag Hammadi codices may have escaped pressures against them by withdrawing into the monastic movement in the desert. One of the writings they preserved, Silv, contains a section of a sermon by St. Anthony.[6] It is a wisdom passage warning against the deceits of friendship and counseling that it is better to walk with God alone. The passage represents an admirable statement of the ethos of withdrawal shared by all the desert solitaries. However, the Gnostics among them would hardly escape the fourth- and fifth-century moves to domesticate the monastic movement: the introduction of monastic rules and the creation of an ordained clergy subject to the local bishop. The free asceticism of earlier days became subject to some semblance of ecclesiastical order.

GNOSTICS AND ECCLESIASTICAL AUTHORITY

Gnostics also focused their mythological condemnation of the tensions and aggressions of imperial society on the ecclesiastical hierarchy that began to develop in the second and third centuries. Pagels has given extensive examples of how the Valentinians use the demiurge and his archons as ciphers for the orthodox bishops.[7] We would suggest that the Gnostic stories about the demiurge had already sensitized Gnostics to the negative facets of social life and hence contributed to their refusal to accept such patterns when they began to emerge in Christian communities. The Gnostic stories of the Creator and his archons antedate the real consolidation of hierarchical power in othodox circles and hence cannot be attributed to that conflict.

---

[6] Silv CG VII 97, 3–98, 24 = Apa Antonios mss. 979a fa+b; cf. appendices to the Rule of St. Anthony, *PG* 40: 1077, 1–20.

[7] Pagels, "Demiurge," 301–24.

We have seen two lines of resistance to developing ecclesial structures in the Gnostic dialogue. First, there is rejection of the use of "Law" to formalize Christian community life. Christians had shifted to using the Old Testament as a source of ethical norms and ecclesiastical models. Gnostic rejection of the Old Testament would make them allergic to much of what Pelikan has called the "re-Judaization" of Christianity. ApocPet and GMary show that apostolic authority was being invoked to bolster this trend. Gnostics reject such developments as counter to the express command of Jesus.[8]

ApocPet is the only dialogue which attacks the hierarchical structure of the Church directly. The polemic section is set up to suggest that there are many different groups opposing the Gnostics. But the motif of a multi-faced divided opposition is a standard rhetorical topos. The unity of one's own group is always opposed to the controversy and divided opinion of the opposition. ApocPet makes it clear that Gnostics are presently subject to the authorities of the larger Church. They are subject to disciplinary action by these authorities. ApocPet says of the bishops and deacons, "There will be others of those outside our number who call themselves bishop and deacons as if they derived their authority from God" (CG VII 79, 23–29). The ecclesiastical office has been endowed with divine authority. This development goes beyond the more modest claims that episcopal office is the guardian of apostolic tradition set forth in the preaching and life of the bishop promoted by Irenaeus.[9] If ApocPet reflects a consensus about Church office in the orthodox community, then it must derive from the consolidation of the Church in the third century. This hypothesis gains further support from the remark "not of our number." It seems to imply a distinction between these officials and other Christians, which is uncharacteristic of the second-century Church but quite typical of the third.[10]

Historians have had more difficulty clarifying the development

---

[8]Pelikan, *Emergence*, 97, remarks that the Gnostic impulse is in some ways closer to the earliest tradition of the common orthodox picture of Christ as law-giver.

[9]See Von Campenhausen, *Ecclesiastical Authority*, 173; Pagels, *Gnostic Dialogues*, 52–72, has a tendency to oversimplify the account so that it appears as if the third-century structures were implied by second-century authors.

[10]Von Campenhausen, *Ecclesiastical Authority*, 175–77, 265–81.

of penitential discipline than that of Church office.[11] For that reason, it is difficult to date the combination of references to Hermes, disciplinary action against the Gnostics, and judgments rendered by authorities, who claim the "power of the keys," that we find in ApocPet (CG VII 78, 1–30). This combination is missing in second-century authors but appears full-blown in Tertullian. ApocPet is the only dialogue which seems to be taking issue with the established hierarchical structures of the third century. It suggests that these developments in orthodox Church life were proving an effective weapon against such deviant Christians, though they had not yet been forced out of the larger community. Unfortunately, we are not told what the issues are on which the Gnostics had been forced to submit to orthodox authority and for which the Lord would later forgive his "little ones"—that is, negate the so-called power of the keys.

PetPhil represents the more open situation of the second century. We have seen that Irenaeus and others had reacted to the issue of the true interpretation of Christian tradition by appealing to the universal testmony of the apostles as a group.[12] PetPhil also claims to present their unified testimony. A similar position seems to be implied by the other dialogues in which the revelation is to the whole group of disciples. The initial discussion of apostolic unity in PetPhil is the most explicit of the group in its acknowledgment that apostolic tradition has to have been revealed to all the apostles together and not to individuals in secret, just as Irenaeus himself insists (e.g., Adv-Haer I 27, 2; III 14, 2). Some of the individual revelations are also tied to this requirement. Both John and Mary convey their revelation to the whole group of the apostles, though in GMary that revelation is accepted with reluctance by Peter. At the same time, the introduction indicates that Jesus had also instructed the whole group in gnosis so that the reluctance of the apostle cannot be interpreted as defense of Jesus' teaching against new innovative doctrines. Thus, at least half of the dialogues appeal to a common apostolic tradition. Therefore, one must conclude that the Gnostic position on apostolic

---

[11] *Ibid.*, 215–37.

[12] See the discussion of Irenaeus and apostolic tradition in Von Campenhausen, *Ecclesiastical Authority*, 149, 170; Daniélou, *Gospel Message*, 141–46.

tradition is much closer to the general second-century view than is sometimes admitted. The Thomas and James traditions are the only ones in which we find a claim to transmission from a single disciple past the others to the Gnostic. The latter view of Gnostic tradition is the one condemned by Irenaeus and adopted as historical by Von Campenhausen. He then goes on to argue that it was responsible for the introduction of verified chains of succession into Christian ecclesial rhetoric.[13] The Gnostic dialogues should cause us to reassess this interpretation. Even the Thomas tradition was not set on the "secret succession" concept. Within the same tradition we have transmission to a single disciple, Thomas, recorded by another, Matthias, and transmission to the whole group of disciples as in DialSav. As in the case of the combination of revelations in GMary, the latter concept may still be the ruling one: gnosis is Jesus' teaching to all the apostles and is their true legacy to the Church. Strict adherence to a secret line of transmission only emerges in the James material. There it clearly is in response to orthodox polemic, perhaps even that of Irenaeus himself. Both ApocryJas and ApocPet acknowledge another charge made against gnosis: that it appeared later than apostolic times. This charge also appears in Irenaeus (AdvHaer V 20, 1). It seems likely, then, that Gnostics picked up the language of an authenticated succession of teachers in situations in which the orthodox attack against their claim to represent true apostolic tradition had begun to make some headway. The opponents of gnosis also used a similar tactic in reverse. They created a negative genealogy of Gnostic sects, tracing them back to the rival of the apostles, Simon Magus.[14]

Toward an Authoritative Text

We are so used to appealing to the text of Scripture as Irenaeus does that we find it difficult to attach credibility to Gnostic claims of apostolic succession. In order to appreciate second-century claims, it

---

[13]Von Campenhausen, *Ecclesiastical Authority*, 158–62.
[14]See the discussion of Irenaeus and his sources in my "Irenaeus and the Gnostics," 197–200.

is necessary to recognize that the Christian community's relationship to its own past was still largely oral. The Old Testament was the only authoritative text for Christians in this period.[15] New Testament writings were perceived as witnesses to the tradition embodied in the community at large. This feeling is typical of oral societies. The common memory is the guarantor of all knowledge. Though Christians lived in a world which mixed oral and written media, the authority of common memory and testimony remains strong. Even Irenaeus, who has a strong feeling for New Testament writings as text, shares this predilection. He assures his readers that even if the Gospels had not been written, the authority of apostolic tradition in the community would have preserved true teaching (AdvHaer III 4, 1–2). One must also remember that what is felt to be in continuity with one's past has much more fluidity in such a situation than is the case today when a variety of "documentary" media fix the past in its particularity almost as soon as it happens. The basic story remains in the oral setting, but traditions are constantly modified in the particular situation of recital without the auditors perceiving that modification as departure from what has always been the case. A written tradition, on the other hand, creates a distance between the situation of the reader and that of the "text" which is the foundation of having a past.

One must be mindful of the oral context of tradition when one is evaluating patristic charges that Gnostics all interpret the common tradition to suit their own whims. That objection is particularly frequent in authors like Irenaeus and Tertullian who have a sense for present reality and the Christian "past" as embodied in the text of canonical Scripture. We have seen that Irenaeus made careful appeals to the text of Acts as evidence for apostolic preaching. But for many Christians, Gnostic and orthodox, in the second century such consciousness was quite foreign. PetPhil is an excellent example of an oral representation of the tradition. The story of the apostles is normative but not binding as a fixed text. It can be retold in such a way as to emphasize what the author and his community know to be the truth of the tradition without anyone feeling that "the past" was

---

[15]Von Campenhausen, *Formation*, 103–121.

somehow distorted. However, the shift toward textual fixation of the tradition is not even complete in Irenaeus. His basic response to the Gnostics still fits the pattern of authority in an oral tradition. What he does is to limit the community which can be evoked as witness to the tradition. He begins with the first community, the apostles,[16] and then moves to the "community" of bishops of major churches as the true successor to that apostolic community (AdvHaer III 3, 1–3; IV 33, 8). For many Christians the words of Jesus considered authoritative were not those written in Gospels but those handed on in the living memory of particular communities. Irenaeus insists that the apostolic tradition is the same everywhere, but the dynamics of such a religious tradition should warn one against interpreting that to mean verbal identity between the normative traditions of the various communities. Without the controlling presence of a canonical written text, such identities are not even an issue. What is transmitted is saying or story with interpretation. We have seen that some Gnostic dialogues testify to the important role such interpreted sayings of Jesus played in their communities. A similar statement might be made about orthodox communities. Papias, for example, does not consider the canonical record of the sayings of Jesus to be the final and fixed form of the Jesus tradition.[17]

The difference between a canonical Scripture and the embodiment of tradition in a community becomes even clearer when one considers the different exegetical methods applied to the Old Testament and the New Testament respectively. The former is subject to rigorous criticism and interpretation. Most of the Christian hermeneutical reflection in this period did not even deal with the New Testament. The text which had to be brought out of the past into line with present reality was the Old Testament—whether one defended its truth as the orthodox did or rejected it as Marcion and many Gnostics did. With the notable exception of Marcion, the New Testament was not subject to the same kind of analysis and critique.[18]

---

[16]In such an oral context, the apostles are the first ones who can count as witnesses. It makes no sense to contrast a tradition beginning with the apostles and one beginning with Jesus as modern historians tend to do; so Von Campenhausen, *Formation*, 169ff; Daniélou, *Gospel Message*, 146.

[17]H. E. III 39, 4–17; Von Campenhausen, *Formation*, 130.

[18]*Ibid.*, 136–42.

However different their readings of different passages may be, Gnostic and orthodox Christians are similar in this regard. Marcion, on the other hand, tried to apply a theological critique based on his interpretation of Paul to the New Testament writings to create an authoritative canon. But before him, and even for some time after, most Christians still belonged to the age of "primitive Christianity."[19] Their religion was shaped by an authoritative oral tradition, not by an authoritative text.

Though the situation with regard to the New Testament canon remained fluid throughout the third century, pressures for a normative textual embodiment of the tradition were moving Christians toward adopting a canon.[20] Irenaeus seems to have been the first to realize the potential of such a canon as a way of embodying and stabilizing the tradition. Gnostic exegesis had made him aware that one could not win an argument over the true interpretation of the tradition by debating various interpretations of the dominical sayings. After all, the Gnostics considered the same sayings and Pauline letters to be authoritative, as did orthodox Christians.[21] Irenaeus responds to Gnostic claims that the apostolic tradition itself is Gnostic by inventing a counter-genealogy for Gnosticism and by treating the Gospels and Acts as an authoritative historical record of the actions and preaching of the apostles. He also insists that the narrative setting of canonical sayings, parables and stories be taken into account when they are interpreted. Thus he might well be considered the first biblical theologian, that is, the first person for whom the New Testament as text is a normative source for the teaching and tradition of the community. His textual orientation is immediately apparent in his account of the arguments from Scripture—for Irenaeus, primarily the New Testament—brought against the Gnostics. He tells us that the Gnostics make the following arguments:

(1) they claim that Scripture is not correct.

(2) they claim that Scripture is not authoritative.

(3) they claim that Scripture is ambiguous; it can mean different things.

---

[19]*Ibid.*, 147–59.

[20]*Ibid.*, 170–72.

[21]On testamentary disputes see G. Kennedy, *The Art of Rhetoric in the Roman World* (Princeton: Princeton University, 1973), 86ff.

(4) they claim that the truth cannot be discovered by someone who is ignorant of the truth, which was handed on orally (AdvHaer III 2, 1).

The first three arguments have parallels in legal rhetoric. They are used in disputes over wills and other documents. The fourth, on the other hand, belongs to the world of oral tradition and its authority. Even Irenaeus has not totally rejected that line of argument, since he has tried to make the bishops the necessary community. His way of formulating the first three, on the other hand, bears all the marks of someone who thinks of Scripture as binding text. If they are also an accurate reflection of the arguments of Irenaeus' opponents, they show that some Gnostics had also begun to respond to the pressure for a normative Christian text. They have accepted some canon and then gone on to appeal to established legal procedures in disputes over texts to justify their interpretations.

If we are to look for signs of this increased pressure in Gnostic writings, we must distinguish appeals to the New Testament based on oral traditions and those based on interpretation of the New Testament as a fixed, normative text. It is possible to see the disputes over interpretation of Jesus' sayings, over the interpretation of the passion, and even over the missionary efforts of the apostles as part of a "primitive Christianity" founded on oral tradition. The story is not a set of fixed words, so it may be retold differently. This approach seems to be that of most of the dialogues. But the James tradition presents us with a different situation. We have already seen that it is the only tradition which would support patristic charges that the Gnostics claimed a non-apostolic transmission of the tradition. The James apocrypha account for the non-apostolic character of the chain by having the apostles reject gnosis and the express command of the Lord. They also acknowledge the relative lateness of gnosis in Christian preaching.

The two dialogues give slightly different accounts of this situation. 1 ApocJas sets up a strictly controlled chain of transmission. Note, however, that this chain involves handing on a written account of the revelation. It does not involve the kind of oral instruction mentioned in Irenaeus' fourth point. ApocryJas is also very much concerned with written transmission. Its opening scene may well be a Gnostic version of the creation of that very canon to which the orthodox are beginning to appeal. The disciples are sitting around and individually recording what the Savior has said to the group as a whole and to each one privately (CG I 1, 23—2, 15). Thus there is no unified, completely public apostolic tradition such as Irenaeus claims. Each account is a mixture of the public and private teaching of Jesus. Irenaeus had also claimed that the apostles transmitted their teaching to all simply and ungrudgingly (AdvHaer III 14, 2). The concluding interaction between James and the apostles contradicts that picture. At first, the apostles accept the revelation given to James and Peter. That acceptance might be said to authenticate the "apostolic" claims of gnosis. But then they all, including Peter, refuse to wait in Jerusalem to enlighten the Gnostic race for whom the teaching was intended. James is forced to send them away because of their resentment. Thus, an imperfect and partial revelation comes to be spread abroad as apostolic tradition (CG I 16, 3–11). ApocryJas has given narrative authority to the picture of the New Testament which underlies Irenaeus' list of objections. Its narrative shows that New Testament writings are individual, mixed with error, not authoritative and out of touch with the tradition which the Savior wished to be passed on to all his beloved followers.

GNOSIS AND THE AUTHORITATIVE TRADITION

Despite the evidence that Gnostics responded to increasing pressure for canonical texts, they still lagged behind the orthodox community in appreciating the religious significance of the change slowly taking place around them.[22] Our tendency to call some Gnostic writings "gospels" or even to refer to the Gnostic dialogues as the equivalent of "gospels" gives the misleading impression that the Gnostics followed the orthodox canon with one of their own. It should be apparent by now that nothing could be farther from the truth.[23] These Gnostic writings reflect the liturgy, teaching, preaching and polemic of their respective communities. But they never

---

[22]Von Campenhausen, *Formation*, 182–200, agrees that Gnostics lagged behind in the development of the canon.

[23]In this respect, our Gnostic groups differ from the Manichaeans who propagated their gnosis through writings.

claim to do more than to embody true tradition. They never claim to be the textually authoritative source of reflection, authority or even contact with the divine. The revelation about which they speak may put an individual in touch with the truth about God, about the cosmos, about himself or herself, or about salvation, but that truth is not definitively embodied in any inspired text. Gnostic interpretation is still the hermeneutic of an oral tradition. It does not provide the formalized interpretation of a text that would sponsor a systematized and rational account of Christian theology such as that proposed by Irenaeus or Origen.

There are Gnostic theologians, to be sure. Like their orthodox counterparts, they engaged in speculative reflection on matters of belief. But they do not have a normative text that might dictate the limits of or sponsor a wider expanse of systematic reflection. Irenaeus' predecessors were unable to root out the Gnostics in their midst because they all argued on the same basis. The *Epistula Apostolorum*, for example, represents an orthodox attempt to use the same weapons as the Gnostics.[24] There, orthodox convictions about the life and death of Jesus and his bodily resurrection are related in a dialogue between the Risen Lord and the twelve. This dialogue is introduced by a cover letter presenting it as a work of the apostolic council to combat heresy (c. 1). It includes the standard commissioning of the apostles to preach the doctrine given by the Lord (c. 19). Though the contents of this dialogue are closer to the canonical Gospels than in most Gnostic examples, the author still feels free to harmonize these traditions with each other and with a variety of apocryphal acounts. EpistApost may have been intended to be the true, orthodox "revelation dialogue" in contrast to the false ones of the Gnostic Christians. But, in principle, it proceeds as they have done. The Jesus tradition is assembled in an apocryphal and interpretative narrative in which the

---

[24]See M. Hornschuch, *Studien zur Epistula Apostolorum*, PTS 5 (Berlin: Walter de Gruyter, 1965), 4–7; 92–97. His early dating of EpistApost—first half of the second century—would require that the revelation dialogue had become an authoritative form for the propagation of Christian Gnostic teaching very early in the history of the movement.

dialogue between the Risen Jesus and his disciples sets the true tradition of the community.[25]

The brilliance of Irenaeus' counterattack was to see that such arguments have no conclusion and to move the locus of authority onto new ground. This move required that the teaching community be associated with a smaller group which had come to have responsibility for Christian churches. It also required what they were to teach to be regulated by a fixed, normative text that would be subject to certain standards of interpretation. The full flowering of this move was not yet realized in Irenaeus' time. But it fit into the larger pattern of religious developments that would dominate the third through the fifth centuries. In contrast, Gnostics were insisting on their own version of what had been the common pattern of religious association and tradition in the earlier period. Both the missionary thrust of many of the Gnostic dialogues and the patristic warnings against the ubiquitous Gnostic threat remind us not to picture gnosis as a secret society carefully hidden away. It seems clear that the primary—if not the only—target of Gnostic preaching was the larger Christian community.[26] It is also clear that Gnostic and orthodox Christians remained together in the same ecclesial circles into the third and perhaps even the fourth centuries.[27]

The basic Gnostic ecclesial models are of undifferentiated unity, a Gnostic seed from a heavenly pleroma. Gnostics viewed themselves as an inner circle of Christianity.[28]

However much their resistance to ecclesiastical pressure led some Gnostics to insist on more universal access to the divine than was being permitted by the new move to draw boundaries and to cut down on the fluidity of Christian tradition in various areas of life, this same resistance may also have been responsible for the eventual demise of this religious option. The social and religious patterns of

---

[25]Von Campenhausen, *Formation*, 142, points out that even with orthodox acceptance of canonical narrative, one still finds appeals to the authority of freely formulated sayings and traditions.

[26]Koschorke, *Die Polemik*, 222f.

[27]*Ibid.*, 228–32, assembles the patristic evidence for the continued presence of Gnostics in later Christian circles.

[28]*Ibid.*, 220f; ExcTheod lviii, 1; AdvHaer III 15, 2; TriTrac CG I 122, 13–123, 22.

the empire as a whole were shifting out from under them. Brown has observed that by the end of Augustine's life, Manichaeism—the great Gnostic threat of his youth—no longer presented a threat to Christians. It was unable to move into the new world of stable, local Christian communities. These local communities had to take on themselves the responsibilities of ordering their larger social milieu as well as of developing theoretical and intellectual insight into the nature of human life, society and government that could supplant pagan philosophy.[29] Augustine, the Manichaean, could never be the bishop of *City of God.* The demise of gnosis is apparent already in PS. There, neither the narrative power of Gnostic myth nor the speculative reflections of Gnostic theologians find a hearing. Instead, the truth that the apostles have waited twelve years to learn comes down to a tradition of formulae and interpretations for the heavenly journey of the soul. The larger context of reflection on God, the cosmos, and human bondage in the material and psychic world has been dissolved into a quasi-magical, esoteric sect—a sect that might be appealing to some, but hardly the dangerous hydra perceived by Plotinus, who defended the old classical order against it, or by Irenaeus, who set the emerging Christian order on a different course.

---

[29]P. Brown, "The Diffusion of Manichaeism in the Roman Empire," *Religion and Society in the Age of Augustine* (London: Faber, 1972), describes the demise of Manichaeism as the unavoidable fate of a missionary religion in a world of shrinking horizons: 107f, 111–115.

EPILOGUE

Gnosis and
the Modern Spirit

In her popular account of the Gnostic/orthodox conflict, published with great fanfare by Random House, Pagels portrays the Gnostics as the champions of individual creativity against an increasingly repressive and unimaginative orthodoxy. She claims that gnosis represents the form in which Christian symbols continue to inspire great creative artists, otherwise alienated by a rigid orthodox Christianity. Gnostics insist on the rights of the autonomous, creative human self.[1] The preceding section has already taken issue with the historical inaccuracies in such presentations of the Gnostic/orthodox relationship. We have seen that Gnostics did not have the picture of the autonomous, differentiated, creative self presupposed in this argument. Such a view of the self is largely the product of modern thought and presupposes a consciousness of self and world radically different from that of second- and third-century people.[2]

Gnostics lagged behind their orthodox counterparts in adapting to the larger cultural changes of the third and following centuries that demanded reshaping of religious traditions. Whatever its value as heresiological weapon, the emergence of a canon responded to a deeper shift toward the priority of written over oral traditions. The same shift made it possible for more and more people to appropriate the analytic, cognitive tools made possible by literacy. Those tools of

---

[1]Pagels, *Gnostic Gospels*, 179f. Also see my review in *Commonweal*.

[2]See W. Ong, "World as View and World as Event," *American Anthropologist* 71 (1969), 634–47.

philosophical analysis forced more and more of the religious traditions to answer to different standards of intelligibility and adequacy.
Insofar as Gnostics stayed with the more amorphous religious perception of the oral tradition of the second century, they would lose
their place as a deeper interpretation, because that place was coming
to be taken by another mode of apprehending the tradition, that of
the great theological symbols and syntheses of the third and following centuries. For example, both second-century Christians and
Gnostics shared a soteriological language of the soul's liberation
from cosmic powers. But it is only the Christians who put the pieces
of that story, with its equation of the powers and the passions, together with a psychology of inner transformation, that made the shift
of the metaphor to one of inner mystical ascent possible.[3] A century
later Augustine and his Manichaean friends provide an analogy. The
hearers, the young ambitious intellectuals, are attracted to what appears to them a more "profound" understanding of Christianity.
They are not beaten out of it by orthodox opposition. They "out-
grow" it when they encounter a Christianity capable of a more adequate and universal response to the spiritual and intellectual needs of
the time than the Manichaean teachers provided. And Augustine
himself would be in no small measure responsible for the further development of the Christian tradition into a more precise rendering
of human social and spiritual development. With the demise of
Manichaeism, ancient gnosis died. It was not carried on in an unbro-
ken esoteric chain as some writers suggest.[4] Peter Brown has pointed
out several reasons for its demise: the world became a more settled
and traditional place in the fifth century; towns had collapsed
around their bishops—not as a result of some power takeover but because of a genuine gap in leadership and administration in much of
the empire; the wide-ranging merchants had also begun to settle
down; the Church in both the West and the East (Nestorian in Syria)
was increasingly assimilated to society; Manichaeism continued to
embody primitive modes of asceticism that were simply "out of

---

[3]Jonas, "Myth and Mysticism: A Study of Objectification and Interiorization in
Religious Thought," *JR* 49 (1969), 315–29.

[4]Against Pagels, *op. cit.*, 179, and Voeglin, *New Science of Politics* (Chicago: University of Chicago, 1952), 124–27.

date." Manichaeism does not revive until the twelfth century puts an end to the rigid and parochial structures of society.[5]

The transformation in consciousness from ancient to modern times means that the modern fascination with gnosis is often with something quite different than the dimensions of the ancient dialogue show gnosis to have been. Moderns now read its images of rebellion as the grandeur of a human spirit, which refuses to be guilty of evil that derives from divine ignorance. Passing over the limitations of ancient Gnosticism, they see it as sponsor for all protest against the all too visible defects of the orthodox Christian synthesis. Reading Gnostic texts through the glasses of modern subjectivism and delight in "creativity," they mistake a genuine oral mysticism and the free variation of its tradition as the celebration of individual inventiveness. But it is such readings of the Gnostic phenomenon which seem to have sponsored an intellectual stance in modern thought that many have referred to as modern Gnosticism. It is not entirely analogous with its ancient ancestor. For modern Gnostics, the victory of the human spirit is ambiguous. Both utopianism and nihilism can be tied to the same impulse, because any order that is to be created must be imposed by the human spirit. Modern gnosis lacks the dimension of radical transcendence so crucial to the ancient perception. Without the source of order and revelation, the modern can either impose order or champion variants of the nihilistic declaration that one must stand firmly in a cosmos where there is none at all.[6] Though we cannot study the so-called modern Gnostics in detail, a survey of some "Gnostic trends" in literature, psychology and political thought will indicate the loci of the contemporary Gnostic dialogue.

GNOSTIC HEROES: THE REFUSAL TO BE GUILTY

Cleanth Brooks compares the heroes of Walker Percy's novels to the "modern Gnostic" described by political philosopher Eric

---

[5]See P. Brown, "The Diffusion of Manichaeism in the Roman Empire," *Religion and Society*, 116f; E. Voeglin, *Order in History IV: The Ecumenic Age* (Baton Rouge: Louisiana State, 1974), 19–22, links the emergence of Gnosticism to the phenomenon of imperialism.

[6]Jonas, "Gnosticism, Existentialism and Nihilism," *Phenomenon of Life* (New York: Harper & Row, 1966), 224f, 233.

Voeglin. These heroes live in a world dominated by mutilated Christian symbols. These symbols are so twisted from their origins that they can no longer provide a coherent framework for human life.[7] The Christian view of humanness runs counter to the modern view of the human as an organism in interaction with an environment, not a spiritual being who is in some way responsible for his fall from the divine order of the Creator. Human attempts to wrest satisfaction from that environment frequently fail, sometimes in crude, ugly bumbling, sometimes in unexpected eruptions of violence—unexpected because moderns have quite lost their bearings where evil is concerned. Humans know that all is not well with themselves and the world, even at the height of success when they are most satisfactorily "adjusted" to the environment. They feel alienated and guilty but refuse to accept a story which puts them at fault.[8]

While Percy's earlier heroes won through to some personal redemption that could be considered Christian, his most recent incarnates Gnostic rebellion. Lancelot is played off against a doctor-priest friend who appears only as "listener" while the tale of Lance's encounter with evil in the form of his wife's adultery and his own rebellious torching of their plantation unfolds. Lance protests that the world is built on a systematic cover-up of the violence hidden in sexuality that has forced women into so perverted a consciousness that they will accept violence/rape as pleasure. Such a world cannot be allowed to stand. Lance punctuates his "true understanding" of the world with a reinterpretation of Genesis, which he says would have shown the truth about the world if only the orthodox had gotten it right. Original sin is not something that man did; it is something that God did to man.[9] (Our ancient Gnostic Genesis stories agree.)

The themes of death, revolt, violence and perverted sexuality appear in other "Gnostic" novels. One can turn from the southern

---

[7]C. Brooks, "Walker Percy and Modern Gnosticism," *The Art of Walker Percy*, ed. P. R. Broughton (Baton Rouge/London: Louisiana State, 1979), 260–79.

[8]See Percy's philosophical discussion of modern alienation in *Message in the Bottle* (New York: Farrar, Straus & Giroux, 1975), 19–28. Percy argues that, for the alienated, apocalyptic speculation is a relief, since the impending destruction gives focus to their anxiety. The real question, which is not faced, is what if the world is not to end—p. 84.

[9]W. Percy, *Lancelot* (New York: Farrar, Straus & Giroux, 1977), 222–24.

mansion of Lancelot to the decaying Avignon of Durrell's *Monsieur*, for example. Durrell's novel exploits his fascination with ancient Gnosticism. Orthodox Christianity is represented by the decaying symbols of the medieval papacy. But even with ancient Gnostic inspiration, these modern Gnostics have hardly achieved a liberating sense of cosmic order, of freedom from the psychic bonds of passion and anger. The principals in the tale—the career diplomat Piers whose family estate in Avignon is as decayed as the papacy, his sister Sylvie, and their friend, the doctor, Bruce—are locked in an incestuous triangle whose seeming innocence may have driven Sylvie mad. Years ago their relationship had led them to a Gnostic "mystery" in the deserts of Egypt. Now Sylvie is in a local asylum, Piers has died a mysterious death, and Bruce has come back to unravel the peculiar circumstances of his friends as he sifts through the mists of their past with the help of the dead man's papers and notes.

Durrell paints pictures of pseudo-intellectual decadence that is drawn to the mysterious Gnostic shaman Akkad. Perhaps not surprisingly, the gnosis they encounter is equally decadent, that of the magic formulae and mystic interpretations of the Pistis Sophia which are chanted and commented upon in a strange Ophite ritual. One suspects that Durrell's imagination has painted as good a picture as any of the esoteric ritual of such a form of gnosis. Piers is the only one who attains Gnostic enlightenment. Eventually we learn that liberation of the soul, for this strange sect, requires a ritual death. But the initiate never knows his or her time until the messenger appears with the letter in Akkad's hand. Piers had seen the sign. Was it delivered by his sister, the last one to see him? Perhaps. One neither knows nor cares. No one is the better for his strange gnosis. All the characters in the tale drift off to their solitary fates. Nothing is either resolved or transformed. One wonders perhaps if the decay of modernity is so pervasive that there is no esoteric truth or wisdom that would save Durrell's characters.

Both Percy and Durrell have tried to unravel the spirit of the modern age. Gnosis speaks of the decay of that spirit. Critic Harold Bloom is much less successful with his first novel, *The Flight to Lucifer: A Gnostic Fantasy*. He mangles Gnostic myths and characters into a mixture of science fiction and Gothic romance that is supposed to represent a novel. But there is too much intellectual juxtaposition of Gnostic tales and mythic symbols to make a good story. No one's imagination will be gripped by these characters and their fate. Valentinus and the aeon Olam have taken the hero Perscors in a strange craft to battle the star world on Lucifer. There, he is left on his own to find out, if he can, what gnosis is. This world is peopled by Gnostic sects and various entities from Gnostic myth, the evil creator Saklas, and two dangerous and murderous female seductresses, the lower Sophia, Achamoth, and Ruha, Semitic for "spirit." As one expects of the modern Gnostic, all elements of the liberating transcendent are gone.

Bloom has peppered his story with twisted quotations from Nag Hammadi writings. The conflict with the archons from the introduction to NatArc becomes a challenge to the hero to discover whether his soul belongs to the powers or not. Valentinus, meanwhile, is engaged on his own question to remember the Gnostic story which he has forgotten. But he learns that he will never remember,[10] and at the end he "daydreams" himself into the pleromatic rest something like a senile old man. The depths of the pleroma give no one peace. Olam arrives only to find that it is empty. There are no Gnostic brethren; he must return to estrangement. In fact, the cosmic war between the Abyss and all that is below is endless.[11] Perscors, meanwhile, goes from one Gnostic tribe to another possessed by lust for the demonic temptress and violent anger as he constantly battles obscure demonic forces. Finally he abandons the search for knowledge, having decided that he neither belongs to the archons and creation, nor to the aeons and their pleroma. He proclaims himself the glorious primal man whose glory had been stolen by Saklas and Achamoth.[12] His gnosis might seem superior to the abandonment of knowledge that also came upon Olam and Valentinus,[13] but what has he been freed for? Nihilism? One can be the primal man; one can take vengeance on strange powers who have stolen one's glory, without purpose as Perscors does. So what? The war is endless, and none of the heroes

---

[10]H. Bloom, *The Journey to Lucifer* (New York: Farrar, Straus & Giroux, 1979), 234–40.

[11]*Ibid.*, 237.

[12]*Ibid.*, 209.

[13]*Ibid.*, 240.

have been freed from it. These modern heroes can thrash, fight, lust, search or daydream, but there is no rest, no reconciliation, no fellowship. In that respect, they are just as ethereal as Durrell's characters. The modern Gnostic hero is much more like the pre-gnosis humanity of the older stories, caught in an obscurely felt revolt with no one to rescue.

GNOSIS AND THE PSYCHOLOGIST:
THE SOUL DISCOVERS ITS UNITY

Not all modern readings of gnosis latch onto its symbols of alienation. Those influenced by Jungian psychology have quite a different reading. One novelist may serve as a transition to this type. Quispel has shown that Hesse was influenced by Jungian reflection on Gnosticism when he composed *Steppenwolf* and *Demian*.[14] He then abandoned gnosis for the symbolisms of the East and Boheme. Jung emphasized the inclusion of the feminine and the ability to integrate evil into his interpretation of Gnostic symbols. Like other moderns, the transcendent Father hardly appears. Jung is more interested in those figures which show Gnostic awareness of the dark, instinctual underside of the divine, since he thinks that moderns can only attain wholeness by integrating those dimensions from the unconscious into the psyche. Hesse's heroes are faced with that task of psychic integration. In *Steppenwolf*, the fallen Sophia, "whore," appears as the prostitute Hermine. The hero must come to terms with the "despised female," the instinctual, if he is to attain peace. *Demian* was explicitly recognized as Gnostic, since it proclaimed discovery of a new god, the Gnostic Abraxas, the source of both good and evil. Psychic healing and the end to schizophrenia come with the inner vision of the archaic Eve, and reconciliation of opposites comes through this new divinity. Quispel points out that such modern gnosis is quite different from its ancient counterpart. The former gnosis insisted upon separating the opposites of fullness and deficiency. The modern wants to unite them in a larger whole.[15] But the new source of transcendence for these modern Gnostics has

---

[14]G. Quispel, "Hermann Hesse and Gnosis," *Gnosis. Fest. H. Jonas*, 492–507.
[15]*Ibid.*, 501.

emerged from within the psyche, not through revelation of a higher external order.

The reconciliation of opposites in transcendent symbols of Self founds Jung's understanding of healing psychological transformation. At the same time, one would badly misinterpret Jung's picture of Gnosticism if one concentrated solely on the dynamics of individual psychic processes. Although Jung himself often speaks as if that is all he intended, he never goes on for long without introducing the larger problem of the spiritual and psychological transformation of humanity—or at least Western humanity—as a whole. This perspective saves his insistence on the psychological interpretation of religious symbolism from naive subjectivism. Jung's particular interest in Gnosticism fits into his larger attempt to understand why traditional religious symbolisms do not seem to meet the spiritual needs of moderns and yet patients continue to call up religious symbols and images to focus psychic growth and distress.[16] Jung thinks that the Gnostics were able to bring forth symbols crucial to psychic growth because they were still in close touch with the instinctual dynamics of the unconscious. When he calls them psychologists, he is not—unlike some more recent interpreters—mistakenly attributing to them the awareness that belongs to modern "psychological man." He does think that the Gnostic refusal to accept a salvation based simply on faith and to undercut human self-valuation forced them to explore dimensions of the psyche often ignored by others. Similarly, the scientific revolution obliges moderns to demand the evidence of their own and others' experience. In addition, unlike the ancient Gnostics, moderns cannot accept a stance toward self and world which rejects the created material order and its associated passions, the instinctual foundations of creativity itself. One must rebel against a constraining religious symbolism, insist upon human worth, and defend the right to search out the meaning of all religious symbolism.[17]

Jung's most extensive discussion of the problem of God and consciousness comes in his discussion of Job, *Answer to Job* (1952). One is tempted to call it "a modern man's biography of God." Much

---

[16]C. G. Jung, "The Spiritual Problem of Modern Man" (1928), in *The Portable Jung*, ed. J. Campbell (New York: Viking, 1971), 461–67.

[17]*Ibid.*, 468–78.

of its portrayal of Yahweh would be congenial to an ancient Gnostic. He is hostile, jealous, envious, ignorant and largely unconscious. Humanity's emergence into consciousness provokes his wrath. But Jung will not take the unknown Father of Gnosticism as a serious alternative. This lower God himself will have to attain consciousness not only through incarnation but through the continuation of that incarnation in humanity, through the work of the Paraclete, through the transformation of men into sons of God.[18] What is at stake is no less than a cosmic reconciliation of the forces of evil and destruction. Humanity now has these forces in its own power in atomic weapons. Therefore, unless it can attain spiritual transformation as a race, it stands to unleash all the violence of the apocalypse.[19] God will not transform the world from without; humanity must be spiritually transformed from within. Thus, the eschatological dimensions of the older Christian and Gnostic religious language have been given a psychological counterpart in the spiritual development of humanity as a whole. How this "biography of God" turns out rests squarely and none too certainly in the human balance.[20] The modern description of the psyche as locus of the new, critical transcendence leaves humanity terrifyingly alone, unless one assumes that all will be brought to a harmonious conclusion by the inherent dynamics of the racial unconscious. But such an assumption could hardly be founded on evidence or experience.

Even Jung's treatment of Christian, Gnostic and alchemical symbolisms of the Self in Aion quickly move outward to this global perspective. He argues that individual psychic transformation requires a shift in the psychic center from ego to Self. This Self may be portrayed in a variety of symbols. Jung suggests that Gnostic language about the unknown Father refers to the attraction of the numinous unconscious, which motivates the necessary expansion of consciousness. The psychic symbols for this transcendental structure

---

[18]Jung, "Answer to Job" (1952), *The Portable Jung*, 583–605.

[19]*Ibid.*, 638f.

[20]E. Neumann's history of consciousness assigns gnosis to the stage of hero myth, struggle against the world-parents: *History and Origins of Consciousness* (Princeton: Princeton 1954), 118f, 178, 188f, 254. This view does not explain the remarkably "unheroic" character of Gnostic stories. The transcendental, luminous power of revelation defeats the powers without a struggle.

of consciousness take the form of quaternity, the genuine wholeness of opposites. It is important to remember that Jung is not suggesting a lapse back into the unconscious, to pre-psychological stages in which religious symbols guided the psychic life of persons through its dynamics. No, the divine which emerges from the modern must also be changed by the process of becoming conscious; the God-image itself is altered.[21]

Examples of this fundamental image of wholeness appear in Gnostic symbolisms of the divine Anthropos or of the Fallen Sophia who must win her way back to light out of the darkness of creation.[22] Jung is not interested in exegeting the dynamics of ancient Gnostic consciousness but in the appropriation of their spontaneously generated symbolism to address the psychic crisis of modern people.[23] The crisis of the modern world demands of reconciling symbolism: God-/humanity; good/evil; male/female. This symbolism must bring such opposites into a wholeness that can be effective not only in the religious vision or psychological integration of a few individuals; it must be effective on the psychic level of cultures as a whole. The ancient Gnostic was in an entirely different situation. Consciousness was still so mired in the material and caught in the realm of passion that the overwhelming thrust upward to spiritualization did not need to be reminded of its roots. It took all the force of revelation and the numinous that could be mustered to focus the large-scale movement of consciousness toward the spiritual.[24] Jung argues that this great outburst fostered the eschatological expectation that materiality would be destroyed and all would become spirit. When that failed to materialize, attention turned back from the realm of God/the divine as center to that of humanity. He sees the orthodox God-Man Christ symbol—not the Gnostic revealer Christ—as a crucial reminder of the inseparability of opposites.[25] But even that symbol is not complete, since the "negative side" of the divine-human Christ has been

---

[21]Jung, *Aion: Researches into the Phenomenology of the Self* (1951) (Princeton: Princeton University, 1968), 194.

[22]*Ibid.*, 196–215.

[23]*Ibid.*, 255.

[24]*Ibid.*, 255f.

[25]*Ibid.*, 41.

split off into another figure, the Antichrist. And even that figure was weakened by a dogmatics that treated evil as simply the privation of good. One must recognize the genuine power of evil before one can attain its reconciliation.[26]

Thus, the Jungian picture always looks toward the problem of the spiritual development of humanity. It does not seek to capitalize on Gnostic symbols of revolt and alienation. Unconscious projection of psychological realities onto the world will no longer work healing transformation for modern consciousness. The novelists are right; we cannot go back to being ancient Gnostics or Christians simply. All religious symbols must pass through the scrutiny of psychologically differentiated modern consciousness.

GNOSIS AND POLITICS:
THE VIOLENCE OF ALIENATION

Jung's concern for the spiritual situation of humanity ties him to the discussion of gnosis in modern political and philosophical speculation such as we find in Hans Jonas and Eric Voeglin. But both see gnosis as serving the forces of alienation and destruction, not of reconciliation. Like the other examples of modern gnosis, the focus has switched to man himself as the center of all possible order. Modern Gnostic thinkers also reject the dimension of transcendence characteristic of the ancients. What they commonly appropriate in turning to "Gnostic speculation" is the symbolism of knowledge as key to the eschatological transformation of a reality whose disorder and evil are not man's fault but can only be set right—if indeed that is possible—by human intervention; order is not given in revelation or discovered in receptive reflection but is imposed from without.[27] Or, lacking any certain source of order, the modern Gnostic may become a nihilist, denying all sources of truth or value.[28]

Voeglin has consistently labeled such perversions of consciousness "Gnostic." He argues that this perverted eschatology dictates

---

[26]*Ibid.*, 53–62.
[27]Jonas, "Gnosticism, Existentialism and Nihilism," 213–19.
[28]*Ibid.*, 224–34.

much of modern politics.[29] He would agree with Jung that the spiritual survival of humanity depends upon its abilty to overcome the seduction of polarized and hence potentially—and actually—violent imaginative constructions of reality. Humanity cannot escape living "in-between" the material and the divine. It must be willing to accept not only its scientific insights but a further intellectual and spiritual insight that recognizes a transcendent that reaches out to humanity, that both founds and demands *caritas*.[30] Voeglin sees modern political ideologies as clear examples of the violence inherent in the alternative: the human attempt to create order by imposing the systematic construction of its own imagination on reality.[31] This false eschatological consciousness may take a variety of forms, but they are all based on a desire to force reality to bend to the human construction of how things ought to be.[32] Voeglin interprets ancient Gnostic systems as manifestations of the same disorder of the spirit, though the more detailed evidence from the Nag Hammadi corpus suggests that they are a lot more sensitive to the limits of the human situation than they are often given credit for. Nevertheless, Voeglin, like Jung, comes to the traditional Christian symbol of incarnation as a more adequate expression of human rootedness in the world than the Gnostic divine revealer.

Modern Gnostic speculation is more dangerous than its forebear because the dimension of revelation as divine gift and liberation has been lost. All eschatology is to be played out in this world. Modern Gnostics find the transcendent source of order and salvation in their own consciousness. But their philosophical critics insist—and their forebears would doubtless agree—humanity cannot engineer its own salvation. Imposition of such consciously and falsely constructed systems will only breed more of the dangerous violence that so torments modern political life. The spirit cannot live on the self-assertions of

---

[29]See my discussion of Voeglin on Gnosticism, "Gnosis and the Life of the Spirit: The Price of Pneumatic Order," in J. Kirby and W. Thompson, eds., *Eric Voeglin: A Theological Appraisal*, forthcoming.

[30]Voeglin, *New Science*, 77–79; *Ecumenic Age*, 251.

[31]Voeglin, *New Science*, 121; *Science, Politics and Gnosticism* (Chicago: Regnery, 1968), 83–88.

[32]*Science, Politics* 22–34; *New Science*, 167–72; *Anamnesis* (Notre Dame: University of Notre Dame, 1978), 108–10, 184.

ideologies that are thin covers for nihilism. Voeglin would not accept Jung's solution either. Transcendence mediated through the psyche—however lovingly received—will not correct the perversion of modern Gnostic consciousness. Transcendence always speaks from without, from beyond, guaranteeing an order greater than humanity's psychic or intellectual apprehension of it. One is left then with a question: Can the balance of classic religious symbolism or philosophy open to the transcendent bail a disoriented and alienated humanity out of its spiritual dead-end? The ambiguity of modern Gnostic novels provides little hope. Yet it seems that the biography of God continues to be written in the spiritual history of humanity.

Selected Bibliography

Complete bibliographies of materials pertaining to Gnosticism have been published by:

Scholar, D. M. A NAG HAMMADI BIBLIOGRAPHY. 1948–69. NHS I. Leiden: E. J. Brill, 1971,

———, "Bibliographia Gnostica" nos. I–VII. *NovTest* 13–20 (1971—77).

Selected Studies:

Arai, S. "Zur Christologie des Apokryphon Johannes," *NTS* 15 (1968/69), 302–18.

Bauer, W. DAS LEBEN JESU IM ZEITALTER DER NEUTESTA- MENTLICHEN APOCRYPHEN. Tübingen: J. C. B. Mohr, 1909.

Böhlig, A., and P. Labib. KOPTISCH-GNOSTISCHE APOKALYPSEN AUS CODEX V VON NAG HAMMADI. Sondesbd. Wiss. Zeit. Martin-Luther Univ. Halle Wittenberg, 1963.

Brown, P. THE MAKING OF LATE ANTIQUITY. Cambridge: Harvard, 1978.

———, "The Religious Crisis of the Third Century A.D.," RELIGION AND SOCIETY IN THE AGE OF ST. AUGUSTINE. London: Farber & Farber, 1972, 78–84.

Bullard, R. THE HYPOSTASIS OF THE ARCHONS. PTS 10. Berlin: Walter de Gruyter, 1970.

Collins, J. J., ed. APOCALYPSE: THE MORPHOLOGY OF A GENRE. Semeia 14. Missoula: Scholars Press, 1979.

Daniélou, J. GOSPEL MESSAGE AND HELLENISTIC CULTURE. Philadelphia: Westminster, 1973.

Festugière, A. J. LA REVELATION D'HERMES TRISMEGISTE, Vols. I–IV. Paris: Gabalda, 1949–54.

Havelock, E. THE GREEK CONCEPT OF JUSTICE. Cambridge: Harvard, 1978.

Janssens, Y. "L'Apocryphon de Jean," *Muséon* 83 (1970), 157–65; 84 (1971), 43–64, 403–32.

Jonas, H. "Delimitation of the Gnostic Phenomenon—Typological and Historical," LE ORIGINI DELLO GNOSTICISMO, ed. U. Bianchi. Leiden: E. J. Brill, 1967, 90–108.

———, THE GNOSTIC RELIGION.[2] Boston: Beacon Press, 1963.

————, "Gnosticism and Modern Nihilism," *SocRes* 19 (1952) 430–52.

————, "Myth and Mysticism: A Study of Objectification and Interiorization in Religious Thought," *JR* 49 (1969), 315–29.

Kasser, R., M. Malinine *et al.*, eds. TRACTATUS TRIPARTITUS. pars 1: De Supernis. 2: De Creatione Hominis. 3: de Generibus Tribus. Bern: Francke, 1973/75.

Koester, H., and J. M. Robinson. TRAJECTORIES THROUGH EARLY CHRISTIANITY. Philadelphia: Fortress, 1971.

Koschorke, K. DIE POLEMIK DER GNOSTIKER GEGEN DAS KIRCHLICHE CHRISTENTUM. NHS XII. Leiden: E. J. Brill, 1978.

Krause, M. "Der *Dialog des Soter* in Codex III von Nag Hammadi," GNOSIS AND GNOSTICISM, ed. M. Krause. NHS VIII. Leiden: E. J. Brill, 1977, 13–34.

————, "Das Literarische Verhaltnis des Eugnostosbriefes zur Sophia Jesu Christi," MULLUS. Fest. Theodor Klauser. Jb. f. Ant. un. Chris. Erganzungsbd. 1. Aschendorff, 1964, 215–23.

————, "Die Petrusakten in Codex VI von Nag Hammadi," ESSAYS ON THE NAG HAMMADI TEXTS IN HONOUR OF ALEXANDER BOHLIG. NHS III. Leiden: E. J. Brill, 1972, 36–58.

Layton, B. "The Hypostasis of the Archons," *HTR* 67 (1974), 351–425; 69 (1976), 31–101.

MacRae, G. W. "The Ego-Proclamation in Gnostic Sources," THE TRIAL OF JESUS, ed. E. Bammel. SBT ser. 2, 13. London: SCM, 1970, 122–34.

————, "The Jewish Background of the Gnostic Sophia Myth," *NovTest* 12 (1970), 86–101.

————, "Nag Hammadi and the New Testament," GNOSIS. Fest. H. Jonas, ed. B. Aland. Göttingen: Vandenhoeck & Ruprecht, 1978, 144–57.

————, "Sleep and Awakening in Gnostic Texts," LE ORIGINI, 496–507.

Malinine, M. *et al.*, eds. EPISTULA IACOBI APOCRYPHA. Zurich: Rascher, 1968.

Ménard, J. E., "La Lettre de Pierre à Philippe: sa structure," NAG HAMMADI AND GNOSIS, ed. R. McL. Wilson. NHS XIV. Leiden: E. J. Brill, 1978, 103–107.

Pagels, E. "The Demiurge and His Archons—A Gnostic View of the Bishop and Presbyters?" *HTR* 69 (1976), 301–24.

————, THE GNOSTIC GOSPELS. New York: Random House, 1979.

————, THE JOHANNINE GOSPEL IN GNOSTIC EXEGESIS. Nashville: Abingdon, 1973.

————, and H. Koester, "Report on the Dialogue of the Savior," NAG HAMMADI AND GNOSIS, 66–74.

————, "Visions, Appearances and Apostolic Authority: Gnostic and Orthodox Tradition," GNOSIS, 415–30.

Pearson, B. "Biblical Exegesis in Gnostic Literature," ARMENIAN AND BIBLICAL STUDIES, ed. M. Stone. Jerusalem, 1976, 70–80.

————, "The Figure of Norea in Gnostic Literature," PROCEEDINGS OF THE INTERNATIONAL COLLOQUIUM ON GNOSTICISM, ed. G. Widengren. Stockholm: Almqvist & Wiksell/Leiden: E. J. Brill, 1977, 143–52.

————, "Jewish Haggadic Tradition in the *Testimony of Truth* from Nag Hammadi (CG IX, 3)," EX ORBE RELIGIONUM. Studia Geo Widengren, ed. J. Bergman. Leiden: E. J. Brill, 1972, 457–470.

Perkins, P. "Deceiving the Deity: Self-Transcendence and the Numinous in Gnosticism," PROCEEDINGS TENTH ANNUAL INSTITUTE FOR PHILOSOHY AND RELIGION, BOSTON UNIVERSITY, 1979. Notre Dame: Notre Dame, 1981.

————, "Gnosis as Salvation—A Phenomenological Inquiry," AUFSTIEG UND NIEDERGNG DER ROMISCHEN WELT. II, 22, ed. W. Haase. Berlin/New York: Walter de Gruyter, forthcoming.

————, "The Gnostic Revelation Dialogue as Religious Polemic," *ANRW* II, 22, forthcoming.

————, "Irenaeus and the Gnostics," *VigChr* 30 (1976), 193–200.

————, "On the Origin of the World (CG II, 5): A Gnostic Physics," *VigChr* 34 (1980).

————, "Peter in Gnostic Revelation," SOCIETY OF BIBLICAL LITERATURE 1974 SEMINAR PAPERS, Vol. 2, ed. G. MacRae. Cambridge: Society of Biblical Literature, 1974, 1–13.

————, "The Soteriology of the Sophia of Jesus Christ," PROCEEDINGS OF THE SOCIETY OF BIBLICAL LITERATURE, Vol. 1. Cambridge: Society of Biblical Literature, 1971, 165–81.

Robinson, J. M. THE FACSIMILE EDITION OF THE NAG HAMMADI CODICES. Leiden: E. J. Brill, 1972–77.

————, "The Three Steles of Seth and the Gnostics of Plotinus," PROCEEDINGS OF THE INTERNATIONAL COLLOQUIUM ON GNOSTICISM, 132–42.

Rudolph, K. DIE GNOSIS: WESEN UND GESCHICHTE EINER SPATANTIKER RELIGION. Göttingen: Vandenhoeck & Ruprecht, 1978.

————, "Der gnostische Dialog als literarische Genus," PROBLEME DES KOPTISCHEN LITERATUR. Wiss. Beitr. Martin-Luther Univ. Halle-Wittenberg, 1968/1 [K2], 85–107.

Save-Soderbergh, T. "Holy Scriptures or Apologetic Documentations? The 'Sitz im Leben' of the Nag Hammadi Library," LES TEXTES DE NAG HAMMADI, ed. J. E. Ménard. Leiden: E. J. Brill, 1975, 3–14.

Schenke, H. M. "Bemerkungen zur Apokalypse des Petrus," ESSAYS ON THE NAG HAMMADI TEXTS, ed. M. Krause. NHS VI. Leiden: E. J. Brill, 1974, 272–85.

————, "Nag Hamadi Studien I; Das literarische Problem des Apokryphon Johannis," *ZRGG* 14 (1962), 57–63.

————, "Nag Hamadi Studien III: Die Spitze des dem Apokryphon Johannis und der Sophia Jesus Christi zugrundliegenden gnostischen Systems," *ZRGG* 14 (1962), 352–61.

———, "Nag Hamadi Studien II: Das System des Sophia Jesu Christi," *ZRGG* 14 (1962), 263–78.

Schoedel, W. "Topological Theology and Some Monistic Tendencies in Gnosticism," ESSAYS ON THE NAG HAMMADI TEXTS, 88–108.

Sieber, J. "An Introduction to the Tractate Zostrianos from Nag Hammadi," *NovTest* 15 (1973), 233–37.

Till, W., and H. M. Schenke. DIE GNOSTISCHEN SCHRIFTEN DES KOPTISCHEN PAPYRUS BEROLINENSIS 8502. TU 60.[2] Berlin: Akademie, 1972.

Turner, J. THE BOOK OF THOMAS THE CONTENDER. Missoula: Scholars Press, 1975.

Unnik, W. C. van. "Gnosis und Judentum," GNOSIS, 65–86.

———, "The Origin of the Newly Discovered 'Apocryphon Jacobi,'" *VigChr* 10 (1956), 146–56.

Wisse, F. "Gnosticism and Early Monasticism in Egypt," GNOSIS, 431–40.

———, "The Nag Hammadi Library and the Heresiologists," *VigChr* 25 (1971), 205–23.

———, "The Sethians and the Nag Hammadi Library," SOCIETY OF BIBLICAL LITERATURE ONE HUNDRED EIGHTH ANNUAL MEETING SEMINAR PAPERS, ed. L. McGaughy. Society of Biblical Literature, 1972, 601–607.

Index of Nag Hammadi Citations

Index of New Testament Passages

Index of Patristic Sources

Modern Authors

234

Index of Subjects